ISBN 978-1-331-82923-2
PIBN 10214070

This book is a reproduction of an important historical work. Forgotten Books uses
state-of-the-art technology to digitally reconstruct the work, preserving the original format
whilst repairing imperfections present in the aged copy. In rare cases, an imperfection in
the original, such as a blemish or missing page, may be replicated in our edition. We do,
however, repair the vast majority of imperfections successfully; any imperfections that
remain are intentionally left to preserve the state of such historical works.

1 MONTH OF
FREE
READING

at
www.ForgottenBooks.com

By purchasing this book you are eligible for one month membership to ForgottenBooks.com, giving you unlimited access to our entire collection of over 1,000,000 titles via our web site and mobile apps.

To claim your free month visit:

www.forgottenbooks.com/free214070

English
Français
Deutsche
Italiano
Español
Português

www.forgottenbooks.com

Mythology Photography **Fiction**
Fishing Christianity **Art** Cooking
Essays Buddhism Freemasonry
Medicine **Biology** Music **Ancient
Egypt** Evolution Carpentry Physics
Dance Geology **Mathematics** Fitness
Shakespeare **Folklore** Yoga Marketing
Confidence Immortality Biographies
Poetry **Psychology** Witchcraft
Electronics Chemistry History **Law**
Accounting **Philosophy** Anthropology
Alchemy Drama Quantum Mechanics
Atheism Sexual Health **Ancient History**
Entrepreneurship Languages Sport
Paleontology Needlework Islam
Metaphysics Investment Archaeology
Parenting Statistics Criminology
Motivational

LOCH ETIVE

AND

THE SONS OF UISNACH.

WITH ILLUSTRATIONS.

London:
MACMILLAN AND CO.
1879.

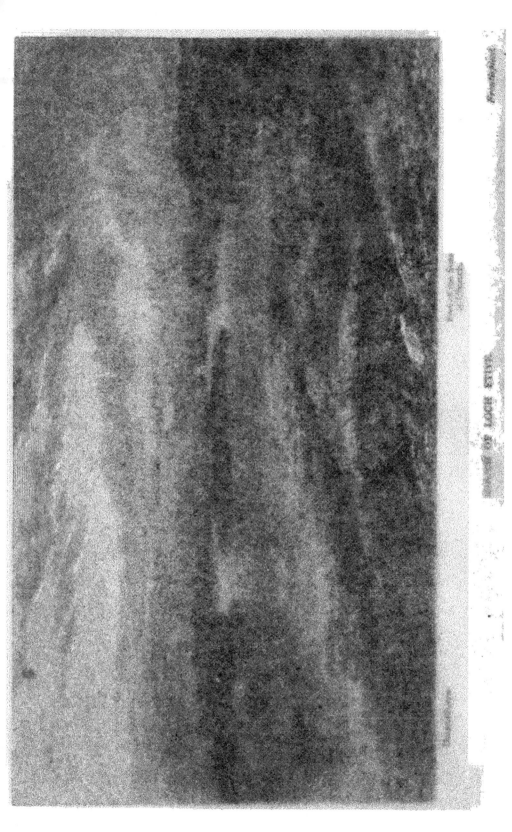

LOCH ETIVE

AND

THE SONS OF UISNACH.

WITH ILLUSTRATIONS.

London:
MACMILLAN AND CO.
1879.

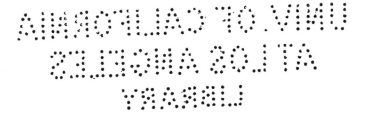
GLASGOW:
PRINTED AT THE UNIVERSITY PRESS
BY ROBERT MACLEHOSE.

PREFACE.

THIS book was begun as the work of holidays, and was intended to be read on holidays, but there is not the less a desire to be correct. The primary object is to show what is interesting near Loch Etive, and thus add points of attachment to our country. There is so much that is purely legendary, that it was thought better to treat the subject in a manner which may appear preliminary rather than full, going lightly over a good deal of ground, and, from the very nature of the collected matter, touching on subjects which may at first appear childish. It is believed that to most persons the district spoken of will appear as a newly discovered country, although passed by numerous tourists. The landing of the Irish Scots has held a very vague place in our history, and it is interesting to think of them located on a spot which we can visit and to find an ancient account of their King's Court, even if it be only a fanciful one written long after the heroes ceased to live. The connection of Scotland and Ireland, previous to the Irish invasion, is still less known, and to see any mention of the events of the period by one who may reasonably be supposed to have spoken in times which for Scotland can scarcely be called historic, excited much surprise and interest in the author of this volume, and it is believed will be pleasing to those who for the first time read the account of the children of Uisnach.

These two eras belong to the earliest notices of our land. The first mentioned has generally been noticed by historians, but little has been said to make us think it real. The other has not passed into history, and it stands at present as our very first account of a connection between Scotland and Ireland which seems to be authentic, although despised as belonging only to Bardic legends. The dreamy state in which the accounts come to us, has led to a desire not to use either the historic or severely critical style in this volume. In the discussion relating to places the wish has been to avoid arguments well known, and as friends have in some cases communicated new ones, these have been chiefly retained as more interesting. The importance given in the main legends to Bards and Druids has led the author to say something of them. It has been his aim whilst beginning with the more distant allusions native to these lands, to describe, after frequent visits and investigations, the remains of antiquity of a pre-historic character as they now appear near Loch Etive, connecting, by historic theories, the larger body of Celts in Europe with the people who were the actors in that region. He wishes to shew that it has required several races to make up the population of countries called Celtic, judging either from their early history or from their present condition.

The slightness of the older materials affected in various ways the mode of treatment, and it was decided to bring together several persons to represent the various views. A Highlander, of course, was necessary to shew part of the ground, but an Irishman was equally required—indeed nearly all the Celtic literature quoted is Irish. A Lowlander was brought to give unbiassed opinions, and he brings three of his family to vary the tone of thought or mode of observation. All, however, take interest in the district, and are supposed to have given to the subject some previous attention. A few of the names are spelt in various ways by writers of good standing, and the author sometimes thought it well not to confine himself to one form, when it does not shew any quality that gives it prominence.

CONTENTS.

CONTENTS.

CHAPTER XX.

CHAPTER XXI.

CHAPTER XXII.

CHAPTER XXIII.

CHAPTER XXIV.

CHAPTER XXV.

CHAPTER XXVI.

CHAPTER XXVII.

ILLUSTRATIONS.

LOCH ETIVE AND THE SONS OF UISNACH.

ERRATA.

Page 134, line 4, instead of "Doruadille," read "Dornadille."

,, 180, ,, 7, ,, "Colmar, Cuar," read "Colman Cuar."

,, 272, ,, 14, ,, "Achnaha" read "Achnaba."

,, 279, ,, 10, 33, ,, "*Cameron*" read "*Loudoun.*"

,, 321, ,, 16, ,, "Druimachothais" read "Druimachothuis."

LOCH ETIVE AND THE SONS OF UISNACH.

CHAPTER I.

DUN ADD.

"They passed away from us
 With the splendour of swiftness,
 To dwell by valour
 In the land of the country beyond Ile "[1] (Islay).

LOUDOUN.—We shall sail to the fastnesses of the sons of Uisnach, and to the islands where they hunted and fished. We shall visit the woods and bays which they frequented, and speak of their history, the romance of their doings, their well-known traditions, and the fancies relating to them. And this I at least do, not merely because of them, for after all they are little known, and much, if not all, is in uncertainty; but they are links of union with early days, and they present a human interest with which to adorn our mountains. We rejoice in the hills, but have too little to say of them. Their natural features are large. We like some thoughts that lead us more into details, and besides on a

---

[1] From the additions, Irish and Pictish, to *Historia Britonum.*— Skene's Translation. Said of the Picts from Ireland.

holiday we require easy thoughts, and these seem for most
men, and certainly for most women, such as refer to persons.   By linking our wild hills to the history of persons,
we have a mode of enjoying them and a reason for loitering
among them, and if we search out the homes of the legendary names, we have places to visit more interesting than
the best of modern houses.   But still, as I was taught, I also
take a delight in our Highland hills for themselves, and in
our Highland air.   The Highland archæology supplies grave
studies, and even labour, when we return home.   The sail
to Oban is rapid, and through scenery too beautiful for such
swift steamers, and I propose that we stay at Crinan.

Margaet.—Of all places on the route, Crinan I would
have chosen last.   Everybody leaves it as soon as possible.
There is a rush from canal-boat to sea-boat and dinner,
and are five minutes not enough for its little pier and the
general waste around it ?

O'Keefe.—I am sorry to hear this.   I wish you had
known and remembered the great cauldron that cooked for
as many persons as were to dine there, and gave everybody
enough and according to his requirements.   No place in
the world was better supplied with food ; hunger was less
there than anywhere else, with a few similar exceptions in
Ireland ; and, if things have changed, at least sympathise
with the past, even if its greatness has departed.

Sheena.—Oh ! that alters the case.   I thought Crinan
had no romance, and people fancy it has no beauty ; is it
not common-place in appearance ?

O'Keefe.—By no means.   Row after row of islands defend
it from the Atlantic, large and little, rugged and flat, whilst

rocks innumerable rise out of the waves, and dangerous currents frighten the reason. They are ramparts and guardians for many quiet bays and towns, whilst their various forms are themselves a wild story and a constant wonder. Steamboats and hotels do not make it easy to dwell there long, but we shall stay a little, and even the sons of Uisnach will not hurry us, since we shall halt at the earliest seat of the Dalriad Scots, and look at their first fortress also, which is passed unheeded as a mere stony heap, instead of the beginning of a great history.

Sheena.—I did not know that it had a history.

O'Keefe.—You may be sure that the English Government that made the canal were not the first who found the value of this narrow passage from sea to sea, nor were the present Scots the first to see that a fine palace might be built in this valley: many a one must have come from the raging sea outside, which cannot reach Crinan until it spends its force upon Mull, rages on the Islands of Saints, roars through **Corrievrecan**, and calms itself down at the Dorus Mor—the "Great Door." The Dalriad Scots came from Ireland here and settled. I dare say some of them knew the way long before. We can imagine the expedition avoiding Cantire and Jura, as there is a long line of coast which would too clearly show their coming. I dare say they knew also that had they taken earlier landing places on the mainland they would have been as much isolated as if in islands, for the long peninsula of Cantire stretches far south, and is the inner breakwater of the calm and cheerful Clydesdale seas. West Loch Tarbert would entice them, but they probably thought that which a later king asserted, that the narrowness of the isthmus made the land an island. At any rate we shall imagine the Dalriads sailing to Crinan from Mull, and one of their earliest establishments was on that island ; we can think of them avoiding the rough rocks outside Scarba and the violent currents, and coming down south of Eilean-na-naoimh to look for a calmer opening between Scarba and Jura, and finding a whirlpool. And we can imagine them shouting with no small fear, "This is Corrievrecan" (Corrie Bhrecain). Brecan was the son of an Irish king, and he had nothing to do with this coast, but when he was sailing between Ballycastle and Rathlin he got entangled in the terrible sea commotion or whirlpool there, and went down with his ships and men. It was then named after him. The name of the Scotch Corrie must have been given to it by men familiar with the Irish one, and about the Dalriadic times Brecan was fresh in the minds of men from the West. St. Columba knew óf King Brecan, and had an interest in him, since it is told of him that one day, when sailing through that rough passage at Rathlin, the wind made such terrible troughs in the sea that he saw the bottom of it, and bones lying there, and it was revealed to him that these were the bones of Brecan and his companions. The saint was glad and prayed for their souls, and he had the pleasure of seeing the soul of Brecan rise before him at once from purgatory up to heaven. The death of Brecan was in 440.

This whirlpool would frighten the Dalriads, and they would turn north again and try to make their way among the numberless little islands and rocky points that defend the entrance to Crinan, and we can imagine the next shout

to be much more cheerful, "This is the way," "this is the
door," and to this day we go in to the bay by the *Dorus
mor*. We may imagine Fergus the son of Erc coming in
this way, and Gabhran after him going backwards and
forwards, and still more, Aedan making permanent the settlement and keeping his power in the islands. We must
imagine few at first, since the valley is small.

But do not suppose that they landed on a desert or lived
in peace; if so, you are far wrong. We shall get a boat
here, and good rowers will in a few minutes take us over
to Duntroon, that old castle which was built by a branch
of the Campbells in later but still in dangerous times. Now
a peaceful clergyman has brought his southern learning
gained among people then unknown here, but when the
Scots landed we have no reason to believe that any building
occupied that spot. In those days the people could not
build a wall closely knit and standing perpendicularly on
a bare steep rock. They went farther back, and there in
the wood we shall find the remains of their fortress in the
form of numerous vitrified heaps in the direst confusion.
The invaders would see a black wall on the hills, the
stones of the lower part melted sufficiently together to keep
them united; having no mortar to bind them the builders
resorted to fusion; and having no tools probably to cut
them into shape or to quarry great masses, they used the
pieces as they found them and thus bound them together. It
was not easy to vitrify the wall to a great height, and they
probably raised it higher than the vitrified part by masses
of loose stones forming a dry dyke which would enclose
small stone buildings. The lesser people would live out-

side in huts built sometimes with loose stones only, and sometimes with interwoven branches or wickerwork.

Sheena.—I should like to know the names of the people and the places, and what kind of people lived in vitrified forts.

Loudoun.—You ask difficult questions, but I suppose Picts lived here—Cruithne. The vitrified forts seem to have come from the north-east of Scotland to the west, and to have made an inroad into Ulster, but only for a little way. It was a curious invention, and it may have been obtained from other countries. There is a fine one in Bohemia, but whether men came to commence it in Scotland from the Continent we do not know; it is most probable.

O'Keefe.—If the people were Picts I should have expected them to live in Picts' towers, and is it not the case that Mr. Anderson of the Scottish Society of Antiquaries speaks of seven of these towers or brochs at Craignish close to Crinan?

Cameron.—Yes, but he says also that we cannot go beyond the fifth century for them, and if they began in the north and east they would take some time to come south and west. Now Fergus came only at the end of the fifth century, and probably did not see these forts, which were a new step, an advance on the vitrified. At any rate there are the remains of a vitrified fort, and we hear of no Picts' towers in the same valley. But the Picts may have continued near; we know that as a nation they were not for a long time conquered, and we can readily suppose them bringing in the new style of building for their defence. The Dalriadic kings did not adopt the broch, but some of the chiefs may have used it; still we may fairly picture the invaders looking at the black line of the old fort with its half melted wall, and the few people living in comparative abundance on the chase, with protection from storms in their abundant material, and protection from cold in an ample supply of wood and peat. We might even say more by help from Irish analogous living, but we must not imagine too much, and I dare say you would like to hear how the strangers landed.

Sheena.—We should like first to know what the people were like.

Loudoun.—I think we shall speak of them some day when we have more time, but I may say by the way that they were mixed even then. Do not suppose that the world began with the people immediately before the Dalriads, or magnify the events of this little part of our world. There are dark people in Argyle, and most are either dark or inclined to dark, but there are light also; now the greatest inroad known to us of people from north and east has been of the light class. This, I think, is a sufficient reason for believing that there were dark people then.

Sheena.—But you said they were mixed, meaning, I suppose, that there were light people also even then.

Loudoun.—Yes, I said so, and for one simple reason. The Caledonians of the North-East are said by Tacitus to have been light, or at least red-haired, and as it is evident that north-eastern habits, especially as to building, came to Argyle, it is probable that the people sent specimens of themselves also. Besides, Celtic Ireland was peopled in the earliest times by light and dark people, as we shall see some day, and the opposite coast much resembled it in population in all probability—we might say certainty. There were small men in Ireland and large; it is probable that there were so here also then as now, but this is less easily shown. The existence of the small is considered certain by most, but whence came the large? We cannot suppose that the small changed rapidly; we must bring in a tall and dark people.

Sheena.—Then, do you think they were exactly as now?

Loudoun.—Not in the same proportion. We have not decided what the Picts were like. The people of Ulster had been communicating with Ireland before the time we speak of, and even if there had been a pure Pictish race in Argyle at one time, it would have become mixed. But the dark and small race were very numerous at the time in Ireland, under the name of Firbolgs, and they seem to have come over to the West of Scotland also. The Irish traditions would lead us to think of other races of Ireland keeping a close communication with Scotland. Cuchullin, for example, is said to have gone to Skye for education. There may have been as the chief people in Argyle the Picts or at least Cruithne, and a considerable mixture. These Picts are not to be supposed as all coming immediately from the North of Scotland. They had a settlement in Ireland, from whence they went to Galloway, and they are well known as opponents of the Romans farther south. Where they came from we do not know, but they had a peculiar dialect, which Mr. Skene has investigated from the few words remaining, concluding it to be somewhat between Gaelic and Cymric. If we want to picture to ourselves these **Cruithne** we shall find many difficulties. Scottish folklore makes the " Pechs" small men, but perhaps this does not deserve attention. Had the whole of the Pictish region been peopled by small Firbolgs—called by some Iberians—more traces would have been left. Even the fearfully murderous times that the Norsemen brought and continued long could not have destroyed them all. If so, the Norsemen would have left only themselves, and we do not find such proofs of extirpation ; on the contrary, we find in the very Pictish Northern regions a tall people with long faces and abundant specimens of dark hair, which Norway, Sweden, and Denmark could not brighten or redden, although there is everywhere a tinge of red, reminding of old Caledonians. These red Caledonians had made advances in civilization. Four hundred years previously, according to Pytheas, no such men had appeared in the North of Scotland. They were invaders evidently. A proverb in Lorn says, " Better to be brown haired than black, better to be black than fair (ban), better to be fair than red, better to be red than bald (carrach), better to be bald than headless." I can only say that I think the races at Crinan were mixed, but the Picts dominant ; this is not proved.

O'Keefe.—Well, however that may be, we must suppose them to be on the shore as we are, and the old black fort frowning upon them. If Duntroon is *Dunt-Sroinc*—the " Dun of the point" or nose—the old fort would not be so called.

Sheena.—You have told us of the fort and the people. Was the land the same as now ?

Loudoun.—I fear the sea has made some inroad, as the

plain was called the great moss or great peat bog, and this is probably in part washed away, and in being washed there would be a great deal of black muddy looking material, which caused later men to call it Poltalloch or the dirty pool. Then there has been found on the plain a stone coffin the bottom being 45 feet above the mean sea level, according to Mr. J. Lawson, R.E. The place appears to me swampy, and one would imagine they would not bury there unless in haste, whereas this was not a hasty burial, and, on the contrary, seems one of the most careful, as there are carvings of hatchets, flint or otherwise without handles, and lines very like Oghams, on the stone. This would point to the spot being at least as dry at the time as now, and not being washed by the sea. The Oghams are imperfect, and it has been doubted if they are Oghams, but this is probably because the people who try cannot read them. Still this burial may have been rather later than the time spoken of, and the argument is imperfect. [1]

Enough to say that the evidence points to a little change of shore from very early times, but to no geological upheaval having taken place. We may suppose this grave to have been made when Oghams were in use, but written badly in this distant place. If they went out in the west of Britain, as Professor Rhys thinks, in the eighth or ninth century, they must have been in use some centuries before, probably in some places, later. Styles did not change rapidly in early times, and languages change slowly in all times; a few cases excepted, for there really are exceptions.

[1] See account by the Rev. R. J. Mapleton.

Willie.—You have not told us where they landed.

O'Keefe.—I must of course imagine, but when the black fort was on the left, we may be sure that the invaders would take the right side. No army would land under the natives' stronghold if it could find a safer place. They would land at Crinan or as far up the stream as circumstances allowed, and so take solid possession of lodging room. The land is rugged; there are many pleasant knolls giving good shelter, but suited only for a small army, and the men could run up the side of the river, keeping near the present canal line. They would thus take the rugged side of the glen and look towards their enemies on the warmer, sunnier, and better cultivated side. It was fitter for cultivation then as now from natural position. And so we can imagine them working their way round. After having made considerable progress they settled.

Loudoun.—Is there not a conical hill near the modern house, called, perhaps, by an old Christian name—Kilmahonig, at Crinan, and having an appearance of stones placed round like a moat hill or a Thing.

Cameron.—I know what you mean — it seems to me rather like the works of nature as they are in the district, but I did not examine, and at any rate Thingvöllr is Norse, and if the cone be of that class it would be much after the time of our Hibernian friends. And now I wish you to allow that even then the country must have been beautiful—it is so now and it was so seven centuries ago, and we must suppose it so five centuries earlier. An Irish poet says of Scotland in the twelfth century:—

"Beloved to me—it is natural to me,
Are the beautiful woods of Alban.
Though strange, I love dearer still
This tree from the woods of Erin."

This was written by Mac Conmidhe when on a mission
to Scotland: he preferred the one tree or stick from
Ireland to all the fine woods of the eastern land.[1]

O'Keefe.—I will let you have your way there, as it may
be right, but if Duntroon is an old name it might be made
to mean the fort of the Druids, and Crinan or Grianan or Greenan, the sun-place, the place where the sun was worshipped.
The name may have included all the valley, and these great
stones towards Kilmartin may have been the temple.

Loudoun.—I suppose you know that you are talking
heresy. I wish I could make out something so clear. It
is by some believed that there were not any real Druids
in Scotland, but the word with its compounds is well known,
and we may talk of it some day. At present, however, you
may be reminded that although Greenan, pronounced Creenan,
means really a sunny place, it is used for the bright part of a
building, the pleasant part of the residence where the lady
presided, and indicates an important dwelling or palace,
so that we do not require to imagine it to refer to more
than to the fort opposite, as that is near enough to give a
name to the whole. Still your idea is a pleasant fancy; one
likes to think of the religion of a people. In it we learn
the character, the very inner souls of the men; and your
remark throws around the place a still greater air of

[1] O'Curry and O'Sullivan, *Manners and Customs of the Ancient Irish,*
vol. III., p. 272.

romance and of mystery. However, I fear that your derivation of Duntroon is too strained to assist us in forming a true picture. It may be added, not as an argument, that the invaders, however pagan in their notions, were by profession, I suppose, all Christians; not so the people who were invaded.

O'Keefe.—But in any case these invaders landed, and they brought their mode of building with them, and on the top of that rough and rocky isolated *Add* they built a *dun*. Perhaps Add was the name of the river then, and the fort would be called after it. Celts are fertile in etymology and they could derive the word from *adh*, *law* and *joy* in their language, but this might not be in any way true; in so far as I see, it might have been called from *adhbha*, a palace, or from Aedh, son of the king to be spoken of, or better, the king himself, Aedan, the son of Gabran, the true founder of the Dalriad kingdom, as Skene says. It is also called Dunat and Dunaet, which does not contradict the last and natural derivation. We can and we must imagine some hard fighting with the people of the vitrified fort some two miles distant, and many must have been killed.

There were at any rate two parties at the time we are speaking of. The pleasant valley which is now well cultivated would for a while be divided between them, and on the Dun Add side we see great and tall standing stones. If these were erected by the invaders, they would not be for worship; indeed, it is the opinion at present that all such stones were memorials of the dead. When large, in long lines, or even in very great circles, it has long been imagined that something more was intended, although this belief is not at present in fashion. Pre-christian worship existed in some form, although we know not much on the subject.. Stones were with certainty connected with it. Old notices sufficiently authentic show this superstition in France, and the very oldest notices in Ireland indicate the same. I know of nothing equally clear from Alba, although there are signs of it, and beliefs existed in the time of Hector Boece that the large circles were not private graves merely.

We shall go up the valley on the west, but we move only a little before coming to the great modern mansion of Poltalloch. This name is supposed to stigmatise the plain below, but it has a fine sound whatever be its meaning. Here it stands, a fine object in the valley, with a fine park and many trees encircling the prospect. Behind it on the bare rock there are some of those strange carvings called cups and circles; the first are little round depressions cut on the stone, the second sometimes single, sometimes several concentric; sometimes the cups are connected by straight lines; the like are to be seen in various Celtic places, and more or less similar in Scandinavian lands. Dr. Mapleton mentions something very like them on a stone in India.

If we move on by the road we find over the wall at our left a cairn and very complete stone circle made of boulders. It is apparently as first made, and it is very like those found on Loch Etive, near a vitrified fort which we shall see. As we go on towards Kilmartin, a place which had no such name at the time we are thinking of, since there were no churches here and no saints, we find in the field a greater cairn recently opened and showing a gallery which had not

been covered with heavy stones as in Brittany, but comparatively light ones, the remaining scarcely sufficient to
keep the two sides from soon meeting. So much has been
removed, that it is all ready to be destroyed, unfortunately.
Nearer still to the Kilmartin church is another with a long
passage to it lined with boulder walls, showing abundant
care and some power of building.

If we pass down the other side, and towards Ardrishaig,
we soon come to the high stone pillars spoken of, and we
can imagine the two parties, invaders and natives, struggling
long, and burying their dead in different methods, keeping
their own side of the glen. This is supposing the large stones
to indicate burying places—the most favoured opinion. I am
giving, perhaps, a little too much supposition, but each must
judge for himself. We do not go far until the road to the
right leads us to Dun Add. This isolated hill, perhaps 150
feet high, has so many stones irregularly around it that
one scarcely feels sure which have been left by nature,
but after consideration one feels sure that much has
been touched by man. Indeed one may fancy, and even
more, one may almost feel certain, of a passage winding
upwards, consisting partly of rocks and partly of building.
When half way up on the south there is found a less
uneven spot where dwellings may have been, and on the
upper part and near it, certain remains of very definite
buildings, the most definite being at the very summit, where
the lower ranges of stone are in some parts undisturbed.
Here certainly was an artificial fort, and around it
many people may have dwelt ; here the invaders made
their stronghold. In old times the land in the plain could

not have been drier than now. I believe, indeed, the ancient name, as Mr. Skene and Dr. Donovan say, was Dunmonadh, and although there are some arguments for making that apply to Dunstaffnage, they seem quite insufficient, and we are safer to follow the guidance of these Celtic-learned. Dunmonadh means the fort of the peat-moss, and so we may suppose still more peat than now, but not a great deal, as people seldom put houses on peat, at least I have that belief. Men, too, wanted their cattle fed, and required grass; and in the old days cattle were the great wealth, although wild swine and deer were abundant on the hills. Birds were less easily caught, still they were not neglected.

Sheena.—But do you think they had little houses and gardens, and kept cattle, and grew vegetables?

O'Keefe.—Little houses they would have, perhaps some round bee-hive ones, and almost certainly wherever there were trees, wattle cottages, made of sticks plaited together. I do not see that they had raths like the Irish, places surrounded with earth walls, for their cattle; but I believe in later times they used wattle fences for the same purpose, and perhaps even then. Their cattle would probably be in some such enclosure in times of commotion, and they would in some such way take care of their little brown-wooled, many-horned sheep; and surely some of their long-legged pigs would be at home, since it would be difficult to catch them when they had leave to ramble freely in the woods or on the hills.

Of course the brown wool made brown dresses, and I suppose that the men had the short kilt and the women the long over-gown, the upper part of the man's body being often uncovered amongst the poorer.

We must now suppose the Dalriads to have settled here, to have conquered the people of the black fort, and that vitrified fort itself to have begun to decay, whilst several little but ambitious kings, much admired in their time, held their court on this hill, and had still their so-called Druids, perhaps soothsayers of a kind, and their bards certainly, and their fine apparel and their pride of conquest. We must suppose Aedan to have passed away, he who settled the kingdom of Dalriada, and whose power was great enough to lead an army, including Angles, into Northumberland. We have supposed him to have made Dun Add important, and to have given it its name ; we may learn better. His life was troubled, although he was blessed by St. Columba; and perhaps he might have been better at home than fighting in England. I am inclined only to think at present of his successor, the yellow-haired Eochy or Eochy Bui (Buidhe), appointed by the same saint. It is pleasant to have a picture of him in all the glory of his court as painted with the cheeriness of Celtic imagination by an Irish writer or bard. What the foundation was who can tell, but there is generally some for the bright pictures drawn by the class. We cannot say that the account was written in the king's day, and we do not know how late, but it is found in the yellow book of Lecan, transcribed in 1390 according to O'Curry. We must make a great jump, but information exists scantily; when we want to know exactly the extent of purely historic knowledge we must go to Skene's Celtic Scotland.

B

Cameron.—And of what age are you speaking?

O'Keefe.—King Eochy began his reign in 606 A.D., and this may be enough of chronology for the present. The time is not doubted by Skene, and the man is no myth, although he may have been too much exalted by a writer, who, according to Dr. Donovan, wrote of him before the year 1197, or about six centuries after the events. The earlier authorities are lost, and we take our account of his court from the story as it is extracted from the book of Lecan. Let us imagine the valley lighted by the brightness of the company, an invading and successful people, and the king with the yellow hair to be as he is painted, and proud of his warlike sons.

Eochy was the grandfather of Congal Claen, a young man who sought to be king of Ulster, and who felt himself so insulted at the feast of Dun na n' Gedh that he determined to redress his wrongs. He had not been fed as the other guests were, for they had had wild goose eggs on silver plates, and he was left out, and, as he thought, with intention. So he sought his grandfather King Eochy in Dun Add, and took with him a hundred warriors.

A Druid from the Dun met the ships with greetings. His name was Dubhdhiah, but he is elsewhere called Drostan, as we find in Dr. Samuel Ferguson's poem of Congal, where the story is told in the adventures of that fierce warrior, as an incident which led to the famous battle of Moira (spelt Magh Rath). These incongruous spellings often sound sweetly in the modern pronunciation. The Druid's name I do not know how to make soft, but you may leave out the *bh* and the *dh*.

The Druid said—

Margaet.—But before you tell us what he said, what had Druids to do there? I thought the invaders had been Christians, and blessed by St. Columba.

O'Keefe.—That is true; but Druids of some kind we must admit. The Druids, then, if they did come over with the Dalriads, may not have been exactly like Cæsar's Druids, and at any rate all these tales have a thoroughly heathen ring, and seem to have grown out of unchristianized ages. Perhaps Christianity had but a slight hold of the people, and still less of the bards and magicians, who would keep long to their traditions, notwithstanding St. Patrick's great success. We have here our Druid and his welcome, and I consider the modified and so-called Druidism, or witchcraft if you prefer, at the court, much more credible than any real Christianity. The Druid came to meet the boats, and we can imagine him standing on the shore, when he said to Congal Claen in a dignified style of welcome :—

> " My favour was to your bright fleet,
> Which I saw at a distance.
> Declare your race of stainless fame,
> And what your country, whence you came."

Congal said—

> " We come from noble Erin,
> Oh, proud and noble youth ;
> And we have come hither
> To address Eochy Bui."

The Druid—

> " If you come hither
> To confer with Eochy Bui,
> After your arrival over the sea,
> I tell to you my affection."

Sheena.—I do not admire the poetry.

O'Keefe.—A literal translation never sounds well, and Dr. O'Donovan, whose translation it is, wished to be exact.

The King of Alba was sitting in an assembly of his nobles.

Sheena.—Over there?

O'Keefe.—Yes, on the spot contemptuously very early called Dunmonadh, and now disregarded. The king and his men welcomed Congal, and in a right royal way promised him the forces of Alba, and sent him to confer with his sons, who were there in conference. He said, "I have four sons, Aedh, of the green dress, Sweeny (Suibhne), Congal Menn, and Donald (Domhnall) Brec, the eldest of thy maternal uncles; it is they who have command of the forces of Alba." He had promised never to fight against the king of Erin, but with diplomatic duplicity, royal even then, he promised all his forces.

The uncles were all delighted to see the young man from Erin, and all wanted to take him home and feast him ; they had all separate houses not far off, and all these are spoken of as having been well appointed.

Sheena.—One wonders how food could be found for any large number of people here.

O'Keefe.—You forget the abundance I spoke of, and that Eochy the king could entertain any number of guests with abundant food, because he had the great magic cauldron which always cooked food enough for whatever number of guests there were. Aedh, the youngest, in his green dress, asked Congal to stay with him, and refused to fight if this were not granted.

Donald Bree said he was the eldest, and ought to have the guest, and the others put in their demands, until the Druid was obliged to interpose, as Congal did not wish to offend any óne. Dubhdhiah said, " Tell them that you will stop with that one of them who shall obtain the regal cauldron which is in the king's house to prepare food for thee, and that the person who shall not get the cauldron is not to be displeased with thee in consequence, but with the king."

Sheena.—This is rather depreciating the capabilities of the sons, is it not? It supposes that they could not feed Congal well enough.

O'Keefe.—No one would despise the use of such a cauldron. It was able to return its due share to each, and no party ever went away from it dissatisfied, for whatever quantity was put into it, "there was never boiled of it but what was sufficient for the company, according to their grade and rank;" there were other cauldrons in Ireland with this same power.

The sons then sent their wives to petition the king for the cauldron. Aedh or Hugh's wife went first.

I cannot remember all the speeches, but the king asked this Hugh's wife why the cauldron should be given to her, and she said it was because her husband never refused any gift to any man; he had a bounty more extensive than the world, and the jewels of the green-faced earth would not remain an hour on his hand; he would put upon small spits all that his proud brothers would give to guests. But the king said, " I will not give you the cauldron as yet," and turning to Congal Menu's wife, asked her why her husband should have the preference. Because, was the reply, there is no king's son better than he, his shield can shelter a hundred heads, he is brave, not small, and jealous.

That was not enough for the king.   So Donald Brec sent his wife, who gave her reasons for preference—" If the great Sliabh Monaidh were of gold, he would distribute it in an hour ; no king ever ruled better than Donald Brec."

Sweeny's wife then came and boasted of the size of the house—

> " One hundred goblets, one hundred cups,
> One hundred hogs, and one hundred joints,
> And one hundred silver vessels,
> Are yonder in the house."

But after all the old king had the feast in his own house, and so prevented quarrelling ; still it was after asking the advice of the Druid, whose answer was very wary.

The King.—" Let my austere Druid decide
　　　　　　Between the wives of Mogaire's sons,
　　　　　　To what fair-skinned yellow-haired woman
　　　　　　Of them my cauldron shall be given."

Dubhdhiadh.—" If it were a golden cauldron,
　　　　　　With golden hooks to move it,
　　　　　　Oh Eochy of the hosts of men,
　　　　　　It should be given to Donald.

" If it were a cauldron of silver,
　　　From which would issue neither steam nor smoke,
　　　It should be given to the plundering Hugh,
　　　The youngest of the sons of Eochy.

" If it were a cauldron very great,
　　　It should be given to Congal of the beauteous tunic,
　　　That renowned man of great prosperity,
　　　Who makes lawful of unlawful property.

" The cauldron with ornament,
Oh Eochy, oh great king,
Should be given to the host,
To Sweeny in the middle of the house."

The king gave his blessing to his sons' wives, and feasted everybody.

I must not follow Congal; having excited your interest, you may read of his collecting troops in Britain, and his failure in Ireland. [1]

Margaet.—We must now leave Dun Add, and see the valley. But before we go I should like to know what happened to the place, and why it is so solitary.

O'Keefe.—Perhaps a good deal more may be gleaned. I can tell you some little. We shall not go over the history. The Dalriads had four divisions, and one of these was in Lorne, the chief of which lived in the castle of Dunolly, the head of all being at Dun Add. The whole of the power was taken from them again by Angus, the king of the Picts, who laid waste the country, took Dun Add, and burnt Creich, their western centre in Mull. You must read Skene's history to see the order of things till the Picts and Scots were united in Kenneth M'Alpin, and as that king lived at Forteviot, near Perth, and died in 858, the old capital here would go early to wreck, and you see what it has become in a thousand years. It has been difficult to unearth the little we know, and to connect the stories of old with these broken fragments of buildings.

[1] Dr. (now Sir) Samuel Ferguson has written a poem called " Congal," the hero being the Irish sub-king of Ulster. His course is illustrated till his end arrives at Moira.

Margaet.—You said the sons had houses; can you tell where they lived?

O'Keefe.—That is asking much. I told you of cups and circles over at the new castle, and if we go a couple of miles nearer to Lochgilphead you will see a farm house called Achnabreac. This, they say, means the field of the spots. Breac is not uncommon as applied to places; it might mean also in the Irish, the field of the wolves, and this is much more sensible. The word is not given in Scotch Gaelic dictionaries as meaning wolf, but it is in Irish. It means also a trout, which is spotted; but one fancies that it might take its name from Donald Breac or Brec, who became king. He was no mean person, and his power extended far.

Cameron.—Would that be good Gaelic—would not Ach·*na*breac suit the wolves better than the king?

O'Keefe.—That may be, but a similar form might easily pass into Achnabreac when the original idea was forgotten, and that king has been long forgotten here. Another son may be remembered in the names Sweeny, Loch Sweeny, and Castle Swin. One may be fanciful at times, but we must take care to keep our fancies free in the sense of distinct, so as not to confound them with facts. I daresay the cups and circles were old at the time we speak of, and Donald Breac would not know their meaning, and the word would not relate to these spots; but even this is only an opinion. I believe in many old traditions among the Dalriads.

Cameron.—It is getting late. At Carnban, the white cairn, we can see more cups and circles, and we may go back to Kilmartin to stay, so as to dream for a night, and wander for

a morning in this valley of the Scottish kings; for these men
were Scottish invaders, intruding on the men of Alba and the
Picts.

Loudoun.—To-day is fine. We may take a walk up the
valley, and have a peep at least at the tower of Carnassery,
where the Carswells lived, where, I suppose, Bishop Carswell
was born. It is a long step to him, although he was successor to St. Columba after 1000 years, as Bishop of Argyll
and the Isles, after being rector or minister of the parish of
Kilmartin. He did not care for old stories, and tried much to
suppress them. We owe him, therefore, a certain grudge,
although we may thank him for translating into Gaelic John
Knox's Liturgy, which has been so carefully edited by the
Rev. Dr. M'Lauchlan. Bishop Carswell made poems, and
rather melancholy ones, warning us to think of death, whilst the
neighbours made lampoons upon him, and called him greedy;
but his size was great, and his eating may have astonished
people scantily fed in the troublous times of the sixteenth
century. He requested to be buried at Ardchattan; and
he was carried there with difficulty on a wild and stormy
day. We intend to visit the place, but we shall not find
anything to remind us of him, so we shall leave him connected in our minds with the paternal tower standing high
in the wood to our left hand going to Lochawe, and making
a fourth style of building still to be seen, before the old
Highland cottage, which is a fifth, brings us to our modern
varieties.

The steamer will take us to Oban. We can meet it at
Crinan pier. We have scarcely time to look at the little

conical hill alluded to, said to be a Scandinavian hill of meeting, but we can mark the wondrous twistings of the road,
and the scanty arable land among the many prettily wooded
hills.

It needs a poet to describe a sail to Oban.   Swift steamers
run in two hours or little more, but it is a new land to those
coming from the South or East.   There is a new geology to
them ; the hills have changed their shapes, the land is cut out
into forms difficult to remember, places that look inland
are suddenly seen to be sea-ports, and the ocean is sprinkled
over with rocks, whilst it rushes in violent currents.   Old
shores stand up and show themselves, reminding us that
they too in their time had borne the ravages of the waves, and
were glad of rest.   Islands deserted tell of men also who had
suffered and fled ; and the Garveloch Isles at our left, containing Eilichanave (Eilean-na-naoimh), the isle of the saints,
reminds us of terrible struggles that Christian civilization had
in these stormy regions.

Eilichanave has remains of churches and a monastery
nearly as old as those of Iona.   It was called Hinba before
the saints made it famous, and now it descends to be called
one of *mare* islands, a corruption, as Skene thinks, of
Eileann an mhara, isles of the sea,[1] an expression indicating
loss of tradition and fading interest.   This name has been
changed again into Horse Island ; and this derivation may
account for several islands named so.

We are going to Loch Etive, and we cannot wait for all
the visits that these isles tempt us to make ; we cannot wait
where the slates are leading men deep under the sea, and

---

[1] *Life of St. Columba*, by Dr. Reeves, 1874, Appendix, p. 319.

where, I daresay, the workers have frightened the **Gruagach**, who lived about this spot, and who himself frightened so many people long ago.[1] We shall pass the rugged turning of Seil, which stands like a smaller **Ardnamurchan**, and looks to those ever threatening precipices of Mull. We shall pass the great walls of basalt—dykes built by rocks better fused than the walls of the vitrified forts, and outlasting all around, defying the sea and rain when others have been ground into mud and long cleared away.

We are coming into a new district; we may rest and look for the old tower of Dunolly, and the cheerful white houses of Oban, which tell us to be ready to land in its well-protected bay.

[1] I remember this in Campbell's West Highland Tales, but cannot turn to it at present.

NOTES.—This presumes that we do not know the really first arrival of the Scots in Britain, and that we are equally ignorant of the exact boundaries of Picts to the west.

Dr. Fergusson says that the "Brochs" were built by the Norwegians, but this does not affect the arguments here.

Marc is a word for *horse*, and may have been mistaken for *mara*.

CHAPTER II.

TIIE CHILDREN OF LIR.

A land where the past wills to be present, and refuses to yield to the senses.

MARGAET.—And now we have found repose in this hotel, looking over to the hills of Morven ; are we still in the land of the past, and is the country peopled only by shadows ? The very visitors pass through the land like ghosts, scarcely speaking. Do the people themselves become transformed, and to begin, how much of your story is to be believed ?

O'Keefe.—We must admit that the cauldron never existed, and of course the conversation about it must go into the same region of romance; but I fear we must admit more. Even King Eochy did not reign at that time ; he had been dead a few years before Congal Claen came over.

Margaet.—What then is true ?

O'Kcefe.—It is true that you have seen Dun Add, and that the king did live there, that he was chief of the Dalriads in what is now called Scotland, and the achievements are the ideas of a bard who did his best to make the history of his invading countrymen interesting. Let us be thankful for what we can learn.

Margaet.—I am glad to hear the opinions of men who lived at least much nearer the time of action than we do, and who had much probably of the same spirit as the actors had. It strikes me, however, that the love of giving away is inconsistent with the character of Scotchmen, who are always held to be so penurious.

O'Keefe.—Oh, you forget. These were Irishmen; but in both Scotch and Irish you will find the two extremes meeting; it is at least a wise thing for a people to be very careful of their goods when they have little, and both nations have had long struggles with poverty; this was especially felt when they came in contact with nations more advanced in the arts and accustomed to an entirely different style of life. The struggle is not over yet, and some of us have seen a good deal of it in our early life, and when we visited the Highlands. These Scots came as conquerors, and may have had the generous extreme dominant in their excited condition.

Margaet.—For my part, I do not care how much of the story is true. I like to hear the romance, and I like to see the spot where it is said to have happened, just as I should like to look at the summit of Olympus, where Jupiter may be supposed to have sat and judged. I expected to find some romantic places, and I also expected to hear some romantic stories, but I never expected to be ushered into the halls of romance at once on leaving the steamer, or made to picture the tents of the invaders and invaded as soon as we left the banks of the canal. The word "canal" itself is void of romance, and we think of boats drawn by horses, and carrying loads of coal and lime. The canal, as we have seen, leads us through a region of time and backwards in history, and we can scarcely believe our school books which say that time past never returns. For my part I almost begin to fear that we may not return to 1876, or it may be that when we return home, it will be 1976, and no one will know us. Such things are said to have happened in lands not so romantic as this seems.

O'Keefe.—Yes; but we shall at least be as young when we awake as in the century we left, like the seven sleepers, and not like the children of Lir.

Margaet.—Oh, tell us of the children of Lir.

Sheena.—Everybody knows of King Lear and his children from Shakespeare; don't let us have Shakespeare, we really have too much of him at home; we cannot live on honey alone or on beef alone.

O'Keefe.—The Lir of whom I speak was unknown to Shakespeare, and I see I must tell you the whole story to prove it. Lir was a chief among the Tuatha De Dananu in Ireland, and he married a ward of the king of that people, Bodhbh Dearg, and her name was Aobh (I think it is pronounced Aive, perhaps it is Eve), and she died and left four children, when Lir married her sister Aoife (very like Effie, and we may call her so). Now Aoife was very fond of the children until she found the father devoted excessively to them; when one day as she drove them out in her carriage, pretending to go to the king, who was also very fond of them, she tried to incite her attendants to kill them. However, they refused to kill the children, and it then came out what a mighty witch, or rather Druidess, this woman was, for she struck them with a Druidical wand and told them to turn into white swans, and set them afloat on Loch Derryvaragh, in Westmeath, beside which they were. Now, the eldest daughter, Fionnguala, or white bosom, remonstrated, because although she was a swan she had the use of her speech. However, Aoife was rigorous, and condemned them to live for 300 years on Loch Derryvaragh, and 300 years about the Mull of Cantire, and 300 years on the sea at Erris, on the north-west of Ireland, among Firbolgs. The father was enraged when he heard of this, and so was the king, their guardian, and they used to come down to the lake to feed the birds, and to talk to them. The stepmother was not allowed to escape, for the king was decided, and asked her what was the most disagreeable shape to be in, and she answered, " A demon of the air," and so the king used his Druid's wand, and a demon she was made for ever. One blessing the witch did leave them, that they were to keep their reason and not be distressed by being birds, if this was a blessing. But father and guardian died, and the poor swans were left for the rest of the 900 years flying about in all seasons. They used to chant plaintive music, "such as might delight the whole human race," and they could speak the Gaelic language; but they were forgotten not the less by the people. They were especially miserable before their feathers grew, and when sitting on the bare rocks with shoeless feet ; and they made sore complaints of living so long on the Mull amongst the dreadful storms. Sometimes, as at

Erris, a friend used to feed them; and there a young man, who was able afterwards to relate their adventures, found them hundreds of years after their transformation. When the long time was expired they went back to their ancient home, where they found only green raths, without roofs, with forests of nettles, and with no house or fire. They had a time of freedom to go about their old haunts and chant plaintive fairy music; but when St. Patrick came, one of his messengers found them on a little island. The bell, a symbol of Christian worship, was rung before them, and seems to have attracted them, and they came and accepted the Christian religion, worshipping on the altar tied together in pairs, with silver chains. The king of the time wanted to seize them, but their feathers came off, and they changed at once into shrivelled old bony people, who had no more than time to be baptized before they died.

Willie.—It was a dreadful place to live upon. Is not the Mull always stormy?

Cameron.—Very often; but I have slept on a smooth sea exactly opposite it several times, although when the great swells are blown in from the Atlantic upon it, one sees it must be wild, because all the soil is blown off, if ever there were any, and all the crumbling of the rocks that would make soil is removed, and there stand the awful effects of wind and rain playing their game for ages. Imagine how much water rolls up and down the Firth twice a day, filling and emptying, whilst a great deal of it comes by the Mull. But if you want to know about the character of the Mull, read "The Highland Drover"; it is only a little six-penny book, but he was a clever man who wrote it.

Loudoun.—And now I think you have had enough of nonsense. If I have come here to help you to spend a holiday, I have begun well by letting all the sense be driven out of your heads with idle stories, conveying little real truth, although I have watched for it. No hard study here, no wasting of your brains, Willie, by lessons. Perhaps in the morning you may come to your senses; you have a chance of the swan's experience, in the wind and rain which are no uncommon things here. They will help to bring you to a sound state of body and mind.

Cameron.—In this country we all go to bed early, and don't be surprised if you can go without candles at this time of the year. The sun is down, what a glory it has left! but that may not last many minutes, and we must wait till the end. One would think the sun lined all the hills of Morven; it brightens all the tops, and one cannot wonder if it fills all the valleys with fairy tales. Is it not like a land of ghosts? many a one has been seen there.

Loudoun.—If this is not a land of ghosts, I confess that is a sky of glory.

CHAPTER III.

EVONIUM.

"These are but dreams and wishes of our forefathers."

SHEENA.—Again we waken in Oban, the "little bay," a good name.

Cameron.—That definition is from *ob*, a bay, and *an*, a diminutive. Some of my friends object to this and call it the white bay. I cannot consider it white, although the derivation may be made to fit.

Sheena.—It is a sheltered spot, and no one need fear here if in any vessel, at least when there is a good anchor, for one may run aground of course. Oban, at least, is new enough. Imagine it early last century having only one house. One wonders why such a fit spot should be so long uninhabited.

Cameron.—You forget ; look at Dunolly, that old castle. It was destroyed by Selvach in 701, and built again by him after thirteen years. Do not suppose that one of the divisions of the Dalriad kingdom had no inhabitants but such as could live in that tower. When Loarn came over and gave his name to this district, he had to conquer his position as his brethren had to conquer theirs, and it is more than probable that he lived at a spot which had been inhabited by his opponents. Whether their bones were found under the castle, who can tell; but some one's were. We must imagine the little bay filled with **Loarn's** boats, and his people living along the shore, and the same state of things we may look on as continued far down to the times when the older system was broken up by the Norse, perhaps even when the Celtic power revived with the only semi-Norse Somerled and continued with the Macdougalls; but, at any rate, the followers of the Highland chiefs have left few of their dwellings, which we suppose, therefore, to have been slightly built.

Willie.—I should have thought that the chiefs would have lived at Dunstaffnage.

Loudoun.—Tradition and Boece have given much pro-minence to Dunstaffnage, but its origin is obscure.

Cameron.—To-day we are in a hurry to see one great object of our visit, and we shall take a boat and row to Loch Etive. The day being fine, we can at least see the lower part and entrance; some other day we shall see more. Four rowers are waiting for us at the quay, and we may walk down quietly through Oban, looking at its streets and new shops, perhaps seeing faces from home, since many strangers show themselves here, as in a moving panorama, for they are soon gone, leaving no marks.

Willie.—Well, here is something really new. They are actually digging pots out of the ground.

Loudoun.—True enough, Willie, and you are lucky to see one. I have known of thousands, but I never saw one actually emerging. This is an urn, and it is a very pretty one; Was there a cairn here?

Digger.—No, sir, no cairn that we know of, but there was, I dare say, a cairn once. We were digging a foundation for a house, and here we found a stone kist with this in it.

Cameron.—It's many a day since the man who buried that lived, and the man whose dust was in it. But here is Mr. Noble, and he's going to photograph it, so we shall see a good memorial of it when we return perhaps, and it will remain with Captain M'Dougall or Sir Dugald.[1]

Willie.—Did they burn the people here?

Loudoun.—Yes, the old Celts did, and the Romans sometimes did the same, you know, and you will see thousands of urns in Rome put up in places so like pigeon holes that they have got that name in Latin (columbaria).

Cameron.—But we must not stay here, because the boat is waiting, and it is eight o'clock, and the tide turns about nine.

Margaet.—What a beautiful morning. What a pity we cannot paint it and keep it to show.

Cameron.—Yes. Watch that land opposite, it is a long island called Kerrĕra. I hope you observe the pronunciation, and do not fancy it like Carrara, where the fine marble of Italy is quarried. We have no such lofty mountains as the Alps, or even the Apennines, and we have not the forests, but Kerrera is so romantic it requires no trees. The rocks jut up so wonderfully that they take the place of the forests, and the numerous glens are like glades among the woods.

Sheena.—It seems good enough land, why cannot they grow trees?

[1] Campbell of Dunstaffnage.

Cameron.—You will think differently in a while; if all the land were covered with trees how should we see the varied surface, the hills and dales and long grass; and where would the sheep live, and where would men get food? We like the rich sweet grass to look at; under the trees you see nothing; here we live in the weather, and the heaven is our ceiling.

Loudoun.—All very well to-day, but when the ceiling is a black cloud?

Cameron.—Then the grass is sweetened and fattened, and the green rejoices our hearts.

O'Keefe.—There are steamers taking people everywhere, and they are flying over the fine sea among the many islands, whilst we only crawl along the coast.

Margaet.—But how lovely, there are trees as fine as ours on the right, and a beautiful walk and rocks standing up quite straight. And a fine castle is Dunolly on the very edge of a rock; all this where a waste was expected.

Cameron.—Now I won't be a guide book, remember; because it is too systematic, and it will weary you and me, and I shall only tell you little incidents unless you ask questions.

Margaet.—Well, I shall ask a question: what is that pillar? is it built?

Cameron.—No, it is natural, and they connect it with the name of Bran, one of Fingal's dogs, and people say that on hunting days the dogs of the castle were tied there. But that is a fancy; it is far too big to tie dogs to. Finn and his dogs have each been made gigantic, but it is the fate of strong creatures. Bran was the most talented of the dogs.

Loudoun.—The rock is evidently a remnant of the ocean

border; when the sea washed higher up it broke down the rocks, and this would have been broken down too had the whole land not risen up, and so left this mark as a piece of history, the date of which is not found yet. It is an ornament to a fine shore, and had we been in a steamer we should have passed it without time to observe it.

Sheena.—And now I want to know why they built the castle so high.

Cameron—In rough times the great went high for shelter and the poor clung around for the same, and that you find over all the world.

Loudoun.—Before we pass we must remember the little trace of fact. The castle was built in the eighth century by the Lorn leader, Selvach.

Cameron.—Well, if you will, I believe it was only a small castle attached to Dunstaffnage where the kings lived, and this was the Dun or castle of the Oileamh, Ollamh, physician or learned man.

O'Keefe.—I don't think Dunstaffnage was ever so great as to have an official or lawyer so important. More likely it was the Dun of Olave which is a well known Scandinavian name, and we know that these people had great power in the west and were long in fact the rulers.

But some say that the name of this castle is from *aille,* a precipice—the Dun of the precipice. P. W. Joyce says that *aille* takes the form *oil,* and I think this the most probable derivation.

Loudoun.—That sounds well; look into your own annals and you will see that Norsemen did not come till the ninth century. A cave with stalactites was found under the castle.

In this was a number of burials and coins, but although proving it not to be excessively old, we must believe the annals of Tighearnach of your own country, and that it was indeed the place of the rulers of Lorn. Somerled may have lived in it, and the Macdougalls also, for centuries; they are said to be descended from him, and they live still just below in a modern house.

After all it was a foolish thing of these old Highlanders not to have written more; you Irish have beaten them thoroughly, and most of our information is got from your books. Surely we cannot blame the Norse for all the loss of literature, when they have kept so much of their own. If the people here ever had writings they were probably good at their destruction, and by that means they have brought the age of romance nearer to us. Romance belongs to the days of ignorance and uncertainty.

Margaet.—We must receive that cautiously even from you, and my authority is Tennyson, who speaks of "the fairy tales of science and the long results of time."

Loudoun.—I am corrected; I meant the romance of our Romantic ages so called. After a time however every great historic age becomes romantic, and to one who looks widely on history and on the present there is a romance over all time and space.

O'Keefe.—And now that we are past Dunolly, let us look forward, there is an island in the way.

John, a rower.—That is Ellen's Isle.

Margaet.—And who was Ellen?

Cameron.—That question is often asked! There was no Ellen, however, I may tell you. The Gaelic for an island is Eilean, and that is easily turned into Ellen. This is also called the Maiden isle, perhaps by some similar misapprehension. But now look at the view. There is Mull,—and Morven and Appin and Cruachan; if you are not satisfied with this I shall be disappointed, and perhaps return. Still, I will give you another chance, as we do not see so well from a small boat. Macculloch, who was no sentimentalist, was roused to admire the beauty of the view from that small tower on the left. It is on the point of Ardnamuic.

Margaet.—My book spells it Ardnamucknish.

Cameron.—That is very long, and the writer ought to know better. It is a doubled name, *Ard* is point or promontory, and so is *nish* or ness; evidently it was called Ardnamuck by the Gaelic people before the Norse came; it meant the promontory of the swine or boar, and when the Norse came they called it the *promontory of the boar point*, simply because they did not know the meaning of the words. That is a common occurrence in naming places, and it is a good proof of great antiquity. Now remember that when I speak of wild boars.

Loudoun.—This bay is a fine one with that point on the left, and the old castle on the right, and Cruachan before us. Is it not Lochnell Bay?

Cameron.—By no means; and it is annoying to see the names of places changed. Lochnell is fresh water, six miles south of this, but the estate is called after it, and the proprietor built his house on this bay.

Loudoun.—I intended to take you to Loch Etive above the falls first, but as we go close by Dunstaffnage — a name much better known—we may as well land there for a little. There is a fine sheltered bay when we get round these rocky islands. The castle itself is on a rock, a square enclosure. One wonders at the smallness of these ancient castles or palaces. Nowadays we require so much more room.

Cameron.—True, but this is larger than you would suppose. You will find the wall quite broad enough for a good walk. If you go into the court below, you find a comparatively modern house built on one side of it found to be large enough for the abode of the baronets of Dunstaffnage. It resembles the later buildings of Scotland before 1745, when lofty houses were not used as in Edinburgh, but very small solid stone ones.

Willie. — Is not this castle the very first that our early kings inhabited, and the spot where the sacred stone was kept, which is now in the Coronation Chair at Westminster Abbey?

Loudoun.—This can scarcely be the case; at least we recognized Dunmonaidh in Dun Add, and we looked on that as being the seat of the chief king of the Dalriads, so we must seek another history for this.

O'Keefe.—This has always been considered the great deposit of the stone that came from Tara, the Lia Fail, the stone of destiny. That certainly was a wonderful stone; it sounded when the true king stood upon it. It came from Egypt, having been brought by Pharaoh's daughter Scota.

Cameron.—I think your fairy tales are quite as true as all that. Surely we know that the Tuatha De Danaan came from Scandinavia or Lochlan, and brought a wonderful sword, a wonderful spear, a wonderful cauldron, and this wonderful stone to Scotland. They afterwards took it to Ireland, and we know how it returned. Wherever the stone is found a sovereign of Scotland reigns, as witness now the Queen, who reigns by virtue of even the small amount of Scottish blood in her veins.

Willie.—I thought the stone was used by Jacob for a pillow on the memorable night when he saw the angels ascending and descending.

O'Keefe.—Yes, and afterwards it was the judgment seat used by Gathelus in the time of Moses, and after many adventures it was taken to Spain by Gathelus, who was a Greek, and who married Pharaoh's daughter, one of the Egyptians who was not drowned in the Red Sea. Simon Brec, his descendant, took it out of the sea when the chair—for it was then a chair of marble—stuck to his anchor. I have read all this I know, and it was called the anchor of life. Ferchar took it to Ireland, and Fergus took it to Scotland in the fifth century. This seems plain enough.

Loudoun.—So are fairy tales, and not so contradictory. Will you believe me when I tell you that it is all false, and Mr. Skene, than whom I know no better authority, only believes that a stone was found at Scone and was taken from it in 1296 by Edward 1st, and is in Westminster Abbey now. The stone is old, and it was customary for the Celtic races to be crowned on a stone, and there was one at Tara. Some people say that it is there yet, but that which I saw there is not such a thing as any one would sit or stand upon in its present position, or with its present shape. The Westminster stone seems

to have been used by the Pictish kings from time imme-
morial at Scone, their capital—at any rate it was their capital
in 710, when Nectan expelled the Columban clergy, accepted
the forms of the Italian church, and promulgated them from
the Moat Hill.[1] The stone is broken from the red sand-
stone of that district of Scotland, according to Professor
Ramsay. I like to think of it as having belonged to the
old Pictish kings, perhaps also true Caledonians.[2]

You forgot to mention another story that it came from
Iona, where St._ Columba used it as a pillow. But it is
not a stone of that island: the Iona stone is probably there
still, and is supposed to have been found only last year
by digging. I believe in wonders, because nature and history
give us plenty, but let us have true wonders if we must
have them. After all you never mentioned to what place
the stone first went from Ireland; some say it was to a
place called Beregonium, which others have fancied to be
Dunstaffnage, also a mistake.

O'Keefe.—And by what right do you destroy all our
stories?

Loudoun.—I know little myself on this point, but I follow
Skene, because I think he has proved his points. If I follow
our latest authorities, it is because our early ones, like your
own, invented so much; although we had fewer than you
in Ireland, probably because fewer of us could write.

Margaet.—You must not leave us in this confused state
with all these contradictory tales in our ears. I want to
know the exact case as it now stands. I understand you

---

[1] See Skene's *Celtic Scotland*, vol. I., p. 278.
[2] See the volume on the subject by Mr. W. F. Skene.

to mean that the history of the stone does not go farther back than its appearance at Scone, and that it has been taken from the rocks there. As if to increase the difficulty, you have introduced a new name — Beregonium, and I should be glad to hear its connection with our object. Willie seems to have read a good deal about it, and I should like him to give us what he knows. It will at least be the learning of the schools as he is fresh from one.

Willie begins.—As I knew that I was to be brought here this summer on a holiday, and as I was obliged to write a historical essay at school I thought it better to choose this spot, and I was glad because I found it remarkably easy to arrive at the material. There seems to be no historian on the subject, except Hector Boece of Aberdeen, and his translator into the Scottish tongue, John Bellenden. It was also translated from "Scottish" into English, instead of taking it from the "Latin copie which is far more large and copious." Now tourists are an impatient race, and I do not think you would listen to the long account of kings who lived near here. In my essay I shortened the account, I assure you, as much as I dared, and I feel it needful to make it still shorter, knowing how few care for these themes.

We are now in the region that first gave kings to Scotland, in a land where kings reigned in great splendour, when England was barbarous and unknown even to the Romans; a land which had its men of learning, its Druids, its physicians, and its poets, where now there are only ruins and heather; a land to which ambassadors came from Spain before the Christian era. The Picts and Scots, as well as Britons of the southern part of Scotland, quarrelled,

and the Scots sent for aid to their brethren in Ireland, and
Fergus, the son of an Irish king, came over in the year
327 before Christ, and was crowned king, being the first
Scot that ruled in Albion. He made a treaty with the Picts
because the women were powerful enough to demand, with
success, a peace; but Coile, the king of the Britons, attacked
them both, and they met on the river Doon in Ayrshire,
where King Coile was defeated and slain. His tomb is to
be seen at this day, and the land Coilsfield is called after
his name, and the district of Ayrshire also now called Kyle.
Now, Fergus built a great castle in Argyleshire, and I
believe it is only a few miles from us : it was called Beregonium, and in this he reigned. Boece says that it was in
Lochquaber, which is a good deal north, and in which Fort-
William is; but whether it extended so far as this spot, on
which we now are, at any time, I can only take the opinion
of my authorities for concluding. Fergus was drowned in
going to Ireland, and Feritharis, the brother, was made
King. He had a reign of peace, he was wise and great, since
even Charlemagne made a treaty with him. You may
stumble as I do at this chronology, but you may call this
a quotation and wait for the reply at any rate. Mainus
succeeded him. Besides wise laws he made temples of
rings of stone, with one stone at the south greater than the
others, and on these sacrifice was made to the Gods. He
appointed also livings for the priests, and died after reigning
29 years. Dornadille, his successor, made the first hunting
laws.

It would be long to tell you of the attacks of the
Britons, and how they were overcome by a union of the

Picts and Scots under King Reuther, who then came back
and lived at Beregonium, where he died in peace, after
having introduced into Albion many of the arts and
sciences before unknown there.

Ewin was also a wise king, and he lived after his necessary wars quietly in Beregonium, but he preferred the site
of Dunstaffnage, and he there built a castle, calling it after
his own name—Evonium. It is also said that he was
crowned sitting on the marble chair that came from Ireland.

Afterwards many kings lived in Dunstaffnage, until the
capital was transferred to Scone. I might keep you longer,
but I think I have given you a good specimen of one of
our earliest historians existing; he said he obtained the
material from other still earlier writers.

Loudoun.—Now, Willie, I am so far pleased that, you
have given us in few words a specimen, although of course
quite a schoolboy's one, of Boece's early Scottish history, but
do not wonder when I tell you that none of these kings
ever lived. Probably no kings of the name, not even petty
chiefs, have existed, nor could any of the events have
happened in your chronology, which ends about the time
of Julius Cæsar. We may banish it; still some of the events
may have occurred centuries after. However, Beregonium
is a mistake, and Evonium is not known to us, and
Dunstaffnage was not the seat of the kings, and the stone
of destiny was never in Dunstaffnage, neither was it ever a
marble chair—that I told you of already. Where the in-
ventions were made no one can tell. But remember that
the main object of this journey is to see the place called by

some Beregonium, and we must go there and discuss all the themes, this of yours coming up again, of course, among the rest.

Margaet.—I confess it interests me to hear these things. I rejoice to live on a spot which so many generations of men have peopled in their own minds with great kings. It has been no dead place, but one fertile at least in im- aginings, and it has borne many heroes for some centuries at least. I remember when walking about the Palatine Hill in Rome, to have come upon an opening in the rock which attracted the attention of myself and friends. There was no name, no mark to teach us what it was. It re- ceived a careful examination, and then we learnt that it was called the cave in which the wolf lived that suckled Romulus and Remus, and was therefore their first home. Now, you may call that nonsense. I do not know how much is nonsense, but I say that a place supposed to be sacred by a great people for more than two millenaries is one crowded about with so many memories that it be- comes sacred, if only by the amount of human faith, interest, and reverence devoted to it. This reasoning would be enough to make Loch Etive interesting.

Cameron.—You are right, but it needs none. Look at that mountain, and the deep cuts along the side, each, we know, a clear, bright stream or a wide loch ; look at the beautiful woods towards the base, the endless dells and crags that one sees, indicated by slight shadows every- where on the rocks and on the rising heath opposite, and you see yourselves in a land of romance at once. This scene produces imaginary incidents ; valleys are places out

of which people come, and if there are no people we must
suppose their substitute ; and if they came out they must
go in again, and we thus in our fancy pursue them home.
It is an unavoidable act of the mind, and this for these
reasons has been, and ever will be, a land of imagination
and romance.

Loudoun.—True ; but Hector Boece, or rather the people
he followed, had no right to put romance for history. The
place he is said to have called Beregonium is over this
bay ; you can see from this spot a green mound, to the
left of the point of that long hill of Ledaig. I want to
impress you with its situation. It is said that Ewin called
this Evonium ; but the origin of the word may have been
Dun Monaidh or Mhonaidh (*mh* is pronounced *v*), which
place we have looked at as Dun Add. Dunstaffnage is said
by Boece to be called after St. Stephen. It has been
remarked that this saint is not much honoured in Scotland,
and the favourite derivation of the word here is *Dun
agus da innis*, pronounced Dun's da nish, meaning the Dun
and the two islands. It might be called so very properly.
Still one fears the slippery character of Celtic etymology.

O'Keefe.—This affords a fine view, of sea, of island, and
of hills, up towards Fortwilliam and to Morven. It was a
fine place of shelter from English and Scottish power in
early days, a safe station, but not a good position from
which to conquer Scotland. A direct road never existed
till of late, unless it were a road for a few mountaineers.
One sees why the Dalriads kept their centre at Dun Add.
It is probable that the road was over the **Druim Albin**,
which, although, as the meaning shows, a great region of

hills, was practical for armies at Tyndrum. This place was naturally shut out a good deal from Scottish mainland influence, and became more directly connected with the lordship of the Isles under Somerled, whilst Dun Add became secondary and decayed.

Cameron.—It is a pleasant place, and one rambles among these rocks, and finds woods and morasses and fine little bays with shells, and an old church and many recent head-stones, which show that a spot is still used as a sacred burial ground.

As we are here, I may as well tell you of the piece of carved ivory that was found, representing a king sitting in a chair, and it has even been supposed that it was intended as a representation of the fabulous marble chair and the stone of destiny, and so forth. It is in the possession of Sir Donald Campbell of Dunstaffnage, but we do not require to seek far for its meaning. Chess was a very old and favourite game, and a chessman it evidently was ; who carved it we cannot tell.

Loudoun.—I fear you will find that carved chessman very like the Norwegian ones. Some have imagined for it a very great age.

The day is fine, and we have made this only a short excursion ; but as to-morrow we may have a long way to run, we shall leave the boat here and walk, returning here in the morning by the coach.

Cameron.—Unless at high water, we cannot pass Connel, so it will be safer to take the boat whenever the tide is up, and leave it at Ach a Lieven (Leamhan.)

Ian (a boatman).—The tide is up at about nine in the morning, and we can easily pass the boat over then, and either take you in here when the coach arrives, or at Ach a Leamhan.

Cameron.—Good ; then meet us in the morning, and now we can have a quiet walk to Oban.

> " Few here the smooth and rounded rocks,
> These made by nature in her dreams,
> Still bear the marks of sudden shocks,
> And deeply cutting ice-bound streams."

MARGAET.—Now we are at Connel, but there are no falls.

Cameron.—No ; the tide is high and the water is smooth. Connel falls are strange : sometimes the water falls this way, and sometimes that ; sometimes the water here is smooth as at present, sometimes it is a roaring fall of several feet, with a swirling rapid of several hundred yards, and people half a mile off are wakened in the night by the noise. At the south side there is a deep place where vessels can pass at high water.

Margaet.—I see the reason ; there is a bank of rocks nearly across the narrow part of the loch, and the tide makes the fall as it flows out and in.

Cameron.—We often pass smoothly. Many a time have I crossed the loch both above and below with anxiety. The rocks at this gorge narrow the loch so much that here it is only about 150 yards broad, although it is 1500, or nearly a mile, up at Kilmaronaig, and as it is 22 miles long, there is a great deal of water to pass so frequently. The passage between these rounded rocks has probably been made when the sea-beach was lower. The heights correspond.

Cameron.—Many a fine rock cod have I caught beside these shores, and they made many a good breakfast in Lochanabeich. Let us go up the bank. This old sea-beach has been made into rabbit warrens where it is steep, and into cornfields where the slope is gradual. The whole of the plain here is composed of debris, chiefly rolled boulders, not very large, and it seems to have been flattened like a sea-bottom. It is now nearly all covered with moss, and it lies almost a waste, with a few cottages at its skirts. These cottages have only lately been built along the road ; they were put up by General Campbell of Lochnell some forty years ago or so, that he might always have people to help him with his carriage across the ferry at Connel below the falls. Now so many people come with cattle and carts that men are always kept ready ; but the cottages are pleasant companions of the district, and contain cheerful faces to meet us on the road. This heath is wild. Professor Daniel Wilson in his *Prehistoric Annals of Scotland* calls it " The Black Moss." It is no blacker than others, but uncomely places have often more abundant honour, and some have called this the heath of Lora, and Connel the falls of Lora. I who agree to this may explain to you that Lora means a noisy stream, and I may remind you of that beautiful beginning of Cath Lodin (or Loda), generally put the first of Ossian's poems—

"Oh ! thou traveller unseen, thou bender of the thistle of Lora."

That is the travelling breeze, the light wind that shows itself to exist only by the result of its efforts. The very breeze is made into a mysterious agent, and takes its place among the spirits of the hill. And there before you is the thistle of Lora, gracefully bending before the unseen power.

Loudoun.—After all, the moving air, or wind, gave the original idea of spirit, gas, and even ghost.

Margaet.—Don't be sure, it is only one of the unseen things, and the grossest are most frequently alluded to, and are assumed to be the fundamental.

Loudoun.—However that may be, there has been an unseen agency here at work, putting that strange little lake in this beach of boulders. By what power was it made so steep? I have tried to find a cause, but have heard of only one efficient. Some suppose it to have been the lower part of a whirlpool, where a great motion whirled out the boulders, but the water would require to be deeper than it seems to have been here at the time when the former beach was used. Others have supposed a glacier to have lain here, and prevented the water from filling the space with boulders or gravel as you see it.

Cameron.—There is a hollow at Achnaba quite round, and one of the shape of a cow, *i.e.* such as it makes in lying down. I can give you the notion among the people, *i.e.* the fairy tale. It is that the cow belonged to Cailleach Bheir, and

the round form was the cheese mould which she used. A
great cow that was, certainly, more than an acre in size, and
the cheese mould is very deep, with trees at the bottom
scarcely reaching the top.

Willie.—If the cow were so large, how large was the
person who kept it?

Cameron.—Cailleach Bheir means simply, old woman called
Bera, or Bere. The Gaelic aspirates its words, as Beir into
Bheir, and has an inconvenient way of making cases.

Cailleach may mean also *witch.* You must learn a few
Gaelic words. They say that Bera could walk over the
loch in two or three steps; it is a very narrow part which
is only a quarter of a mile wide, and you know it is very
deep.

You need not dispute about the size, you may go and
measure her head, which is turned into stone on the top
of the rugged rocks that form the south-westerly side of
the Awe. There she is, looking quite like an old woman,
some think. Great ideas come down for children to play
with. Beither or Beir is put down as lightning or as thunder
with which great rains come, a spirit of lightning or storms
residing on the hills. The old lady had charge of a
fountain on Ben Cruachan, on which at the going down
of the sun she was obliged to put the lid; but she was
tired one day feeding the flocks and fell asleep, so that
when she wakened, the fountain had overflowed and covered
the plain, drowning man and beast. The place is now
covered by Loch Awe, and the old woman was turned to
stone. The name haunts the tops of hills, the region of
storms. The ancient works of nature have been made into

toys: in this case we have the personification Bera, the daughter of Griannan, which may be a sunny hill from which streams come and on which lightning often plays. I do not know that she was always old, but Cailleach means also a woman of olden times; she must have been active, feeding her sheep on such a mighty scale. 'When that great flood came it broke through the rocks and made the pass of Awe, and it is believed that at one time the Awe emptied itself to the south, so that it would escape at Crinan. It is something of a geological myth, a broken-down theory, perhaps, of ancient geographers.

Loudoun.—The name is found also on the hills between Strathlachlan and Glendaruel,[1] and Bera is said also to have made Loch Eck in Cowal above Holy Loch. Colonel Leslie draws attention to the connection of the word Bera (or, as aspirated, Vera) with the Hindu Vrita. " Indra strikes the earth, shaking Vrita with his rain-causing hundred-spiked Vagra thunderbolt." Certainly both Vrita and Vagra could run into a Gaelic Beir or Veir easily, and the resemblance of the qualities of the Hindu and the old Celtic goddess is interesting. Beir also appears in Ireland.

You can scarcely wonder at the people here attending to mountains, and I wonder rather that we have not more stories. Look now at Cruachan Ben; five minutes ago its summit was clear, now there is a streamer from it and it is actually stretching out before our eyes. It moves onwards; I should think, judging from the land over which it lies, that it must at least be a mile long: it has been formed in ten minutes, and is growing.

[1] Colonel Forbes Leslie's *Early Races of Scotland*, p. 142.

It has ceased. This is interesting; I have never seen one form so rapidly. Now it is actually diminishing, and now after ten minutes more the hill is clear again. No wonder with these sudden changes, Bheir, Vear or Bera, was taken unawares, and the terrible rush of waters followed, and prevented her ever after using her shepherd's crook on the sides of the Cruachan. However, the petrifying is only one part of the tale. She lived as a power long after, and of course such a power never dies.

Willie.—But why did that cloud form?

Loudoun.—That is explainable by a little change of wind bringing a current of very moist air from the sea and cooling it on the peak. We also bring in invisible agents for our theories, but ours are impersonal. I have seen a streamer from a rock floating for ten miles, so far as I could judge, and growing into a mighty cloud, looking at a distance like a great roof supported by pillars of the height of 1,200 feet.

But cold is not the only cause of rain; the vapour comes from the sea chiefly to this place, and the reason of its deposit is not always clear. However, it deposits most where there are mountains. You see that strikingly if you look at a rain-map. Forests also do their part.

O'Keefe.—But we must really move. I should like to have a boat, and fish on this little loch—*Lochanabeich*, the loch of birches.

Cameron.—You would not like it long; the fish are coarse.

O'Keefe.—But I would fish it out, and finer would perhaps grow; they live too long here undisturbed.

Cameron.—We shall walk onwards, and I will introduce you to your first specimen here of prehistoric antiquity. I do not use the word exactly, because, after all, Dunstaffnage may be older than that which we are going to ; but Dunstaffnage belongs to a historic age, and this cairn belongs to a class that is chiefly prehistoric, although I dare say it may have been formed in later times.

Margaet.—It is very difficult to walk over the heather.

Cameron.—Yes ; but we don't go far. You see that gray pile of stones standing solitary in the moss : it is the *carn a' Bharan* (the cairn of the Baron). It is a melancholy object and takes away from the bright natural scenery, but it is a powerful proof to us that men who revered others have lived here. You will observe that it is built on the solid ground, and the peat has grown above the foundation and nearly to the summit of the cairn.

Loudoun.—Do you not think that the stones have caused good drainage here, and destroyed the life of the mosses, so that they decayed and have been washed away ?

Cameron.—There is a certain distance, however, between the cairn and the peat all around, and it looks much as if a place had been dug out of the peat in order to make the cairn. They would never put such a heavy mass on a soft peat.

Loudoun.—But if they had dug, they must have heaped the matter up somewhere, and I do not see it.

Cameron.—This loose matter might have been levelled down in time by the abundance of rain, as the quantity is not very great, and the peat is not above three feet deep here.

But in any case I will show you a new proof that peat was here during the baron's lifetime, if there was a baron, which we may first consider. I cannot tell whether he is a true tradition or a fancy. The name is not common, and I am

disposed to look upon it as correct.   I see no use in decrying
what is probable enough, so I will suppose that the baron
died about here—perhaps was killed and buried in an unusual
place, or we may suppose that this is a simple cenotaph—a
small memorial of a respected man or memorable event.
Barons are not ancient Celtic chiefs, and I suppose him to
have been the bailie of some baron of northern origin; and
here he lived or held his court, or tried to do so.   Let us look
at the court.   We need not go far.   It is a circular enclosure
made by a peat mound or wall, and a ditch outside.   It was
the custom to dispense law if not justice in circular places
among the Norsemen, and Tynwalds are in abundance in
that people's land.   We have no proof that there was
a dwelling here, but there may have been.   In Dr. Wilson's *Prehistoric Scotland* we are told of an ancient hearth
where food was cooked on the ground, and over which six
feet of peat have now grown on this very heath.   Such may
have been old Celtic or pre-Celtic for all I know, but could
have no reference to our baron, who lived, judging from the
size of the mound and the ditch, at the time when the
peat existed, if not so deep as at present.   I do not know
of many such rings as these in the country, but there is
another, a little one, over at the farm of Ledaig, and not far
to the north of the house ; we shall see it when going to
Keills from Connel ferry, about half-way onwards.

O'Keefe.—The circle here is large, and it reminds me of a
"rath," of which there are thousands in Ireland.   They call
them the residences of chiefs, but I think they often corres-
ponded to good farm-houses, having room enough for a garden
and yard for cattle.   This spot is said never to have changed in

To face page 58.

The Baron's Cairn.

the memory of man, but we see that the road from the loch, or at least the ground to the loch, is rather bare of peat, and may have in part been good pasture land not many generations ago. Indeed I am told of a family having lived on it not forty years ago in a small cottage, and I see clearly that the moss differs very much in thickness. I am used to bogs, and think this not an important or great one, and it need not be very old.

Cameron.—It may be so, but I am glad you have seen this circle, as I have not seen this or any of the kind mentioned in the Statistical Account or elsewhere; and as to the Norse having been here, they were not in great force. Somerled was more Norse than Celtic in birth, but scarcely in acts.

Now let us lunch. Sit on the grass in the court of the baron, and refresh yourselves. The men have brought good food from Oban; and see! there is milk from Lochanabeich. Milk! I ought to say cream. In your great towns you have water in the milk; here we have the other extreme—it is cream to begin with.

Willie.—But what is a cairn?

Cameron.—A cairn, or Gaelic *carn*, is a heap of stones; it is applied even to a stony hill, but it is chiefly used for a burial-place, upon which stones were thrown in great numbers. The honour intended to the deceased did not show itself by fine art but by magnitude.

Loudoun.—Still it is interesting to see how art grew. We find some cairns with a row of standing stones about them, others with two rows, some with a deep trench besides. Then we find some with the bones unprotected, others with a stone box made of small boulders; a better art rises to use long stones forming the sides, bottom, and top. Gradually we rise until these become of gigantic dimensions, and the internal space is not merely the size of a body but a chamber; then two or more chambers are united. All these conditions you will see more or less developed on this heath, and I hope you will enjoy this introduction to the times of old.

Margaet.—You have given a very short history of cairns. You might have told us more, and spoken of such chambers being luxuriously decorated, of the dead laid on splendid sofas, with costly clothing and golden decorations, and of their attendants around them scarcely less magnificently attired. But for these you must go to Tuscany and Magna Græcia.

Cameron.—Even here, and especially in Ireland, gold in abundance is found, or has been found, in the ancient Celtic tombs.

Loudoun.—Yes ; and we read of Charlemagne's tomb being opened at Aachen, and the old king found sitting on his throne as if preserving all his glory. That was a true burial of prehistoric ages, urging itself into Christian times. It is not easy to decide on dates from style alone, but it is a powerful aid, because in old times people knew less of foreign habits, and styles were not so mixed as now.

Willie.—If this is really a land of myths and cairns and spirits, and this wild heath produces only the results of their movements, there must be many ghost stories here. Tell us some.

Loudoun.—I think we have had very little else, or at least stories with little reality in them.

Cameron.—Well, I can tell you one. You have often

heard of people who have lived with the fairies. Look over at that white house under the hill; in that house lives a woman whose uncle or grand-uncle, I cannot say which, was for a time among the green people. You see the rocks so precipitous on the side towards Ledaig and behind the house. It was a pleasant day when the man went out to his work, which was near the rock, and he perhaps went beyond it farther than needful, looking for nuts, when he saw an opening in the rock quite near to him. He went in and was welcomed by the little folks, who amused him exceedingly. He had a few dances, stayed a few hours, but when he came out the people were all twenty years older and scarcely knew him; he was very much inclined to go back, and did try, but neither he nor any one else has found the door again. I daresay you never before saw the spot where such a thing happened, although you may have heard such a story. Walk over the moor to the rocks straight opposite Lochanabeich, and you will come to the place of the occurrence, as the tale was told.

Margaet.—Then that is a kind of enchanted hill. The heath is enchanted, and the only visible remains of the greatness that went before us are wild and mysterious. But who knew the man? Did you?

Cameron.—No, I did not know him; but I knew some one who knew the one who knew him; at least she said so.

Willie.—How long ago?

Cameron.—About thirty years.

Willie.—But tell us something quite new, and something seen by people whom you know well.

Cameron.—Of course I can tell you about the Brunie of Dunstaffnage, or of a farm near it, which struck a man in the face in the dark, one evening, for speaking evil of it. And, indeed, I think it did right, because Brunies hurt no one, but do all the work of the house in the night, and happy is the house that has one. They require, too, but small wages, little food, and no accommodation. What do you think of the origin of such a tale?

Loudoun.—I think it is clear. It is in the soul of man, who seeks to be relieved of his great troubles, and paints to himself days without sorrow and creatures that can labour without pain. There are many who require Brunies to work for them, and who would then be comparatively happy, although unfortunately there are others who earn wages too readily, and are degraded by want of absorbing labour.

Willie.—But you have not told us enough. Do you know any one here who ever saw any of these sights?

Cameron.—Oh yes; I know a farmer, whose house I can show you some day; it is not far off. He was coming home very late; it was dark, and he had far to go; and some one came by his side and walked all the way with him from Connel ferry. It was not a human being, and would not speak, but whatever it was it left him at his own gate very sore afraid. Now, you want to know what this was; I cannot tell you, but I may tell you that the man had been at the market.

Willie.—But this is not ghostly enough; you do not tell us what the follower was.

Loudoun.—Well, I can tell you another. It was told

me by a very great man, and the house was over the loch there. A man had gone into a barn, and in it he saw an immense number of deadly serpents. He was quite persuaded that if he let any out, the whole population would be destroyed, and he made a great noise. His friends outside wanted him to open the door, but he would not, because he said they would all be killed; better for him alone to be killed. He, you see, was a brave and unselfish man; and he was saved, but I could not tell how.

Willie.—This is also an unsatisfactory story, and I do not like it.

Loudoun.—Most of the stories are, but I cannot explain them so easily as that. I believe that last man had also been at the fair.

Willie.—Are the people very drunken then?

Cameron.—No, I do not think so. Most of the people keep no spirits in their house, and taste none except when they go to the market, and then sometimes they rejoice too much with their friends. They do not drink above a very small portion of the amount drunk by many sober men in our towns, *i.e.*, men who never were drunk, and would be horrified at the imputation. They do not even drink so much alcohol as some ladies do who will tell you that they only take a little at dinner, but do so daily. Would you like to see some of the people?

Loudoun.—Yes; we may walk to the cottages.

Cameron.—This is often called Connel moss; it is also called Ledaig moss, because that farm is Ledaig; but many names for one spot are confusing. The people here are uncertain on that point, but not so uncertain as in a town, where I have known people call the stream passing through the centre, *the river* and *the old river*, and knew no other name, as if one should call his father *the man.*

And now, here is the first cottage quite near ; it is higher than the others. The builder has evidently made an advance, and he has put slates on it, leaving the old ways. I can tell you something interesting about that. The owner of that house built it himself, not only with his own money, but his own hands. I saw him one summer after his usual daily work bringing these big stones, and putting them on in the way you see them. He was no mason, but he had sense. I saw him next summer, and he was doing the same. I think on the third summer he had got beams from the landlord for a roof, and now he has a pleasant house and a garden, and a field of oats with one of potatoes ; and I daresay he looks on it with pride, and looks out on the loch with pleasure, and over the loch to the moorland, where he sees Dee Choimhead, which will always remind him to ask a blessing on his labours while it stands there, as it is continually saying " God bless "[1] according to one explanation.

Margaet.—Innovations are appearing, and here is the telegraphic cable emerging from the loch. We may ask one of the owners of the croft a few questions.

Cameron.—Well, I will introduce you. But this house is too dirty for any one to enter; let us call the owner out. How are you, Mr. B. ?

Mr. B.—And how are you, yourself ? It is long since I

---

[1] See under Glen Lonan.

did not see you. I am afraid you would scarcely like my house, so I need not ask you to come in.

Cameron.—I believe you are getting a new one.

Mr. B.—Yes, this is old, but I do not object to our style of house—the old Highland one; it is very suitable to us, and we are only glad when we are allowed to stay.

Cameron.—Surely no one wishes to turn you out.

Mr. B.—No; but many a good man has been turned from home to my knowing, and now good men are wanted back. Who cares for the land like him who has grown out of it?

Loudoun.—But you old Highlanders never made much of it.

Mr. B.—We kept more people on it than your system does, and the men loved their country more, and had more character in old-times. But I am not complaining. I have been favoured, and my house is perhaps better than my father's was. I think after all we were too idle in old times, but now we have too little vitality—at least, there is no excess, we spend it all in work, and I doubt if in old times we did not live better when we spent more in pure rejoicing as the fools do.

Cameron.—These are hard questions.

Mr. B.—I know they are hard, but if you had seen the glen I came from in early days, with a score or more houses and good strong men and fine hearty honest women in them, you would be sad enough if you went up that glen now, and, excepting the big farmhouse and one or two shepherds' houses belonging to it, saw only one cottage and an old woman in it nearly ninety years old—the only one of all that grand company. The houses are small and there is not much in them ; but, do you think that

the men in great houses are really better? I think they
see more and know more, but they don't enjoy what they
have.   My son's children came to see me from Glasgow,
and they are very sharp lads, but they think a great deal
of themselves, and they are always wanting something.
Still, they know more and can do more—that is true—
than we who have always stayed in our glens, and if the
world needs such people it must educate them so.   It
may be good for the country, but these poor lads are not
happier than I was, although as poor as a bee among the
heather.

Cameron.—It is not easy to contradict you, and you have
given us all something to consider.   Good bye!

Now you have seen a cottar.   He is not learned, he is
not read, but he is a gentleman in the sense of refinement
of feeling and manner, and if he behaved thus in any
society in the kingdom he would be accepted, supposing
he had wealth or anything external to give him a position.
There you have the true Gael.

Margaet.—Is it true that you have here the character of
the Gael?   Have we not accounts of the Highlander as very
savage in old times, and even from late times as told of
by Sir Walter Scott, do we not see traits of their ferocity?

Cameron.—Everything about the character of the Gael
found in history can be contradicted by history.   The
"wild Irish" is a common expression, the ferocity of
Highlanders is not unknown, and it has been an opinion
that the courtliness which we now see must have come
from the Norse—but this is not clear.   We have the same
courtliness brought out with richer surroundings, and with

careful development, in France, it is true, where there is (in the North especially), both Celt and Norman; but we have it not in Germany, scarcely in Scandinavia, so far as I know. Old poems certainly give it to the Gael of Ireland and Scotland in great fullness. Nothing can prove this more than the account of Finn, in the book of the Dean of Lismore, but you may say that the MS. is only three hundred and fifty years old, when the songs were caught dying out. Still we must consider that the poem was old then.

> " Poet and chief,
> Braver than kings,—
> Generous, just,
> Despised a lie,
> Of vigorous deeds,
> First in song,
> A righteous judge,
> Polished his mien,
> Who knew but victory,—
> All men's trust,
> Of noble mind,
> Of ready deeds,
> To women mild,—
> Good man was Finn,
> Good man was he ;
> No gifts ever given
> Like his so free."

There is more worth reading. I do not know that any man so refined lived in the days of Finn, but this is at least a very early Celtic idea agreeing with others still earlier.

Loudoun.—On the other hand, are not the Celtic annals dreadful records of blood. I do not say that the two cannot be reconciled. War and killing were the enjoyment of the most refined knights of romance, and I suppose this was the idea of those who lived in reality.

Cameron.—Now we shall walk to the boat, and row up the loch. There we come to another smaller set of rapids and rocks. Some people call that *little Connel.*

Loudoun.—I have tried hard to make the glaciers move which made both this and the chief Connel, but cannot without gigantic sizes; down there we may see the rocks smoothed as the ice crushed its way through, and the whole plain is probably covered by the remnants of a moraine smoothed down by the sea. I think we must alter the levels, this we may manage.

Cameron.—The present is better than that age of ice. Here the water swells into an inland sea, and the trees cover the banks and crown that hill above Achnacloich, on the south side opposite to us.

Margaet.—I heard some one call that Stonefield.

Cameron.—I am in favour of Achnacloich. It is unsafe to translate proper names. I remember a German asking me about Neuschloss. I had no idea where such a place in England was, but he said we called it Newcastle. Suppose we were to call Greenock the *Sunny place*, who would know it? And who would be at the trouble of thinking where Little Bay or White Bay was, if we used these terms instead of Oban? Achnacloich means the field of stones.

Margaet.—I see a little church, but it is very ugly for such a beautiful place.

Cameron.—It is as ugly as they could make it; but at a little distance you see a house among the trees farther up the loch; there the minister lives at a beautiful spot, and near it are the ruins of the old priory; the visible outside parts are very small, and ruthless hands have made a private residence on the site, with a few old walls and the buttery built into it.

Sheena.—Is it a ruthless hand that has made a peaceful home out of such a spot, and converted to abundant use and happiness those blessings prepared by the ancient saints of the place? Holy walls, fine trees, lovely views, a fine old garden—nothing but fine taste can have admired and loved such things. Still, could they not have built their house except out of the walls of the old priory?

Loudoun.—Don't be too severe on the moderns; have they not built that simple church which you notice there at Achnaba, much nearer to the centre of the population than the old priory was? Besides, they have built others at Muckairn and Taynuilt opposite, and modern people like to save time.

Cameron.—It is very well to say so, but there is no church now at Keills or Ledaig, and there was one formerly, so that both ends of the plain were suited.

Margaet.—Still there is one now at Barcaldine over the hill, and there used not to be one; and, besides this, there is one quite recently built at the priory.

Cameron.—Both these are of the Free Kirk. It shows that some kirk was needed, and the reason for removing the Ardchattan one is shown to be a desire to be more central. It was not seen that the day for such long walks was disappearing, and that one church would not be found sufficient.

Let us row on; we cannot land, because if we go up the little **Sruth Mona** or mountain stream at Achnaba we shall

see cromlechs that will take too much time, and if we go into
the woods we shall see stone circles that may enchant
you too long; and if we go up the hill at Ardchattan we
may be too long detained by the old church of St. Modan,
where once perhaps there was a town, and so we shall
move on and try no more than to have a blink up the
inner part of Loch Etive.   People think they have seen
the loch when they have come here.   I never yet met
one who had seen the cromlechs and circles, and I have
only met two tourists who had seen the loch.   Loch Etive
is not seen from the top of a coach, or the deck of a boat,
or even from the top of a hill.

Margaet.—Where can you see it then ?

Cameron.—Where can you see Scotland ?   It is a study,
and not a photographic flash, that can show it.   One
vision cannot fill the soul.   We seek sight after sight,
and prefer to know that there is still more than we can see.
That view always seems small in which the known is not
bounded by the unknown.   We might give one hard pull
to Ardchattan and see the priory, and the rowers can have
a rest for a little.

·There is not much remaining, as you see, but it is
picturesque, and the monumental effigies give it a dignified
character.   One has an inscription showing that the figure
represents the abbot Somerled Macdougal, year 1500
(Funallus Somherle MacDougallus prior de Ardchattan,
MCCCCC), to quote the Statistical Account.   Another inscription shows that it was the family burying place, and
that two sons were successively priors :

HIC JACENT NATI SOMERLEDI MACDOUGALL DUNCANUS

ET DUGALLUS, HUJUS MONASTERII SUCCESSIVE PRIORES
UNACUM EORUNDEM PATRE, MATRE, ET FRATRE ALANO,
QUODAM DUGALLUS HUJUS MONUMENTI FABRICATOR OBIIT
ANNO MCCCCCII.

Another inscription, probably the one called Runic, has
not been decisively read. It seems to be imperfect Roman
writing, the letters badly formed originally, but rendered
still more difficult to read by the effect of weather.

Cameron.—Of course you know that the Macdougalls
descend from Somerled, and that this priory was built in
the twelfth century.

Margaet. — Is that the reason that this family always
opposed Bruce, and never could be reconciled . to the
idea of the western sovereignty being lost? Well, people
suffer much when they cannot see the signs of the
times.

Cameron.—And yet it is said that Bruce held a parliament
here, and that Gaelic was spoken in it.

Loudoun.—As to a parliament the idea is too large. He
met here and had some of his friends with him, and I do
not doubt that there was a careful consultation. Most
people in his day spoke Gaelic in Scotland, and I dare
say Bruce could speak it. It was spoken in Galloway,
which is near to Bruce's place, Carrick, and it was spoken
in the west and isles, where he wandered, and certainly it
was spoken at Roseneath, and I suppose also at Cardross,
opposite Greenock, where he kept his yachts! and where
he died. I do not know in how many places he lived, but he
was for a time in all these. I think he may have taken the
shelter of Ardmore for sailing experiments. The ground

would not do for our modern yachts, but I dare say his
boats would more resemble our fishing craft, and would be
Norwegian in shape. The old Norway shape is still in use,
and can be seen preserved in the Orkneys, and even in the
Hebrides, till this day. The water at Cardross would
probably be a little deeper then, but not much.

Cameron.—You must keep to Loch Etive. In mustering
the chiefs, Sir Walter Scott gives many names of men who
cannot be supposed to have spoken English. One is
Barcaldine, who lived just over the hill. Of course, Barcaldine means the chief who lived at Barcaldine Castle.
Farther up there are other reminders of Bruce ; but, first,
we must look at the manse, a good house. The garden
would rejoice you. These monks could choose fine spots,
but choice was not all, they made them fine as the moderns
made this. Consider Barcaldine, just spoken of, not built
by monks. The garden is a wonder where you expect
only a wilderness, and all has been done but lately. That looks
to the north too, and this to the south. Both point to good
hard work. These monks seem to have left the flavour of
their wisdom and learning, as we hear of the Rev. Colin
Campbell thinking in a most original and powerful manner,
whilst minister in Ardchattan from 1667 to 1726,[1] and
only the other day the same manse gave a professor to
the Edinburgh University.

Loudoun.—We may now have a good pull up to Bunawe.
It is a very wide part of the loch which we now cross,
and we can look at the pleasant sides, well wooded, till
we come to a romantic, broken-up little island, called

---

[1] See *Good Words*, May, 1877 ; an article by Professor Fraser.

Durinnish. One can scarcely tell where it begins and ends, since it has been united to the land. The rock above is also called Durinnish, although, as the word means hard island, and refers originally to the low small spot, it· is scarcely correct to apply it to such a connected mass of the mainland.

Margaet.—The road seems quite stopt up by that great block, on which there is scarcely a blade of grass. It is frightful, and surely it is ugly.

Cameron.—Although it be ugly, you in Glasgow. are so fond of it as to cut it down, and break it into small squares, laying all the streets with it. If it stops our way it makes your way clearer, and don't call it ugly. I remember a lady from the south-east of England coming up here one day, and wishing she were away from these " dreadful hills." She was an artist too, but she had lived too long in plains to learn the glories of a mountain scene. It produced awe and fear, showing at any rate power over her mind. Another artist told me that although he delighted in these mountains he could scarcely help crying at the sight. Another name given to this is Macniven's island. They say that after one of the struggles of Robert Bruce, when he was wandering rather helplessly about the west, he ran down to the Bunawe shore and called for a boat. A Macniven came and rowed him over. A Macniven is there still, and will row you if you like, as he has rowed me. We shall go to the south shore at Bunawe; the landing is not very fine, and the walk is long, but we shall see the country, which, after coming down from these wild hills, looks quite plain. I dare say you will call it hilly; it is at least lumpy; but a farmer's wife up the loch was asked if she ever lived in a flat country, and replied, " Oh yes, I lived a while at Bunawe." We do not find it very flat for walking, and this wooden bridge is almost like that in the Vision of Mirza.

Margaet.—I fear people do not read that nowadays, and may not know the allusion. I know it by chance.

O'Keefe.—Here certainly is something ancient; it is surely a Druidical stone set on a rising ground, probably a cairn broken down. The pillar must be 16 feet high.

Cameron.—As to Druidical that is a point to which Mr. Loudoun may object, but it is really an ancient standing stone set up to mark some great event. I believe it stood on an old cairn near and now almost forgotten, but it was knocked down many years ago, no one knows when, and it has now the honour of being the first monument raised in remembrance of the battle of Trafalgar. The people had expected a great battle, and no doubt some of the Campbells here were personally interested, so they got a stone ready and raised it as soon as they heard the news, which was above two days after it reached London. The stone was set up in the evening, in the old way; no writing, no sign, but that inanimate and illegible one. Curious that the people did not consider that no man knew for what purpose it was first set up, and so infer that their purpose would soon also be forgotten; but the stone is of great value as showing the old spirit and habit remaining to this century.

Loudoun.—It is now five o'clock; we have loitered about, and we may as well loiter a little more; we cannot pass

Connel till about nine; as the days are long it will not matter, meantime we shall eat a little at the Taynuilt Inn.

Margaet.—This inn seems a busy one. This spot naturally must have long been a convenient stopping place. It seems trifling to remain here after looking at nature and the past, and I am glad to leave.

Cameron.—Let us walk back to the shore, and for a while wonder why there should be iron works in this secluded place. They actually make iron here, and have done so for 140 years nearly, some people from Lancashire having found this a good place for charcoal, to which they brought Ulverstone ore. That great wood through which the road passes to Oban, great in extent but of small birches chiefly, is cut every twenty-four years, and is soon burnt down by that greedy furnace. But the district cannot supply all that is wanted, although the amount of iron made is very small. Still, it pays, and the reason for this is that it brings fourteen pounds per ton when the coal iron near Glasgow is worth about three or four. That is the wood of Naisi, the *Coille Nāois,* and it ought not to be passed over as merely a coal cellar of some English Company, but I will tell you more of it some day. Naisi was the eldest of the

Loudoun.—Well, and what of that? it is a boulder, and there are many boulders.

O'Keefe.—That stone has a remarkable name, it is *Clach Manessa.* I am not sure of the meaning; but it is very remarkable that Nessa as a name should be found here. Concobhar or Conor MacNessa was the King of Ulster, who caused the death of the sons of Uisnach who lived here, and of whom we are to hear more; it is one of the traditions of the place probably.

Margaet.—Why did they call it after him?

Loudoun.—I suppose we may as well ask, why did they call that large stone in the public road going out of Taynuilt to Loch Awe after Rob Roy? We like to connect remarkable facts in nature with that which is clear to us. It is sometimes a play of the fancy, sometimes a joke, but often an affectionate reminiscence or a mental connecting link, with that in which we have been interested. And thus the outside nature and man are mixed up inextricably; people call these myths, and imagine something mysterious in a myth. This want of clear observation mixing up ideas of eternal nature with those about poor short-lived man, who is so beloved that we are unwilling to let him pass away unremembered, assists in the rise of a silly story, and such the original of the myth often is; but history has given it dignity, because the confused state in which it is produced is one to which the human mind is subject, and all that is human is interesting. Besides, it often happens that the thoughts of man rise high above the original fact, which then becomes a mere kernel for fine fruit, and sometimes a mere symbol of great achievements. If we call the

stone higher up Rob Roy's pŭtting stone, we begin a myth
at once, and we make Rob Roy a giant, and he must do
gigantic actions such as nature only outside of man can
perform.   In an uneducated people, after some years, this
story grows longer and wilder ; among the older Celtic
heroes we hear of Finn and his friends going through the
seas as monsters a mile long would be supposed to go ;
this is an inferior class of the Finn stories.   I am for a
real human origin to myths connected with man, remembering the pleasure we take in giving glory to our saints
and heroes, until they cease to be recognised as mortals
by the stories, even when we know their distinct origin.

Margaet.—But was Nessa a myth ?

Loudoun.—I think not ; my remarks came in connection
with the names given to stories, &c.

O'Keefe.—She seems to have been a very clever scheming
woman as well as a beauty.   She was asked to marry
Fergus, King of Ulster, and she did so on condition that
her son, who was fifteen years old, should be king for a
year so as to give him rank, and so that his children
should be able to call themselves king's sons.   Fergus
agreed, but meantime she obtained very wily counsellors
for her son, and he acted with great wisdom, and with
bribery also, so at the end of the year it was decided by
the people that Conor should continue.   There seem
different accounts of the willingness of Fergus to resign.
Dr. Ferguson of Dublin, in his poem, the "Abdication of
Fergus Mac Roy,"[1] makes Fergus admire an easy and
partly poetical life. He admired the wisdom of the boy-

[1] *Songs of the Western Gael.*

king and judge, when deciding a very tangled case, and
the poem makes him speak thus, in the court of justice,
after the young king had delivered his sentence :—

> "And I rose, and on my feet,
> Standing by the judgment seat,
> Took the circlet from my head,
> Laid it on the bench, and said,
>
> Men of Uladh, I resign
> That which is not rightly mine ;
> That a worthier than I
> May your judge's place supply.
>
> Conor is of royal blood ;
> Fair he is ; I trust him good.
> Wise he is we all may say,
> Who have heard his words to-day.
>
> Take him therefore in my room,
> Letting me the place assume—
> Office but with life to end—
> Of his counsellor and friend.
>
> So young Conor gained the crown ;
> So I laid the kingship down ;
> Laying with it as I went
> All I knew of discontent."

Loudoun.—Is not Moen a stone in Welsh, and would not
Moen Nessa be a stone set up in honour of Nessa? Such
a word was used in this sense in Gaelic.

O'Keefe.—It is a fair imagining. *Clach* and *man* would
then show duplicates, such as Glenburn Water. I suppose
Conor lived, but there are such wonders told of him that I
can imagine people denying him life: they are still more
startled when told that he was king at the time of the
crucifixion. At any rate here you have a stone that con-

must be more than a legend to leave so many traces as I, with Mr. Cameron's help, will show you even on Loch Etive. With Conor begins the story of the chief heroes, known in this district in the earliest days. I mean the sons of Uisnach. He was their enemy, and Fergus was their friend. I am not sorry, therefore, that you have come on some of the traces to-day. Fergus Mac Roy is little known in this country; I may say the same of Conor. We hear a little of Fergus, the son of Erc, but few know of him, although he brought over the Scots; and we hear of a Fergus in Galloway, the hero too of a mediæval old French romance; but our king in Ulster, and the poet of one of our greatest battles, is not known much.

Loudoun.—We have only skimmed the ground to-day as a swallow does; we have seen nothing well; we must do it all again. Still, we must wait a minute at this boulder since it has such a remarkable name, and as it is near Aird's house, where Dr. Norman Macleod lived—a name that we all take pleasure in.

Margaet.—And now that we have had a walk, we sit more patiently and enjoy that wonderful sunset behind the hills of Morven. Did Ossian or Macpherson fancy his heroes in that bright land? It was some one's idea; and as the same land becomes at times densely black with storms, so we must suppose did the mood and condition of the heroes.

Cameron.—I am loath to leave Abbot's Isle and the Eilean Ban, and all my pretty corners; but the tide is up, and we can pass the falls in peace, and now the run is with us, and we have a fair pull to Oban. It is not easy to do it in an hour and a half, but the night is fine, and even at half-past ten it will be light in Oban.

Margaet.—I am too tired to have a belief; the glory of the day sinks, if not into gloom, at least into silence : I do the the same, and will half doze on the way home.

Loudoun.—Some people, when they return home, like to go to bed at once ; I am more friendly. I say, let us have a social cup of tea, and communicate our rejoicings to each other over it again. It is a prolonged good-night, and a pleasant way of ending the day ; we need not get up so soon to-morrow, but may sleep long, and take only an easy excursion when the day is pretty far on, and when we are tired of resting.

If you prefer supper and wine, have it ; I prefer not to have such a meal. It is true that much tea prevents sleep, but a little tea gives a certain activity to the system ; and I am inclined to think that, in moderation, it hastens the process of repair as much as that of waste.

CHAPTER V.

KERRERA.

" Delightful would it be to me to be (in *Uchd Ailiun*)
   On the pinnacle of a rock,
   That I might often see
   The face of the ocean.

     .   .   .   .   .   .

That I might hear the thunder of the crowding waves
   upon the rocks ;
That I might hear the roar by the side of the church
   of the surrounding sea." [1]

LOUDOUN.—To-day let us be idle. We need not go out
immediately after breakfast. We shall stay a while,
and look at the sun brightening the Morven hills, which
were left to blacken under shade last night. We shall
afterwards wander about the town, and see if there is anything to amuse us. I always meet some one here I know,
just as I do at Charing Cross in London, where you are
sure, some time or other, to find everybody that goes to
London. This is a wonderfully well protected little bay,
and is well named. The precipitous rocks near it, especially
on the south, show the long continued washing of water

---

[1] Song by St. Columba.—Skene's *Ancient Alban.*

that has taken away the lower part, and caused the upper
to project so as to form a precipice. It is the sea that makes
precipices by hewing continually from below.

I see that no efforts make this a great fishing station; it
has turned out very different from the expectation. No
efforts can make the fishermen go to the south shore, and
clean their fish in sheds built for the purpose. But gentle-
men have gone there to build fine houses, and the people
have wondered that the place was so much admired. The
Professor sits on the top of his precipice, and looks out on
the northern hills, and delights in the squalls and the sunsets
—both seen in such grandeur; and the artists come from
many cities, and paint the small remains of the Castle of
Dunolly, which are still a rich field of thought, of æsthetic
emotion, and of wonder. The hills near here are small, but
they are numerous, and every one supplies a new scene, so
that one may take a long time to learn all the walks; you
soon learn them on a flat shore. Here every street is a
study, and you need a separate study to know how to enter
those on the hill.

Margact.—Where is the parish church? Is that it?

Cameron.—It is so in reality, the parish having been
separated from that of Kilmore, a lone but pretty place
over at Lochnell, which we shall see. That was the more
important spot, and probably many people dwelt there; at
least many were buried there. Nobody great has of late
lived permanently in the little bay itself, which was probably
only a piece of Macdougall's grounds.

Loudoun.—I think I can tell you where some of the people
who were near this lived; but, first, let us call a boat, and

we may tell the boatman to be ready for us at four o'clock. At present we may take a little walk along the Dunolly Road—a very pretty road; then let us look at the water of the bay. I fear it is becoming very dirty, and people are throwing rubbish into it. I hope no sewage will ever be allowed to enter; the bay is far too small for that; there is not a **sufficient** sweep of the current, and the tide is not enough for the purification required. Oban must think of this in time. It may waken up some day, and find the bay putrid, and all the people deserting it. These things come suddenly to men's sight and not the sight only, and one wonders why they do not come gradually.

Margaet.—Now I am tired.

Loudoun.—Yes; a little ramble tires us to-day, and we shall have a very early dinner which we need not call luncheon, and we may lounge or sleep a little after it.

After all, we are down by four o'clock.

Let us row across to Kerrera, to the northern bank. Now this was the populated portion of the shores here, and I do not doubt that the island was of some importance. There is a little flat portion, on which is a burying ground, called *Cleigh Bhearnaig* or *Cleigh na Bhearn*, the burying place of the gap or notch. And one sees a peculiar cleft in the little hill there, as if a hatchet had cut it open. We do not imagine this to have been merely a place for burying in, as we see clearly the remains of the houses; at any rate I know of no such burying places among the people here. These are evidently oblong dwellings, and the collection of dwellings is surrounded by a wall. More than this, at the extreme north there is a very solid projecting building which

gives the idea of a watch tower, and just on the point where
such a thing would be useful.   We have, in fact, a very great
curiosity here, a little walled city in ruins, and here it lies
beside Oban and no one cares.   It has the name of a burying
ground.   I believe some people have been buried in it, as a
collection of stones in the south-west suggests a grave, and
this suggests again great antiquity for the time of the living,
since the name of "burying-place" is old, and of the people
there is no record.   The style is very much like that of an
ecclesiastical small town, such as Dr. Petrie mentions as having existed in Ireland, formed by a number of small buildings
surrounded by a wall too small for a fort.   But I know of no
church or cell.   That may be destroyed so much that it
cannot be distinguished from a house.

Margaet.—But a watch tower—that looks like fighting.

Loudoun.—It may also have been a round tower, which is
quite proved to be an ecclesiastical structure ; and monks,
poor fellows, needed watch towers as well as less holy men in
these islands.

There seems to have been no church in it in the time
of Columba, and he was of the sixth century.   There is a
story in his life of twelve vessels going to the mouth of
the river Sale (Seil), in Lorn,[1] to bring wood to Iona to
repair the monastery.   On returning they were rowing to the
west when a westerly wind rose which made them run to
Airthrago for shelter.   The rowers said, " Does this please
thee, O saint ? " for they were unfortunately detained, when
immediately the wind changed, at the desire, as we are led
to believe, of St. Columba, and they raised the sails in

---

[1] See Dr. Reeves' notes in *St. Columba's Life*, and the life itself, cap. 46.

self had gone with the monks for wood. I dare say the Castle of Gylen was not there, the present one certainly not, or it would have contained a very fierce occupant one would think. On a stormy day it looks as wild as the rock around, and I cannot believe that the island looked so when this building rose. Indeed, these trees from the Seil district tell a wondrous tale, and we neglect the country by not growing them still. One of the Macdougalls built the present tower of Gylen on Kerrera.

But the island suggested no homely ideas to these men of Iona in the twelve boats, although the name was Scotic, and Dalriads had apparently occupied it. We may, however, suppose that Columba was in a hurry to get home with the wood. Mull, then, must as now have been free from wood opposite Iona; and how could the smooth rounded granite of the Ross of Mull ever bear it? whilst to go to the north was as difficult as to go to Seil in some winds, and to go to the centre of the island would involve a species of carriage rare and difficult, and without good roads impossible. The sea carriage was at the command of the monks.

If we go to a later period, namely to the time of Alexander II., we find that Kerrera offered more accommodation than the Oban side. It certainly has been denied that Alexander II. ever intended to subdue the western isles,

Ach an Righ, the king's field, and we may as well run to it
to-day as we are lazy, and the fine but rather irregular walks
of Kerrera may not attract us. We shall pass the old coaly
hulk that always lies opposite Oban and keeps stores for the
service of the coast guards, fishing boats, and lighthouse
surveyors: and then by no great rowing we shall come to
a sloping field of corn, with a quiet farmhouse above it.   On
some part of this ground the king is said to have died.

Some deny that Alexander died here, because he is said
to have dreamed a wonderful dream which prevented him
coming; others prefer to say that if he did not die here
there is no proof that he ever was here; to some the dream is
rather a proof that he was in the district, and if it was
wonderful it was so much the more like a dream. Some
people are afraid of the wonderful, and so learn little of
nature which is full of it. They are afraid of anything that
cannot be proved by experiment, and so they narrow their
minds very much. The dream merely was that St. Olave, St.
Magnus, and St. Columba appeared to the king, the first in
kingly robes, stern, middling in size, and ruddy of counte-
nance ; the second, slender, active, engaging and majestic ;
the third, largest of all, his features disturbed and unsightly.
This latter told Alexander to go home and not to subdue
the islands.

The dream is a most natural one, and if these three persons would have been unfriendly had they met on earth, there
could be no idea of their fighting in heaven, and we cannot
expect Alexander to have thought of them other than as
saints. His conscience might well conjure Columba up and
the Scandinavian kings also. The combination is natural,

all being opposed to the new interfering dynasty from the east of Scotland.

I hope now you will think well of Kerrera. What a magnificent breakwater to Oban! Plymouth would be proud of it, yes, and any town on a great and stormy shore. Even the great volcanic wave that broke on Iquique and washed away so much of that and of other Peruvian towns, could not, with its sixty feet of height, wash over Kerrera. It has not the sun of Carrara, neither has it the marble, but it has better grass and sheep, and it has a wonderful variety of hill and dale, if these are small.

Cameron.—Let us go home when the tide is flowing in towards Oban. The steamer has long ago given out its passengers; they will have had time to eat, and will soon come out for an evening walk. Oban will be gay then, but if none of our friends are there, we shall go above the bowling green, as a mode of enjoying that oft-repeated glory, the sun over the hills of Morven.

CHAPTER VI.

THE SONS OF UISNACH.

"Who but the sons of Usnoth, chief of streamy Etha?"
"Blessed are the rocks of Etha."[1]

LOUDOUN.—The next journey will be to Dun Uisnach. That is the chief point in the district, and it has been a point of interest and dispute for centuries, more especially for one century. It has been called Beregonium, Dun Mac Uisneachan, Dun Mhic Uisneachan, Dun Mac Sniochan, and Dun Mac Snichan; the name has even been dissolved into Usny, and twisted at times into Uiston. Then by some perverse persons the favourite *h* has been added, so as to become Houston and Mac Houston, until others have believed in nothing. For simplicity I prefer the oldest forms, Uisnech and Uisnach, but may use others. It is really pronounced Uisnyach, the *y* being a consonant. This spelling makes it simple for English ears, which are afraid of Dun mac Uisneachan, as being long and outlandish to them.

[1] Macpherson's *Ossian* is here quoted. Etha does not occur in old writings; it is Etie, so far as I know, and Usnoth is not the name of a man. It is evidently intended to be a soft form of Uisnech or Uisnach.

There are many stories about it. It has been called the beginning of the kingdom of Scotland, the palace of a long race of kings; also the Halls of Selma, in which Fingal lived; the stately capital of a Queen Hynde, having towers and halls and much civilization, with a Christianity before Ireland; whilst it has also been considered to be that which the native name implies, simply the fort of the sons of Uisnach, who came from Ireland, and whose names are found over all the district, and who in the legend are reported to have come to a wild part of Alban. This latter view, I may say, seems to be the common-sense one, raising no obstacles; but every other view may be discussed, and let us give them all fair play.

Now, first, for the story which makes it interesting. It is romantic and old, and creates its own interest; and before we look at the spot we shall ask Mr. O'Keefe to tell it.

Mr. O'Keefe considered that he was in a region peculiarly interesting to Irishmen, because the sons of Uisnach came from Ireland and lived about Loch Etive for a long time; so before any visit was made to the ruins of their house, he told the story, "one of the three sorrowful tales of Ireland," using the version printed by the Dublin Society in 1808, but not giving word for word.

O'Keefe.—There is no story better known in Ireland than "The Death of the Children of Uisnach." We have songs belonging to it and music also, that sounds well on the Irish pipe. It is an old Milesian story, for these sons were of old and good Milesian blood, and had lived at Uisnach, which is in the middle of Ireland. Uisneach or Usnagh was a fine place in old Ireland, because the council of all the provinces met there, and every year the fresh fire was lighted that was conveyed to all Ireland; this was before Christianity. There is a large stone on the hill where the provinces met, or at least there was, and many other things; but St. Patrick did not like the place, and much was destroyed, and no wonder, since it was thoroughly pagan. The stones lately found may be some of those which were cursed. I do not know why the three heroes of the piece came to Ulster; probably it was for the same reason that people go to London; they became important men at the capital in Emania, near Armagh. The place had the name Caen-druim, the head of the ridge, in very old time, but now it has become Usny by a common piece of carelessness. Old habits keep up, and even "in IIII the Synod of Uisneach met, with fifty bishops, three hundred priests, and three thousand ecclesiastics."[1] It was a convenient spot for Christians, as it had been for pagans, seeing the means of locomotion were the same. Conor (*Concobhar*) was king of Ulster: he was the son of Fatna the Wise, son of Ross the Red, son of Rory, and his mother was Nessa, as I told you. He lived in the splendid Eman or Emania, that great city that was built by Macha of the Red Tresses (*Macha Mongruadh*). She took the golden brooch from her neck, and marked the bounds of the rath; and I assure you it was no obscure spot in which the king lived, and large it was, as the ruins to-day testify. I fear I cannot give you an exact description of the palaces at Emania, but I have one at hand that may suit the purpose equally well, giving the idea of a fine house of those days. It is from the Irish book of Lismore.[2] Crede was a great

---

[1] *Cambrensis Eversus*, cap. 31.
[2] *Manuscript Materials of Irish History.* O'Curry, p. 309.

great enough to comprehend its beauty and taste, and to sing of it in suitable poetry. Many tried, and all failed but Coel O'Neamhain (O'Naevan), who succeeded by means of this poem :—

> Happy the house in which she is,
> Between men and children and women,
> Between Druids and musical performers,
> Between cupbearers and doorkeepers.
> > Between equerries who are not shy,
> And distributors who divide (the fare);
> And over all these the command belongs
> To fair Crede of the yellow hair.
> > It would be happy for me to be in her dun.
>
> .   .   .   .
>
> The colour (of her dun) is like the colour of lime:
> Within it are couches and green rushes,
> Within it are silks and blue mantles,
> Within it are red gold and silver cups.
> > Of its *grianan* (sunny chamber, say drawing-room)
> > the corner-stones
> Are all of silver and of yellow gold;
> Its thatch in stripes of matchless order
> Of (birds') wings of brown and crimson red.
> > Two door-posts of green I see;
> Nor is its door devoid of beauty;
> Of carved silver, long has it been renowned,
> Is the lintel that is over the door.
> > Crede's chair is at her right hand,
> The pleasantest of the pleasant it is,
> All of a blaze of Alpine gold,
> At the foot of her beautiful couch.
> > The household which are in her house,
> To the happiest conditions have they been destined:
> Grey and glossy are their garments,
> Twisted and fair is their flowing hair.

> Wounded men would sink in sleep,
> Though ever so heavily teeming with blood,
> With the warblings of the fairy birds
> From the eaves of her sunny chamber.
>
> . . . .
>
> An hundred feet spans Crede's house
> From one angle to the other;
> And twenty feet are fully measured
> In the breadth of its noble door.
> Its portico is thatched
> With wings of birds both blue and yellow;
> Its lawn in front, and its well
> Of crystal and of cormogal. [1]
> Four posts to every bed,
> Of gold and silver finely carved;
> A crystal gem between every two posts—
> They are no cause of unpleasantness,
> There is in it a vat of royal bronze,
> Whence flows the pleasant juice of malt;
> An apple tree stands overhead the vat
> With the abundance of its weighty fruit. [2]

That is enough. You see it is a fancy house, and the writer had very narrow ideas of comfort; still he had the idea of barbaric grandeur, and at least the comfort of soft pillows. And now we shall go on with the story, as this is quite a digression.

King Conor's house, I may tell you, is now only a set of mounds near Armagh, but at the time of which I speak many nobles were assembled there. They had music and poetry, and pleasant histories of great deeds and tales of their ancestry; they had· philosophers—the name is shortened to Fileas; and they had wise and cunning Druids that were acquainted with magic.

[1] Carbuncles.—*Sullivan.*
[2] Some of the words are from Dr. Prof. Sullivan's Version.

Conor was proud of his house; and in old times people who were great were expected to boast and show their superiority to others in unpleasant ways. There were one thousand six hundred and sixty-five persons belonging to the household, and the king thought of this, and instead of allowing others to drink his health, he raised his voice and said, "Did you ever see a mansion better than my mansion?" "No," they said. "Do you know anything that it wants?" "No," they said. But the king thought differently, and said, "I know of a great want which presseth, that the three renowned and exalted youths, the three luminaries of the valour of the Gaels—that is, the three noble sons of Uisnach—should be absent from us." Every one agreed with this sentiment, because these three nobles—Naisi, Ainli, and Ardan—had defended a district and a half of Alba,[1] and their power was lost to their own country, "for sons of a king are they who would assert high sovereignty from the princes of Ulster" (Uladh).

Then Conor proposed to send messengers to Loch Etive to bring them back. He asked Conall Carnach to go and also Cuchullin, but he did not promise good security for the lives of the three nobles, and the two heroes refused. Fergus MacRoy who had given Conor the kingdom agreed to go, and he vowed to kill any man but Conor himself that would do the Uisnachs injury, but the pledge of the king to give them safety is not evident.

And now it is clear that these sons of Uisnach were men of great importance, when· their return was so much

[1] Now Scotland. I do not know how much a district was.

longed for by the whole court of Ulster, and I must tell
you why they were absent.

.

DEIRDRE (OR DARTHULA).

Feilim was a teller of stories; I suppose a historian and
"filea," and he must have had a high position and been very
agreeable. He invited the king to an entertainment, and
many important men were there. Entertainments were long
in those days, and we hear of them lasting for weeks, months,
or even a year. During the time the king was there a
daughter was born to Feilim, and I suppose all the company
looked at her. We hear nothing of Feilim's wife; she could
not have been pleased when Caffa a Druid, who was there,
said that this daughter would be the cause of much loss
and mischief to Ulster, and the nobles proposed therefore
to kill her at once. Conor objected, and said he would take
care of her and bring her up as his own wife. He sent her
into a retired lios or small fort with a nurse, and in time
a tutor and Lavarcam, who was perhaps a gossip; she is
called a speech or conversation woman, but I think it more
likely that she was a singer (cainte) at the court.

Time passed, and Deirdre was looking out on the snow;
her tutor killed a calf, and a raven came to feed on the blood,
when the young lady said to her nurse that she would like
a husband with these three colours: the hair as black as
the raven, the cheek as red as the blood, and the skin as
white as the snow. This is quite against the opinion that
Naisi was a Milesian, but it was a common way of marking
beauty in Ireland, and it is put here rather thoughtlessly.

Naisi must have had brown hair and not black like a Firbolg; on the other hand I have seen him called a Firbolg.

It so happened that Lavarcam brought Naisi, quite unaware of the trick and playing innocently, on a pipe I think, within sight of Deirdre, and I fear she made love to him, and by some adjuration compelled him to go with her. Woman had great rights in old Ireland. "Naisi was quite alone; sweet truly was the music of the sons of Uisnach. Every cow or other animal that heard it used to milk two thirds more than usual; every human being that heard it was overcome with the delight of its harmony. Their valour, too, was transcendant."

Deirdre threw herself in Naisi's way, and he said, "Mild is the dame that passeth by." "It is natural for damsels to be mild where there are no youths," said she. I don't quite understand all the conversation, and perhaps you won't, but she threw a ball at him and it struck his head, and she said, "A stroke of disgrace is this through life's extent if you take me not." "Depart from me, woman," said he. "Thou wilt be in disgrace," said she; then she took his instrument and played. This music caused great commotion, and the "sons of Uslinn" (another spelling) remonstrated with their brother who knew of the terrible prophecies about Deirdre. But it was fated; Naisi was bewitched or in honour compelled, and the brothers went off with a hundred and fifty men and their wives and servants and greyhounds: they were pursued round Erin to Ballyshannon, Howth, Rathlin, and at last to a wild place, Loch Etive. They chased deer on the mountain, and when these failed they took to

harrying and raised enemies, but the King of Alba required
their help, and soon they became important and powerful.
Some people say that the King of Alba, whoever he was,
wanted to kill Naisi so as to steal Deirdre on account of
her great beauty, and that they ran away to a sea-girt
isle, but we hear that they were living at Loch Etive,
when they were sent for, and they seem to have been happy.
The great fort which is still called by their name, the Fort
of the sons of Uisnach, is in a pleasant situation, and there
are numerous proofs of some population all around. They
fished as we hear, and they had a boat which took them up
to the top of the loch when they wished to hunt among
the wild hills of Glen Etive, and they left their names
well remembered on the fields and the rocks. We can go
up to the fort and see one of the finest views in Scotland
from it, and we can go up the loch to Eilean Uisneachan,
the island of the Uisnachs, and see remainders of their
little hunting lodges where they had three apartments—
considered to be a luxury. We can see the great projecting rock half way up Glen Etive, called Deirdre's drawing
room, as a kind of joke, one very old out of all record.
We can also see the field not far below it called after
Deirdre.

It is also pleasant to go to the wood near Taynuilt and
hear it still called the wood of Naisi (coille nāish), where
the family must have had a settlement, and to hear stories
about them opposite Bunawe on a projecting rocky land
called Ruadh nan Draighnean.

As they were a whole clan they would cover much ground,
and we are not surprised that they have left their name

also on the bay near the fort, and looking to the south of Lismore—Cambus Nāish.[1]

Deirdre is supposed to have sung—that is, if she did not sing some one put a song into her mouth, and Mr. Skene has translated it [2]—

> Glen Etive, O Glen Etive,
> There I raised my earliest house,
> Beautiful its woods on rising,
> When the sun fell on Glen Etive.

They did not confine themselves to the glen ; they went over to Loch Awe, and we can fancy them enjoying the sight and Deirdre singing—

> Beloved is Draighen and its sounding shore,
> Beloved the water over clear pure sands,
> Oh that I might not depart from this east
> Unless I go with my beloved.

When they reached Loch Awe it was but a step to Glenorchy, and we who admire it and who look at drawings of Kilchurn at its foot, and rejoice in the Urchay and the Strae, need not wonder at Deirdre singing—

> Glenorchy, O Glenorchy,
> The straight glen of smooth ridges,
> No man of his age was so joyful
> As Naisi in Glenorchy.

They went up to Glenlochy also, and Deirdre could enjoy the chase and the delights of a good dinner after it—

[1] Where there is the Balure farm of Mr. M'Niven.
[2] See the Book of the Dean of Lismore.

> Glenlaidhe, O Glenlaidhe,
> I used to sleep by its soothing murmurs,
> Fish and flesh of wild boar and badger
> Was my repast in Glenlaidhe.[1]

They sometimes from Glenorchy passed over to Lochfyne and down to Cowal, as we find them in Glendaruel, and so we can imagine them roaming about the Kyles of Bute, and, in fact, seeking all the prettiest places.

> Glendaruadh, O Glendaruadh,
> I love each man of its inheritance,
> Sweet the noise of the cuckoo on bended bough
> On the hill above Glendaruadh.

There is a vitrified fort on the Kyles of Bute, and some of their friends may have lived there: it is on a little island, and although the steamer passes near few people know it: it is usually called the Burnt Island.

These Uisnach people went far notwithstanding the want of conveyances. To us it is difficult to enter Glendaruel, as they now spell it. If we run up from Tigh-na-bruaich we are apt to find the upper part of Loch Riddan (Ruel) dry, the tide being out, and if we do not row far we have far to walk, and conveyances are not easily obtained. The round from Loch Striven or Holy Loch is very long, but the glen is a fine broad expanse, and one feels surprised to see such a spot there. Naisi and Deirdre with some of their companions would probably pass from the mouth of the Ruel to the top of Loch Striven, and up the stream to Glenmasan, from which they would easily descend to Holy Loch and Loch Eck. They must have enjoyed Glenmasan—

[1] Glenlochy.—Skene.

Glenmasan, O Glenmasan,
High its herbs, fair its boughs,
Solitary was the place of our repose,
On grassy Invermasan.

This fine poem would tell to a man of Alba the joys of a life in Argyleshire, and it must go to the heart of every man in the west of Scotland who has had the fortune to spend his holidays in that county. I have given the verses in an inverse order to suit our purpose. I sometimes wonder who wrote the whole, as it is evidently later than the time of Deirdre. But let us follow the events in Alba.

Naisi had soon become a great man in Argyle, as he had been in Erin, and he was sent for to help (I suppose, the Picts) up at Inverness. Deirdre seems to have gone also in that direction, and a vitrified fort on the Ness bears her name. But Naisi from one of his journeys, as we hear, did not come straight home, but went down to Duntroon, and he admired very much the daughter of the lord of that place. A later poem, as I suppose it to be, says—

He sent her a frisking doe,
A hind of the forest and a fawn at its feet ;
And he passed to her on a visit,
On his return from the host at Inverness.

This was the only sorrow of Deirdre in Alba which she loved so well—

Upon my hearing of this
My head filled with jealousy ;
I put my little skiff on the wave,
And indifferent to me was life and death.

> They pursued me on the float,
> Ainli and Ardan who uttered not falsehood ;
> They turned me inwards,
> Two that would subdue in battle a hundred.
>
> .   .   .   .
>
> Naisi gave his word in truth.

Deirdre believed in Naisi, and when they had enjoyed the view about Crinan and the hospitality of the lord of Duntroon, who probably then lived in the vitrified fort which we saw behind the present castle, the abode of the Rev. R. J. Mapleton, they sometimes went south as far as Loch Sweeny and could say, "Beloved Dun Suibhne," &c., the Castle of Sweeny.

Now, this I call a very pleasant picture, perhaps the oldest you have in Scotland (said Mr. O'Keefe); let us not look at dates, but attend to our friends in their sorrow.

We have heard that at the feast in Eman, the king sent Fergus to bring back his friends, and Fergus took no followers but his two sons—Illan the fair, and Buine, the ruthless red, and a shield-bearer named Callon. "They moved to the fastnesses of the sons of Uisnach and to the Lake Eitche, in Alba."   Naisi and Deirdre are represented as living in hunting booths at the time.

And when Fergus came into the harbour, he shouted like a hunter.   Naisi and Deirdre were playing at chess ; they had taken King Conor's polished cabinet or chessboard with them.   When Naisi heard the cry he said, "That is the voice of a man of Erin."   Deirdre knew the voice, but avoided the thought, and said, "That is not so ; it is the voice of a man of Alba."   Fergus shouted again, and Naisi said, "That is the cry of a man of Erin ;" but

Deirdre said, "It is not indeed ; let us play on." But a third cry made it certain to all, and Ardan went to meet Fergus.

Deirdre said she knew the voice. "Then why didst thou conceal it, my queen?" "A vision I saw last night, namely, that three birds came unto us from Eman of Macha, bearing three sups of honey in their beaks, and these they left with us, and they took three sups of our blood with them." "And what conclusion do you draw from that, O Princess?" said Naisi. "It is," said Deirdre, "that Fergus comes to us with messages of peace from Conor; for more sweet is not honey than the peace message of a false man." "Let that go," said Naisi; "Fergus is long on the point. Go, Ardan, and meet him, and bring him with you." Ardan went and kissed Fergus and his sons, and said, "My affection unto you, O dear companions;" and he asked them tales of Erin, and brought them in, and Deirdre and Naisi kissed them, and asked them for news. And Fergus said, "The best tale I have to tell is that Conor has sent us under condition and guarantee for you." Deirdre at once said, "It is not meet for them to go thither, for greater is their own sway in Alba than the sway of Conor in Erin." "The land of our birth is better than all things," said Fergus. "It is a cheerless thing to the richest and greatest not to see his own country every day." "True," said Naisi, "and Erin is dearer to me than Alba, even if I have more here." "You may go confidently with us," said Fergus. "We have confidence," said Naisi, "and we shall go with you to Erin." But Deirdre still opposed his going, and Fergus pledged his word and said, "If all the men of Erin were against you, it could not hurt you if I were with you." "True it is," said Naisi, "and we will go with you to Erin."

THE DEATH OF THE CHILDREN OF UISNACH.

They sailed to Erin, but Deirdre looked back after that eastern land of Alba, and said, "My love to you, O eastern land. Grieved am I to leave you; delightful are thy harbours and thy bays, and thy clear beauteous plains of soft grass, and thy cheerful green-sided hills; little did we think to leave you." Then she is said to have sung the song already given—as she mentioned each spot she delighted in.

It was the duty of Fergus to take the Uisnachs to Emania, but Barach laid a trap for him and invited him to a feast, one of those feasts that were to last for months, and to refuse which was war. He was angry, but went, confiding the Uisnach family to his sons; and Deirdre proposed that they should go to Rathlin until the feast was over, and so enable every one to keep his word. But the sons of Fergus insisted on their own valour being sufficient, and the sons of Uisnach were too proud to seek refuge by practising the proposed device, and Deirdre bemoaned the faith of the unsteady son of Roy. She had a dream of Illan the fair being faithful and losing his life, and Buine being faithless and retaining his; and proposed to go to Dundalgan or Dundalk to stay with the great hero Cuchullin until the formidable feast should be over; but the same arguments were used as before, and all went with the sons of Fergus.

There were three great houses, or kingly abodes, in Emania, in one of which Conor lived, and Deirdre gave as a sign to her friends that if they were asked to go there no treachery was intended, but if they were sent to the house of the Red Branch, then it was all over with them. The Red Branch represented a body of men who have been called knights, and we have no better name, men high in the ranks of fighting, and well born men.

They rapped at the door of Conor's house. Conor was feasting and inquired if the Red Branch house were well supplied with food. The answer was in a style that might still be called Hibernian—"If the seven battalions of Ulster would come they would still find abundance to eat and to drink." "Then take the sons of Uisnach to it," said Conor.

Deirdre did not give up. Her character is remarkably consistent and decided. She still desired them to go to Rathlin, but the old reasoning prevailed. "For it is not cowardice or unmanliness that has ever been known of us, and we will go to the Red Branch."

It is true there was enough to eat when they came to the house, but they were tired, and Naisi called as usual for the polished chessboard, and he and Deirdre began to play.

The king had not seen Deirdre for a long time, and he was very desirous of knowing if she were still the most beautiful of women. He was proud of Naisi as one of his greatest nobles, and would not hurt him for nothing, but he was quite willing to break his word and to kill Naisi

if Deirdre were still worth admiring. So he sent his old
confidante, the poetess or singer Lavarcam, and she came
and warned Deirdre and Naisi of the intention of Conor,
and advised them to defend the house against an attack.
She then went to Conor and told him that Deirdre had
lost all her beauty, and was not worth thinking of. Still
he was not sure, and he sent another messenger, one who
was sure to hate Naisi. This was Trendorm, whose father
and three brothers had been killed by Naisi. This messenger
found most of the house barricaded, but he looked in at
one of the windows. Deirdre saw him and told Naisi, who,
having a chessman in his hand, made a *fortunate* throw
and knocked out one of Trendorm's eyes. Of course the
wounded man told Conor, and Conor admired the blow and
said, "The man of that throw would be king of the world
if he had not short life." "Moreover," Trendorm added,
"there is not in the world a woman of face and form
more beautiful than she" (Deirdre).

Then came a terrible struggle. I do not think I shall
tell it all. Faithlessness was mixed with faithfulness. The
story has nothing impossible in it until it comes to the
deeds of these children of Uisnach, who, as in older poets,
have too many deaths laid to their honour. But they died,
and Deirdre alone lived. It was not, however, possible to
kill them without supernatural power, so the Druid Cathbad
came forward, and Conor promised not to hurt the heroes, if
only he could make them yield. Cathbad believed this, and
caused "a viscid sea of whelming waves to come around the
children of Uisnach, so that they swam along the ground."
They did not yield, but the Ulstermen would not approach

them till their arms fell off them, and no one could be persuaded to kill them until a *fellow*, called *Maini Rough-
hand*, son of the king of Norway,[1] said he would do it because
Naisi had killed his father and two brothers. " If so," said
Ardan, "let me be killed first." " No, but me," said Aluli.
But Naisi said, " I have a sword which Mananan MacLir
gave me, and it leaves no remains of a blow ; let us three
be struck together with it, and we shall all be killed at
once." So the three heads were laid on the block together,
and were severed by one blow.

The end is coming for Deirdre. There are different accounts.
One says that she died on the graves of the sons of Uisnach ;
another that she lived a year, and that in rage with Conor
she flung herself from his carriage, head foremost, on to a
rock and was killed.

Cameron.—Let us conclude from a well known version :—
" Awake, Darthula, awake, thou first of women ! The wind
of spring is abroad. The flowers shake their heads on the
green hills. The woods wave their growing leaves. Retire,
O sun ! The daughter of Colla is asleep. She will not
come forth in her beauty. She will not move in the steps
of her loveliness."

---

[1] This mention of Norway shows that the version of the story is later
much than the date given to the events. The Norse get the name of
being rough, as if no gentle Gael could have done such an act. It may
be that Norsemen came in the first century; it has been supposed that the
Fomorians were of that class. The story does not require this discussion,
since this version is unquestionably full of comparatively late additions.

CHAPTER VII.

IS IT A SUN MYTH?

"The sun is the centre of power, and therefore of *life and thought to our earth.*"

" Rejoice then, O sun, in the strength of thy youth."

Macpherson's *Ossian.*

MARGAET:—I am amused, and much pleased with your story, but do you know that I have read about this, and was told that it was an old Aryan ·story out of the Mahabharata? The primitive story sent out from the glowing regions of India has lived among all the race that sprung from the people there, and glows still with all its vigour, sometimes with new tints, sometimes with old. What do you say?

O'Keefe.—Well, we may amuse each other. If the story of a man who kept away a lover from a young woman for some time, but at last was unsuccessful, since youth had its way, is believed by you to be an ·account of that which once happened in India, I will not attempt to prove otherwise. Men do not go far for stories when they can be got at hand. The ground facts have occurred millions and millions of times, and if you do not know several such occurrences among your acquaintances you must be highly favoured. Indeed, I know that it occurred amongst my own relations ; but there was a modern variation of circumstances.

Loudoun.—Do you believe in spontaneous growth ? Do you imagine that stories will grow of themselves anywhere ? You have heard that there are but few of these stories in reality, although they are all made to appear different by change of dressing ? Mr. J. G. v. Hahn [1] tells us that there are only forty classes of stories, each with variations, and this of yours would probably belong to class 27, the Helena form. You do not now require to tell a story in full, but when anything interesting happens you have only to say, " It happened according to form 21, subform *a*," and so on, and the idea is given at once. These names of persons may interest some, but intellectually they mean nothing, and any name may do. As to the names of places, all our shores have been covered with wild romances, and it requires no Aryan beginning to form them ; they grow from the germs which exist in abundance in the human heart, and in human mechanism. We require no proof of spontaneous growth so long as man is one, and if you stop all connection with the past in the memory of man, new Deirdres will rise up to-morrow, new Conors, who will be treacherous and cruel, showing this character according to their stations in life and the conditions of society.

Margaet.—I fear you will speak disrespectfully of the solar myth.

[1] In his *Griechische and Albanesische Mährchen.*

Loudoun.—Yes, if driven to extremity, and of the prin-
ciple that makes men bring this story from Asia. Man is the
most interesting creature to man, and when he looks at the
sun and the sky, he interprets their movements according
to his human interests, having no words at first to express
himself otherwise. We see children doing the same thing.
I have known nurses calling the small clouds lambs, but
they called windlestraws lambs also. Man is the true
beginning, although the motion of the heavens is too
important not to tinge the representation of the acts of
man. The solar myth has been driven to distraction, and
so has Aryanism, but the fundamental ideas as they first
unfold themselves are really beautiful, and commend themselves as true. You have seen children playing with
pebbles. One says, " This is papa and that is mamma,
and this is the coach and the other the horse, and the fifth
the whip." Objects are converted into the ideas which are in
the mind. The objects need not suggest the ideas. A stool
or a table or anything is made to represent a man. As the
" fleecy " clouds are sometimes called sheep (and the
common. adjective is an abundant proof), so are the
whitened curves of the sea waves called fleeces, and similar
thoughts are found regarding the globe and the atmos-.
phere around it. Of course the sun would be held the
highest of his class, and ideas would grow around him
with force ; but new objects continually arise, and especially
new individuals, men of vigour, and these have a powerful
influence on others' minds, I should say the very highest
and most powerful, so much so that human nature has
been exaggerated, and ideas from the heavens have been

transferred to it. For this reason I have great faith in the human nucleus of a so-called myth, but am willing enough to believe in the ideal characteristics caught from the sun's glory, and made use of to symbolize the greatness of the man to be praised. Even when a hero is gifted with divine attributes, I do not suppose him to have grown in the sky, but to have had an ideal life from the sky transferred to him.

When Phoebus mounts his car, we have a very human beginning and a very advanced civilization. It is mere imagery, so far as the car is concerned, exactly as the waves are called lambs and fleeces.

Man and his ways are the beginning of stories. The doings of man are the most interesting stories to man, but the highest expression for all these is got from the heavens. When ideas rise so high they gain in interest: they are human, yet in a certain sense superhuman. In order to exalt man, we take our imagery from heaven. That the highest or strangest images are transferred from place to place, from heaven to earth, is certain, and heaven and earth are intermingled, the human always predominating.

Margaet.—But do none ever begin with the sun?

Loudoun.—I will not go so far, but every one seems to have a solid root in the very common earth, where so many. other ideas grow. In other words, if men find any connection with the sun in the story of the Uisnachs, or any similar tale, the explanation must be that human beings began the greatness, and similar beings have tried to put solar radiance round it; but I do not see a reason even for that. The whole story is possible, probable, natural, and simple.

CHAPTER VIII.

THE ROCKS OF NAISI.

"Are these the rocks of Naisi? Is this the roar of his mountain stream?"
"I will go towards that mossy tower to see who dwells there."[1]

CAMERON.—Your tale is interesting, but notwithstanding all, I believe the greatest resident of the fort to have been Fingal, and I will give you my impressions. Meantime I may say that you have done your best to tell the story fairly, and I cannot complain, but we here make the heroes the real sons of the man Uisnach, who belonged to this place. Besides, we have here a tradition that an Earl of Ardchattan went over to Ireland and ran away with an Ulster princess, and lived up at Ruadh nan Draighean. Then we call the heroine Darthula, and several places are called after her. On the whole, I think you have the best grounds for your version historically. The incidents may have happened before Fingal's time, and no one can deny that the names have a most tenacious hold of the land here. Besides, they occur in no other place as they do here, so that we are not distracted by

[1] Ossian's Poems.

contradictions. Everything is natural but the Druid's wrath and power; these are the only things in the story in the least exaggerated so far as internal evidence goes. I find, too, that the landing at Ballycastle on the return to Ireland is well remembered by tradition. A rock there is called *Carraig Uisneach*. The local pronunciation rather corrupts one name, and the lady is called Gardrei, and it is said that the men were murdered near the rocks, and that she was confined in Dunaveny Castle not far off. Ballycastle is directly opposite Raghery Island, to which Deirdre advised the band to retire. This removes the scene from Armagh where the king was, but it might have been placed there for effect. In any case, it seems a true story, and I confess the name "the sons of Uisnach" is rather in favour of their having come from Ireland. Uisneach is a central place in Ireland, and is in no way to be attributed to Scotland. Still, I consider that Fingal lived here after, if not before that clan, and he is by far the greatest character, so I prefer to connect the Dun with some one of fame.

Loudoun.—He must have been a good Scot that made those poems, and he must have loved this land. I should think Deirdre's poem the first recognition of the beauty of the Western Highlands. Our forefathers in the Lowlands had no idea of it till of late, they seemed afraid of the hills. The writer admires the sons of Uisnach. He has really not a word to say of the sons of Alban. He seems quite impartial. He admires the people of Ireland and the land of Alban. I do not say Scotland; the time claims to be before that name was used here. Fingal's claim is not clear to me at all.

Margaet.—Darthula is a far more beautiful name than Deirdre. I wish you would use it.

O'Keefe.—In Ireland it is never used. I do not know well its authority, but there is some for it.

Margaet.—Darthula must have been a kind of Helen.

Loudoun.—Yes ; a beauty about whom nations fought, places at least quite as populous as Attica and the Troad probably ;. but not quite so far away from Ireland as Troy from Mycenae, although the latter distance is not much above two hundred miles. Deirdre was the Helen of the Celts, and people still say "as beautiful as Deirdre." Do you remark how true and how tender she was ?—truer than any ideal of Greece, and wise and thoughtful. She seems to have been a very noble character, and names of places do not grow from triflers. Even great beauties may have character. We shall meet her again.

Cameron.—You must know I am not so anxious to exalt these sons of Uisnach. I still prefer to give the Castle of Berigonium to Fingal, and to call it by the ancient name of Selma. I see Fingal at the feast of shells on the top of that mound, and I see him stalking down the hill with his great spear. I can imagine him meeting heroes, whom he kills on the plains beneath, and seeing ghosts coming down from the Appin hills or from Morven, for many a dark view have I seen of both.

It may appear strange that the name of the Fingalian hero should not have been distinctly preserved in connection with the palace or city. The latest poems ascribed to Ossian may serve to throw some light on the subject, particularly the piece called "Losgadh Theamhra" or the

burning of Tara. The burning of the home of his ancestors
is particularly referred to and lamented in the sad story
of his old age. He himself was the last of his race,
and Ossian an deigh na Feinne, "Ossian after the Finn,"
has become a proverb. He was an old man, remembering great days. The description of Teamhra given by
the poets makes it exceedingly probable that Dun Mac-
Uisneachan (Selma or Berigonium) was the place meant, and
referred to, and tradition concurs with the poet's account
of the city and palace. Dun Valanree, the king's town, near
the chief Dun, is a name to be remembered in considering
this, the ancient capital Selma.

O'Keefe.—Before you give too many arguments let me
answer those you have suggested. According to our history,
Finn lived nearly three hundred years after Conor MacNessa
and the Uisnach family. It is most natural, certainly, to
take the name from the earliest, but only when in want of
more famous men. If Finn, or Fingal, as you name him,
had lived at this Dun, his superior fame would have put the
other aside, although not quite of necessity. I do not know
Tara as a home of Finn, but of the kings of Ireland. Conor
lived in the time of Christ.

Cameron.—Mr. Skene says that the names Cuchullin,
Deirdre, and sons of Uisnach, were connected with
vitrified forts.

O'Keefe.—I fear the connection is accidental. If in two or
three cases it exists, it only shows the style of building at the
time and favours no side, but the names of the family
are connected with various places, and these chiefly not
forts at all. Deirdre's Grianan is a rock. Eilean Uisneachan

H

had cottages made of boulders on it. The bay of Naisi or Camus Naois has no old building, and so of the wood.

Cameron.—Still, some of the Fingal family have left their name in this locality. We have Tom Ossian near Barcaldine; that was the favourite seat of Ossian.

O'Keefe.—I fear this is not well founded. There is also Carn Ossian at Achnacree mor, and at least three urns were in it. Not that this would prove that Ossian was not there, but it was not sacred enough to be devoted to him alone. Besides, we have several graves of Ossian, and that settles the point so far.

Cameron.—Frequent allusion is made as I remember to the burning of the ancestral home in Ossian's lament for the Fingalians.[1] It may be that the burning of the palace and the extinction of the Fingalian dynasty were remembered in connection with the contest between the kingly and priestly power. There might be a feeling of awe connected with these two events, which would prevent the name of any one of them being associated with the scene of the disaster, in which fire was the means of reducing the palace to ashes and the city to ruins.

Selma, which means *fine view,* had the same meaning as Teamhra, the latest name used by Ossian in describing the ancient palace.

Beregone and Dun MacUisneachan are other names, both of which have been used down to modern times. The locality is clearly indicated in the description of other places in the vicinity, such as Lora or Lora nan Sruth—now called

---

[1] No 'n loisgear aros na Feinne?

Connel, and the favourite Cona in Glencôe, where Ossian spent the evening of his life and composed his most touching lays. The following passages are equally applicable to Selma and Teamhra:—

"In the unruffled sea, with ivy covered rocks, might be seen children gazing with wonder at the smoke of Taura reflected in the deep." [1]

Teamhra must have been very close to the sea when its smoke could be reflected in the smooth water.

"It is the sound of Lora to the stranger groping his way in the dark. . . . He hears at last the sound of Lora, and exclaims with joy 'Selma is near.'" [2]

Again, "A king of future times shall stand on the slope of the hill, once the site of Taura. He can see in the distance the trembling ocean with many green islands. From this lonely spot," exclaims the king, "may be seen many linns and hills." [3] The burning of Tara is minutely described. Fingal was at the time on Ardbheinn, and was

[1] Chìteadh am fè na fairge,
Coillte le'n carraigibh eighinn,
'S clann ag àmharc le ioghnadh,
Air smuidean Thaura fuidhe.

[2] S' amhuil toirm Làoire d'on aineol;
S' gun amas air a shlighe san oidhche. . . .
Chluin e mo dheiradh toirm Laoire,
Se' g' radh le aoibhneas "tha Seallma dlu."

[3] Seasaidh Righ nan laithe 'n ar deigh
Air tulaich an t-sleibh an robh Taura;
Chi e an sin an cuan critheach
Le iomad innis uaine,
'S aobhinn an raon so deir an Righ,
Chitear uaidh gach linn 's gach cnoc.

forewarned by the doleful tones of the harp. "The harp had a doleful tone like the moaning sound heard on the lonely hill before the coming of the fierce storm." "We arrived late at the palace. The flames were flickering low, the house fallen to the ground, and smouldering in the spent fire." "There were in the hall a hundred sets of bows and arrows, a hundred sets of shields, also a hundred bright coats of mail, as many glittering swords, a hundred dogs, and a hundred bridles." Wives, children, and young maidens were among the ruins. "They were surpassing fair, but the flame laid their beauty low."[1]

Dun Lora was the name of another fort near Luath Shruth on Connel. It is referred to by Ossian in the third book of Temora, where Fingal asks, "Where is the chief of Dun Lora? ought Connal to be forgotten at the feast?"

Loudoun.—I shall not enter into the controversy about Ossian, although my mind is quite clear on the subject, but this I may say, that even with the greatest belief in Ossian, Dr. Clerk, who edited the poems, does not see any proof that Selma was at Dun Mac Uisneachan. In a word, the names of the Uisnach family are inseparable from Loch Etive. The Fingalians are everywhere, and have no special connection with this place.

O'Keefe.—I gave you the groundwork of an epic of Deirdre. I leave Ossian and Fingal to others; they certainly come later if our records are of any value. We need not dispute therefore. I may quote, however, from Sir John Sinclair's edition of Ossian, 3rd vol., p. 269, in a

---

[1] Bha iad sgiamhach ach leag an lasair
Am maise, 's an luaithre iosal.

note to Temora, Duan **V.** Speaking of Lora, he says, " There is no vestige of this name now remaining, but a small river on the north-west coast was called so some centuries ago." The phrase "north-west coast" is vague, and can hardly have meant this neighbourhood. And yet in the same edition the name Lora is given also to the hill Ledaig. In the same book, Alex. Stewart, giving his evidence for Selma, says that the white' beach answers exactly the present aspect. Now the beach is not white when compared with other beaches I could speak of.

Cameron.—Well, take that passage—

> "O Snivan of greyest locks,
> Go to Ardven of hills,
> To Selma surrounded by the wave."

O'Keefe.—Who Snivan was we do not know, but we know that the rock in question is not surrounded by waves. It is at the head of the bay. *Ardven* applies to many places, and less to our Dun than to Dun Valanree.

Then we have, "The king . . . . will see Cona's pebbly streams rolling through woods abounding with herds ; he will see at a distance the trembling ocean abounding with many green islands." This seems conclusive against our fort being meant ; we cannot see the streams of Cona or any other streams from it, they are far away. We can see the ocean, but no one would say it was the distant ocean, since one can scarcely creep between it and the rock. True, we can look afar off, but we cannot see many green islands ; although that may be allowed, as we do see islands. It is not a distinctive account that can prove anything.

The description is not exact enough to enable us to identify any time, place, or thing. Of course, if the description of the spot were exact I should then attack the authorship.

Cameron.—Let us look at another poem; it is from the Dean of Lismore's book, the manuscript of which is assuredly above three centuries old :—(English, p. 20 ; Gaelic, p. 15.)

> "All of us rose up in haste,
> Except Finn of the Feinne and Gaul,
> To welcome the boat as it sped,
> Cleaving the waves in its course.
> It never ceased its onward way
> Until it reached the wonted port.
> Then when it had touched the land,
> The maid did from her seat arise,
> Fairer than a sunbeam's sheen,
> Of finest mould and gentlest mien."

Dr. M'Lachlan's translation does not mention the waterfall, which must be Lora, while Sir John Sinclair's edition takes notice of the peculiarity of a vessel crossing a fall.

O'Keefe.—The poem in Dr. M'Lachlan's book does not speak of crossing the fall, but then it depends on the reading. Is it *thir an eas* or *thar an eas?* The first would be the land at the fall, the second over the fall, but it does not matter which, as the poem distinctly says that it was at Easruaidh, where Finn was living in a tent: so it was not near his halls. There are two "Essaroys," but neither fit well the situation. Mr. Stewart seems to wish to make Lora the same as "Cona of Cairns," but this appears to me to strain the meaning very much.

Cameron.—Perhaps you are too precise about Fingal's tent, but I cannot explain Easruaidh. If you read on in that same poem, you will see the death of the fierce Daire, who was killed at the landing; and I was inclined to look at one of the Cairns at Connel as being placed over him. You remember the passage (Dr. M'Lachlan's translation):—

> "We buried him close to the (water) fall,
> This noble, brave, and powerful man,
> And on each finger's ruddy point
> A ring was placed in honour of the king."

I should like to distinguish the Cairn of Daire. He at least had no connection with Macpherson, to whom you are always objecting.

O'Keefe.—I should also be glad. I never remove the traces of history or romance from a place without regret. Still, the evidence is wanting for this point also, but interest enough remains, for these are " the rocks of Naisi," although, that the poet alluded to them when he spoke of Selma, no one, in my opinion, can tell, and even if he did allude to them, the question would still remain, who was that poet?

Cameron.—I think you difficult to persuade. Listen to me again. Let us look at " Carthon "[1] together. I may say, as it is said there, " The murmur of thy streams, O Lora, brings back the memory of the past. Dost thou not behold, O Malvina, a rock with its head of heath? Green is the narrow plain at its feet; there the flower of the mountain grows, and shakes its white head in the breeze; the thistle is there alone, shedding its aged beard. Two stones, half sunk in the ground, show their heads of moss. The mighty lie, O Malvina, in the narrow plain of the rock."

We had, not long ago, the two stones standing in the

---

[1] See " Ossian's Poems."

field below the Dun to the south ; now only one remains. We have the stream in Connel falls, the heath, and the remains of the famous dead. Happy, I doubt not, was the feast on that lonely hill, even when the heroes round Fingal sang of the death of Moina, which happened long before, when Clessammor was obliged to flee in his ships from Balclutha (Dunbarton). But a terrible memorial of that struggle soon appeared. In the morning a mist rose from the linn. " It came in the figure of an aged man along the silent plain. Its large limbs did not move in steps, for a ghost supported it in mid-air. It came towards Selma's hall, and dissolved in a shower of blood." Soon the sun rose, and there was seen a distant fleet. The ships came like the mist of ocean, and the youth poured upon the coast. The chief moved towards Selma, and his thousands moved behind. Fingal was ready to receive him, and drew this picture, in language very gentle in sound, but involving a terrible threat : " How stately art thou, Son of the Sea ; ruddy is thy face of youth, soft the ringlets of thy hair, but this tree may fall, and his memory be forgot ! The daughter of the stranger will be sad, looking to the rolling sea ; the children will say, " We see a ship ; perhaps it is the king of Balclutha." The tear starts from their mother's eye. Her thoughts are of him who sleeps in Morven. Behold that field, O Carthon ! Many a green hill rises there, with mossy stones and rustling grass ; these are the tombs of Fingal's foes, the sons of the rolling sea." A struggle began ; the stranger killed Cathul and Connal ; and this reminds us of the name Connel ferry. Can you not imagine Carthon standing there, looking at the next champion, and saying to himself, " Perhaps it is the husband of Moina, my mother, whom I cannot remember, and who died in sorrow on the Clyde. I have heard that my father lived at the echoing stream of Lora." Clessammor, the father, refused to tell his name, and was mortally wounded, whilst he himself killed his son. "Three days they mourned above Carthon ; on the fourth his father died. In the narrow plain of the rock they lie ; a dim ghost defends their tomb. There lovely Moina is often seen ; when the sunbeam darts on the rock, and all around is dark, there she is, but not as the daughter of the hill. Her robes are from the stranger's land, and she is still alone."

Ossian was sorry for Carthon, and spoke thus in a song : "My soul has been mournful for Carthon, he fell in the days of his youth ; and thou, O Clessammor, where is thy dwelling in the wind ? Has the youth forgotten his wound ? Flies he on clouds with thee ? I feel the sun, O Malvina ; leave me to my rest. Perhaps they may come to my dreams ; I think I hear a feeble voice. The beam of heaven delights to shine on the grave of Carthon : I feel it warm around.

. "O thou that rollest above, round as the shield of my fathers, whence are thy beams, O sun, thou everlasting light ? " . . . .

I cannot finish that address ; it is too beautiful to utter except when I am alone. Is not the whole picture very fine ; does it not describe the spot exactly ?

Loudoun.—The picture is fine, and I confess there is room for a new criticism—esoteric—rather than one relating only to authenticity. Still the scene would suit many places, and Cona is mentioned, which brings great confusion—at least it is a favourite idea that it means the stream of Glencoe. There is no name spoken of known on the ground except that of Connal, and there is little said of him. But you do not prove authenticity by proving that the writer had the plain of Ledaig or any plain in his eye. The poems, which I call Macpherson's, are remarkably atopic—that is, they seldom venture to name a place that we can recognize, and my theory is, that, having a desire to keep to the ancient legends and poems, but being only imperfectly acquainted with the whole of the literature, he preferred as much as possible indefinite scenes. All are vaguely described. The new ordnance map has been formed by the advice of an enthusiast of Ossian. These maps will be used as evidence, but as such they must be put aside whenever they use a name which has been first applied to a place since Macpherson wrote. This must be remembered. It grieves me to say a word against the belief in the ancient Ossian having written or spoken the words quoted ; since you so strongly hold it, I would willingly do so also. Still the change of authorship does not alter the intrinsic character of the poem. I have given some time to the subject, and carefully examined it—with the aid, of course, of the writings of J. F. Campbell (Campbell of Islay) and others, and all doubt or hesitation is removed. Before my careful study I was in difficulties, and feared to decide against Macpherson. When you urge me strongly to believe, I feel it painfully, and I say like " Clessammor with a tear," " Why dost thou wound my soul ? "

CHAPTER IX.

CONOR MACNESSA.

"The bards shall forget them in their song, and their name shall not be known. The stranger shall come and build there, and remove the heaped-up earth. A half-worn sword shall rise before him; bending over it, he will say, These are the arms of the chiefs of old, but their names are not in song."

LOUDOUN.—It seems to me that you are trifling, and talking of fabricated histories and impossible ages. Is there not a story of Conor MacNessa having a ball in his brain for some years, and when he observed the darkness on the day of the crucifixion, and was told by his Druid that the "innocent One" was suffering, he became excited, and cut down trees in his rage; and so violently was he agitated that the ball sprang out of his skull, and his own brains with it, so that he died; and is not this enough to set aside all your histories, legends, and allusions as out of the region of fact?

O'Keefe.—It is quite true that this wonderful story occurs; and I may tell you what this ball was, and how it got into MacNessa's skull.

Connall Cearnach was a great champion, and he killed

Mesgedhra, king of Leinster, and, according to the custom of the time, mixed his brain up with lime and made it into a ball. This ball was kept in the king's house in Ulster on a shelf, and two court fools got it out to play with one day, when *Cet Mac Magach*, who was an enemy of the house, and was prowling about in disguise, got hold of it, and kept it beside him, remembering a saying that Mesgedhra would still revenge himself on the Ulster men. Cet kept the ball for an opportunity, which he made by seizing cattle from the Ulster men, and causing Conor himself to pursue them; when they met, the fighting was conducted with more formality than we should expect. It is rather strange to find ladies at such an engagement, but they were invited, and they had the privilege of asking the champions to show themselves. Conor came forward, and when he saw Cet, who had been hiding, he was inclined to return, but the ball was sent out of a sling and stuck in his brain, causing him an illness, which, however, soon passed away.

Margaet.—What a ridiculous and coarse habit that was of making up men's brains with lime!

O'Keefe.—It was certainly barbarous, but it is not so long since we cut men's heads off. We have in museums some specimens which are thought to be the lime compounds of brains. Those I have seen are white and very small, so that the organic matter must have gone, and a small part of the brain could alone have been used. The brain story may be wrong; the knowledge of the crucifixion, which MacNessa displayed, must be fabricated. Wonderful stories grow around remarkable men.

Loudoun.—Interesting certainly, but not quite answering my question. Does the story not show so much absurdity that we may put it aside altogether, and all its connections, and is the time given—namely, the early part of the first century—not beyond the reach of Irish tradition?

O'Keefe.—You shall not drag me into the whole question of Irish chronology; but I may say that O'Curry gives the dates, and says that Deirdre's story can be traced as having existed as far back as the year 600, and even Campbell of Islay calls it 800 years old, and Skene gives the date of the Edinburgh MS. as 1238. These are long numbers, and when you get back to 600 it is as easy to go on to St. Patrick; and, when at St. Patrick, will any one deny that it is possible to step a few—say, three or four hundred years further, Mr. Loudoun? We know well that traditions may be preserved a few hundred years, and names of places for thousands of years. The identification of names of places spoken of in Scripture has succeeded so often now that we may say that Palestine has remained for thousands of years with the same nomenclature, although there may be some changes of sound according to our ideas of the pronunciation. In Gaelic the meaning of the names of places is often so clear that we know that they must refer to events which are old. Does the fact of the naming of the crucifixion not point merely to an addition made after the time of St. Patrick?

It may be that an error has been made by a too early date, although the actual proof of total chronological error in old Irish writings has not been made clear.

Loudoun.—But is it not true that the genealogies of

Ireland go back to Pharaoh, and even to Adam, and does not that make them all void?

O'Keefe.—It is a pity that we in Ireland are apt, like the Americans, to exaggerate; but this does not contradict the fact that our genealogy may be as old as Adam; and the world is far too old for your little limits.

Loudoun.—Granted; I will allow any age you like to name, but I do not want to be misled by the Celtic exuberance of fancy.

O'Keefe.—Don't be afraid. In the time of Tacitus, Ireland was better known to merchants than England; at least he says so; and if it was not very highly civilized, it was advanced enough to induce people to go there. In the time of Ptolemy, that is the second century, there were cities in Ireland. Aileach is named by him, perhaps in *Macolicum*.

In Scotland you have hundreds of castles, the origin of which has scarcely been mentioned in history, but people have called them Picts' towers, tradition being correct here, as this is being proved.[1] Before them there was another kind of castle, much more formidable, and in many instances larger, but not, so far as we know, so numerous. These were the vitrified forts, about which we conversed some days ago. Tradition fails nearly at the time when these ceased to be occupied. The Uisnach family have their names connected with one great fort of this kind, and a smaller in Loch Ness, also with non-vitrified places, such as the island and farm in Loch Etive. Indeed, nearly all the vitrified forts, if not all except these two, are unconnected, not only with history, but even with tradition, leaving out the

[1] On Brochs, by J. Anderson, *Archaeologia Scotica*, vo .V.

part of tradition which cannot be separated from the purely romantic. Giants, fairies, &c., may be connected with tradition, but we shall not enter into their company in this inquiry.

We know well enough that people lived before our miserable histories, and we see their works. They had some large ideas, as shown both in their remains of buildings and their geographical and descriptive names, as well as general language ; and when these names are consistently assigned to places, we have no reason to deny the connection of the people indicated.

Loudoun.—But are the names consistently put in this case ?

O'Keefe.—I know of no contradiction. I know of no other region in which the names are found in the same relation. The tale agrees with the Irish traditions, and, as said, is natural, and one that would remain long with a people because of its very impressive character.

Loudoun.—But are there not many ways of telling the story ?

O'Keefe.—That of course. Every fine story is told in many ways. Look at our war correspondents ; not two can agree on the same event, although all are there on the same day.

Now, I may tell you finally I am not sure of the chronology ; but the events must have been in the early centuries, and when we get beyond the brochs we cannot be precise. It is consistent to put it before the Dalriad invasion, before the time of Columba, and even St. Patrick. It is a story of heathen times. There is no trace of clerics, and the architecture before us is itself heathen.

Sheena.—I must not let you quite off there. Have you not read Queen Hynde by James Hogg. Here we have the fine young Christian Queen, a descendant of many famous kings of Beregonium, marrying an Irish prince.

Cameron.—I am told that Hogg came and obtained the traditions at the spot.

O'Keefe.—It may be; but they introduce such confusion that I would not even think of them.

CHAPTER X.

QUEEN HYNDE.

SHEENA.—I have heard all your opinions, and now I must give you mine. I have been reading "Queen Hynde," and I find that she was a great and beautiful Christian Scottish Queen, and that she lived at Selma in the time of Saint Columba. The Norsemen came down the sound of Mull, and King Eric intended to seize Queen Hynde and her kingdom, but she sought St. Columba's advice, and he knew that the only person that could save the throne was in Ireland. This man, so predestined, had been put as a child under the care of King Colmar, his grandfather, who lived at Temora in Ireland. Columba went to entreat him to come, but Colmar refused permission, and laughed at all the Christian ways, so that Columba was obliged to leave deeply depressed, and, as he sought shelter from a storm in the north of Ireland, a wonderfully rough, uncouth wild creature came down to the shore, and took charge of the boat, and steered it in all the commotion and storm across to and past the Mull of Cantyre, and laughed and sang and commanded

sternly all the time. Some of the men thought it was a
fiend, and wondered at his song about the sun. He said he
worshipped it, and then he told the rowers that if they
did not work, he would drown them or strike them with a
great oaken club that he had. They sailed up Loch Fyne,
and then walked over to Loch Awe and on to Connel,
where they crossed and passed on to Selma. The two
armies of Eric and Queen Hynde were trying their
strength in games, and the great savage came and beat
them all, even the king. Every one thought he must be
Lok, a kind of evil spirit of Scandinavia. He said his
name was MacUiston.

Columba managed to appease the king so far that it was
to be settled by a combat between three of each side, who
should marry Hynde and have the kingdom. Eric was
killed by a most royal-looking, handsome man in gilded
armour, and this was the hero chosen to be the king; but
the Norsemen wished revenge, and they took Selma, this
very hill you speak of, whilst Hynde and the Scottish party
kept the next hill, Dun Valanree, above the present Ledaig
post-office. The nobles did not wish to obey MacUiston,
but King Colmar came reconciled from Ireland, and
proved that the wild-looking savage who worshipped the
sun and sang among the waves was the same as the handsome
prince who was victor in the combat, and that he was really
Prince Eiden, and that he was the true heir to the Scottish
throne.

However, notwithstanding all attempts, assisted by Colmar, they could not drive away the Norsemen, who were
coarse and cruel, and determined to have a wild feast, and

to sacrifice three times three virgins by burning them in a
pile to ensure further aid from their gods. When the pile
was lighted, heaven was enraged, and a storm of lightning
came and burnt up the whole army and city, so that nothing was left but ashes, and this is the cause of its being
vitrified.

> " All glittered with a glowing gleam,
>   Then passed as they had never been ;
> Walls, towers, and sinners in one sweep
> Were solder'd to a formless heap,
> To stand until that final day,
> When this fair world shall melt away,
> As beacons sacred and sublime,
> As judgment sent for human crime."
>
> " *Queen Hynde,*" *by James Hogg.*

That is a romantic end, and I prefer that story to your
tamer ones.

Loudoun.—Certainly it is romantic, and part of the poem
is well written. MacUiston's sail from Ireland is really fine,
but as to truth it is marvellous how void it is of all foundation. It is not known to us that the kings of Ireland worshipped the sun in the sixth century, the time of Columba, nor
is it known to us that the Scots in Dalriada were Christians
before the Irish. It is not known to history that the Norsemen came to Scotland in the time of Columba, and it is not
known that there was an Earl of Mar there, or earls anywhere
in this country, besides other characters mentioned. We
know nothing in history of a Selma, and we do not know
where Beregon [1] was, if it was anywhere. In short, the amount
of confusion is inconceivable. MacUiston seems some cor-

---

[1] " Beregon " is used in Hogg's poem more frequently than " Selma."

ruption of MacUisnach, and shows that the pronunciation was so far preserved that the *ui* was pronounced and not left out by people so much as now. The whole of Hogg's account is fanciful; as to towers they are poetical, and as to palaces you may see the chief rooms; they are small and not burnt—only the outer walls are vitrified.

However there is no use in proving the whole to be an invention. Had any similitude to truth been kept, the poem might have been worth reading, as a whole. Still, thanks for the tale, even if it is not that of our fort.

CHAPTER XI.

THE BEREGONIUM THEORY.

WILLIE.—I do not feel quite sure that you have done justice to Boece. I don't know much about him, but I told you what he said of **Dunstaffnage**, and now I will read you some extracts about **Beregonium**. They are taken from Hollinshed, but I have also looked at the original and observed differences.

1st. "Fergus was no sooner come into Albion than that, in a Parliament called and assembled in Argile for the purpose, they first consulted after what sort they might maintain themselves against their enemies."

After uniting with the Picts, they fought against the British King Coil at Doon, in Ayr, then "departed to their homes, and Fergus returned to Argile."

Here it is said the places took the names of their first governors; here also Fergus made laws for the maintenance of common quiet amongst them. "He built also the castle of **Beregonium**, in **Loughquabre**, on the west side of Albion over against the Western Isles, where he appointed a court to be kept for the administration of justice, that both the

Albion Scots and also those of the same isles might have their access and resort thither for redress of wrongs and ending of all controversies."

After that came Feritharis, then Mainus, thirdly Doruadille, "who in the twenty-eighth year of his reign departed this world at Beregonium."

In the time of Reuther, Doualus, governor of Brigantia, who had set Doualus up, was routed by Ferquhard, son-in-law of Nothatus, "governor of Lorne and Cantire" (or gentis novantiæ princeps), "they encountered with Doual in battell, whose host, twice in one day, was put to flight near to the citie Beregonium, with the loss of eight thousand men." Brigantia is called Galloway; certainly confusing.

When the Britons rose, they drove the Picts from the Mearns and Lothians, and then passed into the Scottish kingdom, waiting the Scots at Kalender. "This discomfiture put the Scottish nation in such fear and terror, that they utterly despaired of all recovery, where contrariwise the Britons were so advanced in hope utterly to expel all aliens out of their isle, that they pursued the victory in most earnest wise; they forced Reuther and all the nobility of the Scottish nation, that were yet alive, to flee for safeguard of their lives into the castell of Beregonium, where they held themselves as in the surest hold. The Britons being satisfied of the repair of their enemies to Beregonium, environed the castell with a strong and vehement siege, until that the Scots within were constrained for want of vittels to eat each other, according as the lot fell by a common agreement made amongst them."

Reuther then passed to the "iles" and then to Ireland,

afterwards returning to Albion by Loch Bruum, gaining a victory at Reuthirdale. In the end, "Reuther departed this world at Beregonium, in the twenty-sixth year of his reign."

Things then went more quietly, and there are curious episodes about religion and Spanish philosophers and stones set up. We then find that Conanus was made governor in place of a degraded King Thereus ; "when the king died, Conanus renounced the administration in presence of all the estates assembled in Parliament at Beregonium, where by common consent Josina, brother of Thereus, was chosen king."

"When Josina had reigned twenty-four years, he departed out of this world at Beregonium, being a man of very great age."

During Josina's reign, "two men of a venerable aspect, although shipwrecked and almost naked, came to the king at Beregonium, accompanied by some of the islanders." They were said to have been Spanish, and to have been driven out of their way when going to Athens. These people told them not to worship the immortal gods in the shape of beasts and fowls, but putting aside images, to worship the living God with fire and prayers, building a temple without an image ("oportere itaque relictis simulachris viventem cœli Deum igne precariisque verbis, fano ac templo ad id constituto sine forma colere").

Finnanus followed him; after he had reigned long, he went to Camelon, and died when on a visit to "the king of the Picts as then sore diseased." "His bodie was conveyed to Beregonium, and there buried amongst his predecessors."

"Hollinshead" leaves out the ambassadors sent from

Egypt to inquire into the condition of Albion, and I suppose he is ashamed of them.   Still he mentions that some improvements were taken from the Egyptians.

Durstus was disreputable, and the neighbouring princes interfered; he promised better behaviour, swearing before a statue of Diana, and invited many to a feast. "After they had entered Beregonium, and the king had received them into the citadel, an armed ambush came upon them." They were all slain. The wives of the murdered persons came to Beregonium, and aided in raising indignation; after great tumult, Durstus was slain.

Afterwards Ewin, the uncle's son of Durstus, was made king, being brought out of Pictland. He was proposed by Caronus of Argyll, who spoke strongly of the horrors of the last reign at Beregonium.

Ewin was brought from Pictland "in a kingly dress to Beregonium, amongst the acclamations of the people. The guard at Beregonium first denied him entrance; but when they saw such a crowd round the walls, and themselves unable to resist, they came into the power of Evenus," or Ewin. "Evenus was put on the royal seat on entering Beregonium, and at his orders the nobles touched his hand and swore sincere obedience. He was the first of the Scottish kings who required this."

We are told that "he built a castle not far from Beregonium in a very stedy place, and called it after himself, Evonium, now commonly called Dunstafage, or Stephan's camp" (a better sounding derivation than the common one, but not therefore truer). He died at Dunstaffnage, and Gillus raised "sundry obelisks" at his grave near that place.

In the time of **Gillus, Cadall,** the governor of the Brigantes (Galloway, in " Hollinshead "), got into his hands without a struggle both **Evonium** (Dunstaffnage) and **Beregonium.** The young **Ederus** was taken to Epiake, in Galloway. Here we are again curiously brought into contact with the south, and almost doubt our former northern opinions. To choose a king, **Cadall** came " to the continent to Beregonium." He had been among the islands. **Ewin,** the second of that name, married the daughter of **Gethus,** the king of the Picts, and returned to Evonium with his wife.

We are told that he visited the part of his dominion which the Irish Sea surrounds, and in that journey built **Inverlochtie,** a place long frequented by merchants from Spain and Gaul. In the " east " he built Inverness.

Who knows but we may some day find a clue to all these names of kings. If we knew the place to be Beregonium, we should certainly find it interesting.

Loudoun.—Thanks for your account, which might have been longer. I called your attention to the chronology when we last spoke of Boece. It seems to make the whole absurd, and I need not prove the errors, as Mr. Skene has put to flight about forty of the kings. After all, we know of no Beregonium before Boece, and whether it is connected with **Rerigonium** in Galloway or not is not quite proved, but I believe it to be fairly clear. It is quite certain, however, that the **Dalriad** kings in Argyle were connected with Galloway, and that at one time they held both. This may be the origin of the whole mistake. It might be said that **Rerigonium** belongs to the Dalriads, as it did, forgetting that for a time the Dalriadic power had two seats, and we can easily imagine a transference of the name of one capital to the other. This supposes, also, that a mistake occurred in writing, and that Rerigonium was meant. There is no reason to doubt that Ptolemy's Rerigonium was gradually corrupted into Ryan.

Buchanan mentions Bergon as a place in the west of Scotland, but its relationships I do not know, and if we cannot fully illustrate the mistakes of the past, we can keep to our own subject, being assured that no place here had the fame Boece claims for it, and that no such kings could have reigned in the times chosen by him. We find plenty of bones, but no human ones, in the Dun, and vitrified walls, but no trace of dwellings enough to constitute a great city. We have rather the contrary arguments.

The evidence for Beregonium breaks down, and the destruction of the civilization follows. It may be left to be swallowed up in the same gulf that Mr. Skene prepared for the kings, and we can all read his book.

NOTE.—Boece mentions *Caronus*. It is Coranus in my Hollinshead. Hollinshed is the usual spelling of the latter name.

CHAPTER XII.

CHIEFS OF STREAMY ETHA.

" Who but the sons of Usnoth, chiefs of Streamy Etha."[1]

O'KEEFE.—Now that we have heard all your theories let us go to the spot, and as my countrymen from Uisneach were the men who have really given this place fame, I will stand by them, and also be your guide, and first we shall go by coach in the morning to Connel Ferry.

High above Oban, that busy maker of happy summer days, which flow from it in a long stream, I feel that I could sing with Deirdre, " Delightful to look on these islands and bays and harbours, those endless hills and changing forms of land, making us wonder as we turn every corner of rock."

Cameron.—I agree with you that we should give up our time to the Uisnachs. They were our guests many years ago, and you shall be their representative, and we can rejoice as we go along looking at the lofty Cruachan and the rich Lismore, and even turn round to see the distant Mull and the range of Morven.

[1] Ossian's Poems.

O'Keefe.—Yes, this is a day to their memory. We pass Dunstaffnage, and cross Connel. The falls are violent and, I must confess, rather frightful to-day, but it is said that no one has been drowned here in the oldest memory, and this was even said by a writer in the appendix to Sir John Sinclair's Ossian in 1808. It certainly is remarkable, since many people pass at night coming from fairs. Now, having crossed the ferry, we are in Benderloch.

Loudoun.—I think we shall drive from Connel. The Lochnell Arms can give us a dog-cart, and a friend here has left us another until he returns from Oban. If we walk on this warm day we may find ourselves too lazy to go about the Dun, which it is well to see when we are vigorous. Thus, too, we can better carry our lunch, which is a good excuse for us.

Cameron.—Now we come on to the heath, which I greatly admire ; it is too interesting to me to be improved by cultivation. It is the moss of Ledaig in common phrase ; I prefer to call it the heath of Lora, whilst the falls of Connel are to me the falls of Lora, but that you don't sympathize with ; and that overhanging rock is Dun Valanree (Dun Bhaile an Righ), the fort of the king's town, under the Ledaig post office. And did you ever see a more charming cottage? the wall covered with ivy, the front garden full of flowers, the side garden rich in strawberries that climb up to the very foot of that great rock. The rock itself is beautiful in colour, yellow with its lichens, and grey and black in parts to vary the scene.

Loudoun.—We must stop here. This is the entrance to the Fort lands, and the tenant could not allow any acquaint-

Dun Bhaile an Righ or Dun Valanree
extremity of Ledaig.

ance to pass by; but I must tell you who he is—a poet, and well known among the Gaels over all the world. Let us cross the road from his house and pass through the little garden : we enter a room between two great rocks and part of a third, which form the walls ; the rest, with the roof and floor, was made by the poet himself. This is a grotto, a school, a chapel, and a drawing-room, with a window looking to the islands, the shores, and the ocean.

O'Keefe.—I am anxious to visit the Dun. We drive on a furlong and there it is before us, a long rocky mound 150 feet at the highest point, nearly perpendicular at the end on the sea, whilst the eastern end slopes down to the plain. This was the scene of much romance, and nature has made it a centre, an isolated rock, wonderfully defended, being precipitous on nearly all its length, one end only and a part at this side having a somewhat moderate ascent.

Let us first go to the top. We look past the island of Kerrera, the one on which we saw the old and perhaps sacred enclosure, and past the lower end of Mull, along which so many pilgrims and holy men sailed going to Iona; between Kerrera and Mull in the far distance are the islands of Colonsay and Oronsay, both with their sacred buildings and their memories of saints. There, near the shore, and at the cottage we have left, the great rock of Valanree hangs over an old burying ground that formerly went down to the sea and made this place also sacred. The village, or clachan, is called Keills, or Cills, a cell or church of a holy man, and probably Columba himself consecrated the spot.

You see that standing stone in the field, it is one of several I cannot doubt; there were at least two last century, according to Pennant. That stone is worn so much that even the rocks themselves have no such look of decay. That, I believe, stood before the Christians came; we must look to earlier days. But the sons of Uisnach were earlier than Columba's monks; and, if you do not believe me, I will again quote Skene, who says, "The children of Uisnach were Cruithne, and must have preceded the Scots, for the great scene of their Scotch adventures are the districts of Lorn, Loch Awe, and Cowal, afterwards in possession of the Dalriadic Scots," and it is curious that Adamnan's life of St. Columba, speaking of the journey to the king of the Picts, mentions "three localities, near Loch Ness, and these are Cainle, Arcardan, and flumen Nesac." It would seem as if then in the sixth or seventh century, the names were already old, and had attached themselves to places; the men half forgotten.

Loudoun.—I have to remark that the family is called Cruithne in your quotation, elsewhere they were called Milesian, and we were told that they were also called Firbolgs. This is the introduction of a good deal of uncertainty in details.

Margaet.—I suppose we may despair of absolute accuracy; let us drink in the beauty of that varied sea, with islands and lochs and hills; the long romance that has glowed upon them seems only a match to light the glory that so often appears.

Loudoun.—Do not geologists speak of some of the western hills of Ross farther north as the oldest part of the world above the sea, but this too is wonderfully old ; the Himalayas seem half finished and young ; these are venerable, and men must come to them as to a shrine of nature for ages yet to be. Lismore lies beautifully there, and its rich lands brought many quiet people, but pity it is that the Dean did not know more of the value of his work when he collected the poems. He would have told of every habit, superstition, and legend, and we should have thanked him.

Margaet.— Let us be more active and gather every sound from the valley of the past, and write it in music; even that old worn-out standing stone in the field will raise the notes, and the other in the field to the east, both I doubt not remnants of pagan days, seems ready to add to the chorus.

Cameron.—I quite agree ; standing stones and circles were not a few in that plain with the fine background of the Appin hills; but the greater part are now removed, and farmers that waste their good land by carelessness are afraid to lose as much as will allow a standing stone or a circle, if the place suits their fancy. But the past can only live in our memories, for after all it goes and it cannot reappear.

Loudoun.—It seems to me that I can imagine why that standing stone in the field below may have been so much worn. The whole ground was covered with peat, which, we know, dissolves readily some chemical bases, such as lime, soda and potash, which occur in rocks, although it preserves also many organic substances.

Now that Mr. O'Keefe has shown us the ground, I shall

read you from a description of the Dun, which appeared in
the proceedings of the Society of Antiquaries of Scotland.

In the depression between the two divisions of the rock,
and at the south side, the most convenient entrance exists.
We see distinctly the remains on the turf of a zig-zag road ;
five of the angles may be observed. If this place is ever
examined, great care must be taken not to destroy its
present appearance. This road is called Queen Street, or
Sraid a Bhan Righ. It would be interesting to learn the
age of the name. It is, probably, a modern caricature ;
nicknames and fancy names abound there.

The raised beach along the shore to the south is natural ;
but it is said to have had a different appearance formerly,
having had artificial work upon it. The field along the
fort and shore was covered with peat. This was removed.
Duncan Stewart, who was ploughing on the spot afterwards,
was interrupted by great stones, which he thinks must have
been 12 feet long. One of these he broke up. The others,
which did not so much interfere with the plough, were
allowed to lie. He thinks they are about 60 feet to the
south of the standing-stone in the middle of the field.
Still the memory may not be exact, as he says he remem-
bers three standing-stones. When Pennant mentions only
two, he would probably be correct on that point, although
his observations on this place are, on the whole, very
absurd. This field, as well as the circle and enclosures
above, will probably give something new to inquirers, if
any portion will, but the writer found nothing : you will see
that Duncan Stewart had not a memory to be trusted.

The standing-stone gives one an idea of great age. It

is a piece of conglomerate, with the connecting aluminous metamorphic rock a good deal washed out, whilst the hard old pebbles that it had embedded remain. There are no artificial markings but one, and that is a hole little more than an inch deep, as if made not very long ago. Its edges have none of the appearance of being weather-worn like the rest of the pillar. The reason of the stone looking so worn may be that it has been under peat, as has been said.

CHAPTER XIII.

THE FORT OF THE SONS OF UISNACH, COMMONLY CALLED BEREGONIUM.

" Do gluaisedar rompa go daingen Mhac n' Uisneach acas go Loch n' Eitche an Albain."

" They went to the fort of the sons of Uisnach, which is at Loch Etive in Alban."

LOUDOUN.—I think I shall stand on the fort, and give you quite a lecture on the subject. It may be dry, but it will serve for conversation afterwards.

I have ventured to adopt, or at least to hold provisionally, the opinion that the vitrified fort of Dun Mac Uisneachan was inhabited in the early centuries of our era. We need not be desirous to define particularly the date to a century or two. Traditions and the dawnings of history, like the fancies of childhood, are mixtures of the real and the ideal, whilst time and place are not very distinctly bounded.

All fancies about earthquakes, volcanoes, and lightning, go also from the site—fancies which I would not mention had they not been entertained by men whose opinions are to be respected on other subjects.

The hill on which is the Fort is long in proportion to its

Dun Mac Uisneachan from the Shore. S.W.
fancifully called Beregonium, castle of Fergus & Selma.

breadth. The top is pretty well defined, as the sides are almost everywhere either very steep or actually precipitous. The length is from 250 to 300 yards, according to the point of starting; its breadth at the most 50. The broader part is near the west, and looks on the Bay of Ardnamuic, with a magnificent view around. This part is most fitted for habitation, and has been most inhabited; it is also farther from the side where the rise is more gradual and an attack easier. Here about the highest part were the houses built, or at least the more important, and here were the meals, as sufficient remains show. On the north of this part are natural walls, one may say, as well as on the south, and between these, well defended from the storms, the principal dwellings were built. On the west there is a space of nearly 40 yards before reaching the precipice that formed the boundary on the shore. The central living place was 30 yards broad by about 45 long.

The debris was not rich, except in bones of common animals; but here were found the iron brooch which I shall show, also the mica and bronze wire. The mound on the land side seemed to be natural, and only an accident led me to doubt this. It was found to be the remains of a strong wall regularly built, and defending the inner part of the fort even after the rest of the enclosure, or top of the hill to the east, might be taken. About 6 feet high of the debris still remains, but it slopes down gradually, and is covered with grass. The inside was not so high as the outside of the wall. There was an inner wall, apparently more carefully built than the outer, and more fitted for a house than a fort. This inner wall followed the slope of the ground, and

did not form rectangular apartments. The enclosure, however, is not all dug up. There was an entrance to it from
the western court, as we may call it, through a narrow
passage.

Vitrified walls are found along the outer edge of the hill
in most places, and on the western part an inner wall runs
along them, the breadth and space between being about
9 feet. The vitrifaction is never carried inside, where a more
refined work was required. The vitrified wall is not built on
absolute precipices, but on those parts less difficult to scale.
The cross walls, even those defending the central or high
enclosure from the camp, are not vitrified.

At a point of the northern wall there was dug up a piece of
enamelled bronze, 1¼ inch in diameter. It seems to have
served as a cap or cover, as there is a hollow on one side
into which something may have fitted. On the other are concentric circles, the hollows being filled with enamel, and that
of a red colour, whilst the centre piece is of a slight yellow.
It belongs to the class called *champlevé*. Ornaments of concentric circles are by no means uncommon in the drawings of
Stockholm bronze objects by Professor Montelius of Stockholm, and there are many in Mycenæ, but the enamel points
rather to Celtic art, without determining the century. I
should be glad to have some indication of the origin. Coneen-
tric circles are ornaments on many works of art; they are
found on the ancient sculptures of this and neighbouring
countries, as well as on the remains in Schliemann's Trojan
Collection. Schliemann gives figures of them in his volume,
p. 137, and on plate xlvii., English edition, where also
circles of depressions are seen, although on a small scale,

not unlike northern cups and circles as on p. 235. The red oxide of copper gives the colour to the circles on the ornament found here. The yellow central piece is very like that used a good deal by the Japanese, and said to contain silver. This centre piece is so small that I am unwilling to destroy any for examination; besides, it is entire, whilst the enamel of the circles round it has come out to a large extent.

These points are made out:—

(1.) The weaker parts of the dun were walled, the outer wall, or part of wall, being vitrified.

(2.) The wall of the western part is double; the outer being vitrified, the inner built in layers of flat stone, 9 feet being the distance from surface to surface.

(3.) The interior walls were built without mortar, whether they were cross walls or formed a lining to the outer wall.

(4.) The eastern wall of the inhabited part had been rebuilt in a ruder way, partly at least, by using some of the waste of a vitrified but broken down portion.

(5.) The occupation was continued after the ruin of the chief structure, perhaps by stragglers, or as poorer cottages now linger about ruins.

(6.) The occupants of a vitrified fort were not necessarily the builders. This fort may have been built for the Uis-nachs, and as more than one of this kind is connected with their name, this may possibly be a style which they preferred, although they had other dwellings not vitrified.

(7.) Vitrified forts are not common in Ireland, and the improbability of the Uisnachs bringing the plan or custom over is great; indeed, we may say that they certainly did not. It is probable that the forts were built for them by the people of Alba, and that this was the fashionable mode of building at the time for important persons. I am not inclined to see anything mythical in the name when more than one is called after Deirdre.   The word *myth* is not a very definite one as used by antiquarians, and often denotes merely a fact which has lost its original clearness.   ·

(8.) The vitrified fort was introduced by men who quite understood the mode of putting dry stones together in layers.   A part of the vitrified mass *in situ* was overlying a built portion of a wall.

Here is a plan of the surface, and a drawing from a photograph of the isolated hill itself.

The surface is so unequal that I cannot give a good idea of it without a number of contour lines and such care in survey, that I do not think I can give it that time or attention necessary, even if I were accustomed to that class of work ; probably enough will be shown on the Ordnance Survey map, which is not yet published.

Vitrified walls take us far back, but not necessarily beyond the early centuries of the Christian era, since one existing near St. Brieuc, in Brittany, was evidently built after the Romans had shown their skill there.   To the earliest possible date we have no clue further than this, that it would appear as if it were when both iron and bronze were used.   Of the latest date we have a probable negative indication.   Such forts would cease to be built when the country was laid bare of wood, and that certainly would be after the Roman occupation of the east of Scotland; in the west the habit would last longer.   It is probable that they would cease in the east of Scotland before the west, because new ideas came there to break up the life of the earlier times; the habits in the west remained longer allied to those of Ireland. The forts them- selves were a fashion brought from the east of Scotland to the west. The later influx of people from the west, or Ireland, was accompanied by no such mode of building, although previously the east, perhaps by way of the north, had inoculated the Western Highlands with the habit, and slightly touched the opposite coast of Ireland.

The vitrified forts are the work of a rude people learning to emerge from the ruder state indicated by building loose stone walls, if we may judge from this of the Usnachs.[1]   When I say the work of a rude people, men without much external civilization are meant.   I have continued to disconnect more and more, as already said, the style of the dwelling and the character of the inmate, except in some particulars, and one of these is that there is often not energy enough to improve the dwelling even when there is knowledge.   We see also frequently that there is energy enough to make an imposing house, and not character enough to live up to it.   However, the builders of vitrified forts have not shown themselves far advanced in archi- tecture.   They had no mortar for the flat stones; still the vitrified method was by no means the only one known, since vitrified parts are found over the built portion.   We do not know how much of the fort under notice was covered with dwellings, but the eastern part had many loose stones; these were taken down and used for building the houses now standing below.   The most important portion of the fort was that on the highest point, B B (see Plate I.)   Nature had provided a hollow be-

---

[1] I purposely spell the name a little differently here, so that it may be seen that there are various methods.

tween rocks to the north and south of this spot and partly
to the west, whilst a thick wall of loose stones was made to
the east. A good deal of this wall remains, and has been cut
through. This had fallen partly down, and was raised up by
using the material around, some of it consisting of vitrified
masses which had broken down. It shows a second occupation.

Near the middle of this were apartments with loose stone
walls about two feet thick. The drawing scarcely tells how
broken down they are, and how difficult it is at times to follow
them. Four, however, were fully made out, each rectangular;
they are not vitrified, but follow the rule in all these cases—a
rule I mentioned before—not to vitrify internal walls. The
stones chosen are flattish, and no mortar was used. South of
these chambers are broken down walls with vitrified pieces lying
irregularly as if some walls had early fallen; a less careful
class of men had made their habitations there for a time,
living roughly, and leaving abundant evidence of their food in
the bones of sheep, pigs, and cattle.

There is a long passage from the western side of this enclosure shown at *a a*, and various confused evidences of other
buildings are also found. The passage is very narrow, and
leads out to a fine open space at A looking out to the sea,
well protected by precipitous sides and by vitrified walls in
most parts, probably at all parts originally.

We may imagine the central rooms to have been the
apartments of the chief. Near the surface were found querns
very rude, and on the north wall at *b*, the bronze ornament
which I have already described. At the north-west was found
part of an iron sword, at *c*.

A sloping road exists up the so-called Queen's entrance (Bealach-na-Bhan-Righ). I suppose the whole to have been surrounded with a vitrified wall, or one extending along the edge of the less precipitous part. The outer walls have to a large extent fallen down the hill.

G is a large vitrified mass, not connected apparently with any building, and I have supposed it therefore to have been a tower. It is midway between the two elevations into which the summit is divided by a natural depression, although it does not itself stand in the most depressed part ; in reality it stands on a prominent part, by no means the highest, although the most central.

C is a varied green slope, on the edge of which near the precipice is a well, concerning which romantic stories have been told, which stories I was unfortunately compelled to prove to be founded on fancies. D is varied, and gives a variety also of small knoll and dale with rock. At E there are indications of enclosures less formal than at B, BB. At one spot there seems to have been a stone circle. F is a steep green slope before the precipitous part begins.

It will be seen that the digging was not continued all round, but in places sufficiently numerous, I believe.

Here are a few photographs, taken from different points, in order to show the style of building. The view is put by the side of the plan to show the relation of the parts, but is not so exact as the photograph from the same point.

After all, the best general observations regarding these forts are found in the small volume by the discoverer of the first, John Williams, Esq., Edinburgh, 1777, and in the letter of the celebrated chemist, Dr. Joseph Black, then Professor in

Edinburgh University. The difficulty of cementation by heat
I have never seen, and I believe it need not be much considered. Where basalt is abundant, and where so many
mixtures of silica with bases are readily found and made,
abundance of fuel will do the rest.

So far my task has been to illustrate one fort only. I believe this is the first time that a regular dwelling has been
found in a vitrified fort, or vitrified walls over "dry stone"
ones. Of course we can always distort every kind of
evidence and speak of previous occupation as being wonderfully far back, and no man can give a reply; but I
certainly find no evidence of anything existing in this fort
to prove that it belongs to very remote antiquity. Every
trifle that has been found points to times that need not
have preceded European history, so far as the skill is concerned, and it is unscientific to imagine an age that is not
demanded by the evidence. It would be equally unwise
to feel certain that the objects and the walls are of the same
date, but, taking the whole evidence together, I rather think
that a similarity of date is most probable; and when I
read of Mr. Anderson's searchings in the Picts' towers, and
of the introduction of strong thick walls of stone built
without mortar, I naturally think of them as made by people
accustomed to thick walls, and, either by imported advice
or skill, beginning a new system, seeing that wood was
failing, and the old reckless use of it for vitrifying purposes
was impossible. That, of course, is a conjecture, and as
such it must be left for the present. It is a reason for the
Pictish towers following closely on the vitrified.

Since I examined these remains I have looked at those

Top of Dun Mac Uisneachan & View from it.

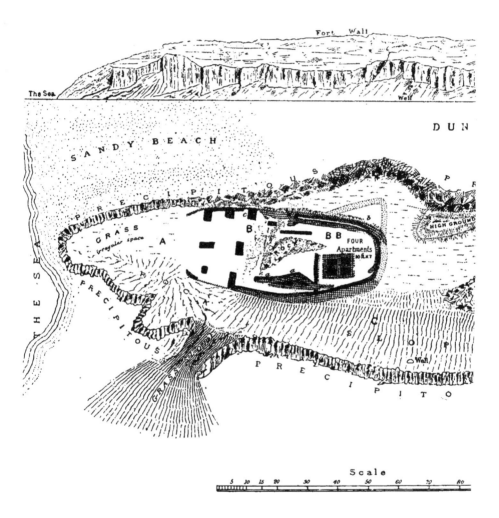

Fort Wall

The Sea

Well

D U N

SANDY BEACH

P R E C I P I T O U S

HIGH GROUND

T H E · S E A

GRASS
irregular space   A

PRECIPITOUS

R O C K

GRASS

B   B

BB   FOUR
Apartments
10 ft. X 7

ROCK

S L O P

Well

P R E C I P I T O

S L O P E

G R A S S

P R E C I P I T O U S

Scale

5   10   15   20   30   40   50   60   70   80

VIEW FROM

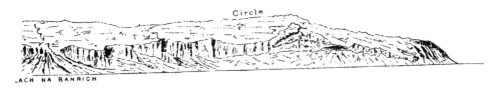

UISNEACHAN

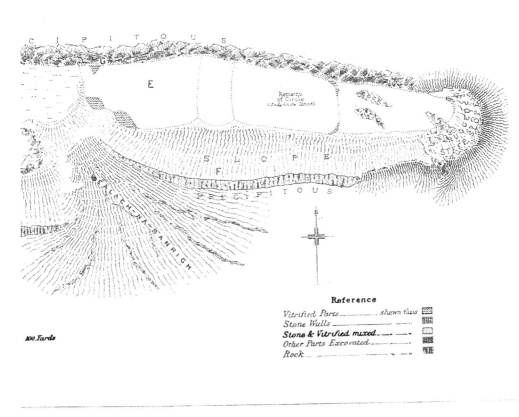

MACUISNEACHAN.

in Rome, and it has surprised me much to find how much
that great city in imperial times was built of rubble. Great
buildings that astonish us, baths of Caracalla, palaces of the
emperors, great arches high and wide, were of concrete and
broken masses, and the half spans still hang with the mixture
hardened into one stone, almost like natural conglomerate ;
remains of former houses broken up, with remains of statues,
and pieces of bricks, stones, marble, or otherwise, are all
smashed together, and the older Rome forms the material
for the newer. The buildings, to the very centre of the walls,
are a type of the empire itself, where nations were crushed,
annihilated, or converted into Romans, to all external appearance, until the outer form broke down, and the real
material showed itself. We may thus make these walls a
good lesson for the ethnologist.

The vitrified walls, like the Roman walls spoken of, are a
kind of rubble work, and this way of building has a dignity
which seems not to have been considered sufficiently. Now,
in modern times, it is coming again into use, and we seem
to be learning, as the Romans learned, that it is extremely
expensive to build with quarry stone, or even with burnt
clay or bricks, and some of our largest engineering works
are being done with rubble and cement, or concrete. Some
may think the use of rubble to have arisen from the primeval
habit of making a mound of earth as a protection, a habit
common among the Zingari of Hungary at the present day,
and seen abundantly in the raths of Ireland. These form
walls of enclosure, as common, probably, as the walls to our
farmsteads and gardens, and, as a culminating point, ending
in the earthworks or walls of the latest fortifications. We

can see here the natural growth of ideas, and it needs no communication among nations to cause ideas to grow when the materials and the wants, as well as the machinery, are the same in each to an obvious extent. To determine to what extent they are the same is not easy, but we cannot doubt that the use of earthworks would occur readily to many. The use of cement, however, implies invention; the early Romans did not use it; it became common only when the greatest amount of building was required; we have not used it until lately, when the demands upon us for building material had put us in a position similar to that into which the Romans were driven when building increased so rapidly under the emperors.

If people were accustomed to build with loose stones, it would be a very natural wish to make them keep together; and if ever a beacon fire raged unusually and burned a part of the wall into one mass by melting, the discovery would be made. Still it requires invention, or at least good observation, to see the value of such an accident; and who can say if some wise stranger did not first find it out and show the example,— some wise man coming from the East, and who had lingered with his tribe in Bohemia, where also a vitrified fort has been found? or shall we account for that Bohemian fort by imagining some soldiers from Caledonia sent by the Romans over the Rhine, and driven farther than was agreeable to them, making use there of their old habits learned at home?

I throw together a number of ideas, but cannot give yet a full examination. I am more inclined to attribute the influx from time to time of the new ideas to the immigration of strangers, whether wanderers or conquerors, than to invention.

Marauding has always been a favourite pursuit, and it comes before merchandising. Some one probably came and showed that the Caterthun system of building with loose stones was a bad one, and showed how to build firmly, as on the Tap-o-Noth, and the invention seems to have spread from near that part. Had these new men come as great conquerors, they would have brought many people, and we should probably have had some indication of them; but if they came as wanderers, either marauding or selling, there might be few. I am more disposed to think of a few dropping in at a time when there would be little to steal; besides, at a later time, we have new ideas coming into the east of Scotland, and resulting in the peculiar Scottish sculptures. It is too much to suppose all to have originated on the spot. It was most natural for people from Continental Europe to come to the east of Britain first, because of the distance of the western coast, and even from the Mediterranean, it was more natural for navigators who kept near to the land to find Kent than Cornwall. It was probably not until after a long familiarity with the seas that the inhabitants of the Iberian peninsula found out that it was really shorter to go to Ireland than to the north of Britain, and probably, almost certainly, this would apply to Cornwall and Wales. Ireland, in the time of Tacitus, was apparently pretty well known, although that historian has not taken much trouble to describe it.

It is to be remarked that the decided advances in the north of Scotland came after the time of Pytheas, who leaves us an idea of great desolation and poverty; whereas in Tacitus we have iron chariots, which indicate many great strides in civilisation. It is quite possible to believe an immigration to have taken place abundantly in those very early times without our historic knowledge being affected, but it could in that case be of only two races, Celtic or Scandinavian, if language is to be our only guide. Small numbers would account for new ideas and habits without change of tongue.

I did at one time imagine that considerable numbers might have come and brought the face so peculiarly Scottish, which is seen in considerable perfection in the north-east, or rather from Aberdeenshire to Ayrshire; but now I am more inclined to look at the great extent to which that face is spread in Scotland, and especially to see it prominently in the Pictish districts. It may be an ancient Caledonian peculiarity; where obtained is another question.

There is, of course, a certain amount of fancy in these discussions; but there are a few more reasons which I hope to be able to make clearer for some of the opinions. New ideas and habits seem to have come in along with the peculiar physiognomy which characterizes so much of Scotland that it may be called the Scottish. If the features referred to are Caledonian, they separate that tribe from the Irish Scot and the Kymry very distinctly. I hope I may be excused for giving this in such hurried sentences; it is a subject that deserves much more minute treatment, but one must only feel the way.

Numerous photographs are very much wanted to illustrate Scottish ethnography. Many varieties of face are seen in our country villages, but there is one which a photograph only can explain, more frequently found in Scotland than else-where, and perhaps nowhere else distinctly.

CHAPTER XIV.

KEILLS—CONNEL AND ITS CAIRNS, ETC.

LOUDOUN.—Let us go again to Keills. I think I shall keep to the old and familiar word. The post-office has taken the name of Ledaig—the name of the hill and the farm to the south. I prefer to call it Keills—the name of the little church, of which scarcely a score of stones remain, and of the churchyard.

Cameron.—You still refuse to yield to the name of Selma; although there is both Selma and New Selma. Is that not rather unfeeling?

Loudoun.—We have argued that point before, and I must keep to my principles. Keills is an old and respected word, Selma is the embodiment of a fanciful theory.

Cameron.—Why do you try to remove the romance from this spot? Look only at that heath we are passing. I cannot see it without covering it with the spirits of the heroes that lived here. I have already referred to the "traveller unseen, the bender of the thistle of Lora." Excuse me returning to this topic which is so dear to me.

O'Keefe.—That translation, if it is one, is not quite clear enough. Dr. Clerk renders it so—

> " Thou genial breeze, for evermore unseen,
>   Swaying thistles round Lora of storms,
>   Wandering through narrow glen of the wind,
>   Why so suddenly forsake my ear ? "

I confess, however, the word " narrow glen " does not
suit this broad heath of Connel or Ledaig.

Loudoun.—That is one of the passages that seem to me
more beautiful and natural in the Gaelic, if I can judge;
there may be thousands of the same of which I cannot
judge.   That is the first sentence in Macpherson's Ossian.
It is a fine poetic impersonation.   I shall try to translate
it simply—

" Thou pleasant but ever unseen breeze, bending the thistle
of Lora of storms; thou that art wandering up the narrow
glen of the wind, why so suddenly hast thou left mine ear ? "

That is my picture: it personifies the breeze travelling
along, a lonely visitor, never seen but by its effects, and it
comes at once like a weird spirit that we can never escape.
I seldom now see a thistle bending without a mysterious
presence seeming to make itself partially known.

Cameron.—I should like you to prove that Lora is a name
associated with the falls and the moss and the hill.

Loudoun.—I would gladly prove it, if I could, but first I
see no narrow glen, and next I see no reason for calling the
peaceful plain " Lora of storms."   The scene suggests some
place in the mountains.   Glencoe or upper Glen Etive would
suit better; many other places would suit also.

Cameron.—But is there not an Ossian's cairn over there
among the trees, and can you not prove that he was buried
there ?

Loudoun.—I fear we cannot. There are many claimants, and this has only of late come into notice. I fear it is a name given for want of a name, as one might say, "Giant's grave," and very much as people give names to their houses in Glasgow or in London, the names that are dear to them, however remote in romance or in reality. The mere name is not a proof without the examination of circumstances. Lora seems to me as hard to find as Loda's Hall on Cruachan Ben. This does not destroy the fine feeling of the lines or the deep significance which these vague forms have, as shown in nature here, and in the soul of man, who must so often bend in awe in contemplation of its effects, as well as before its occasional violence. You see therefore that I have sympathy with the feeling, whoever the author may be.

Margaet.—I scarcely like to think of the time you spoke of when glaciers filled the valleys; it would be dreary, and the loch would be impassable. Surely no one could have lived here; it would be a cold desert.

Loudoun.—That is not a fair conclusion. We like to go to Chamouni, which is most pleasant in summer if not very pleasant to most men in winter.

Cameron.—I think people must have lived here even then, because they say that the Dun was an island, and. that may be a tradition.

Loudoun.—People say so without reason. It would appear that man did not live here in the glacial period of this island, and certainly not advanced man, but after all we do not know if that age was very long ago. The Dun of Uisnach was not an island when the oldest remains were set up in the plain. The standing stone in the field is very old and weatherworn,

apparently older than the Dun. It was not put up when the
Dun was an island ; it might have happened that the sea
came in on the north side and extended pretty far, but not
a quarter of a mile ; we have another standing stone barring
its progress, if we may so speak, and pointing to the fact
that people do not put up standing·stones in the sea.

Cameron.—Well! look at Ledaig Hill, on the south-west
there seem to be cliffs caused by the sea.

Loudoun.—Yes, that may be, and quite in accordance with
what has been said.

Cameron.—Besides that there is a place at Ledaig, very little
south from the hexagonal school-house, called Tir nan
biorlinn, the place of boats, as if it were usual to put boats
up there. Biorlinn is a very ancient word, meaning a boat
made of one log of wood.[1]

Loudoun.—That suggests a difficulty, but I may give at once
a reason why even in very early times the sea can be shown
not to have come so far in all probability.   South of the
clachan of Ledaig, and not far south of the point where the
roads from Connel Ferry and Achnacree meet, a few yards
from the road on the west side and in a gravel mound,
there was found a little stone coffin, one of the smallest,
roughest things that could be imagined, as if for a small
infant. For rudeness and simplicity nothing could sur-
pass it. It was only about two feet long, made with the
boulder stones abundant there. The interior resembled the
section of an egg lengthways, and to cover it were two
pieces of the clay slate of the district, of the length of the
exterior. No remains were found, and no charcoal. It was

---

[1] See *Armstrong's* Dictionary.

out of the usual confines of Christian burial, and we can imagine that at a time when only the chief people were buried in cairns or stone structures, some mother had determined that her little one should also have a similar honour, and put up this small one to its memory. It could be built in half an hour. Unfortunately when it was once opened, people, who had left it all their lives unheeded, disturbed it too much to allow a drawing to be made, even a few days afterwards. Besides this, there was the cairn at the school-house, where many urns were found.

Cameron.—All these on the level of the moss and bank at the Dun, I suppose? Still there might have been an inlet of the sea reaching to the spot for the boats.

Loudoun.—That is true enough, but at the same spot may be seen a pretty deep peat bog, and this, in all probability, covers an old lake, on which people rowed or kept boats in rough weather. It may have been part of the same in which the lake dwelling was found. That is a little farther south, not far from the junction of the roads, and a little east. But we shall spend a day there.

O'Keefe.—We may as well walk on to the ferry. That little stream has made a deep bed which is pleasantly green.

Loudoun.—Yes; and it shows you what the whole land here is made of—rounded boulders, of a small size, with earth intermixed. I dare say the sea is heaping up a little more in certain parts where the tide rolls in most violently. I referred you once to a curious circular spot here when, at Lochanabeich, we had a conversation about a supposed Thing-wald, a place for a court according to Norwegian fashion. It is a little south of Ledaig farm-house. I may be wrong.

and others might prefer to call it a **rath,** but it seems too small for any defence. It is more like a place for a baron's court, if such were ever held here but that might be doubted.

Cameron.—The idea of a baron's court rose from the name given to the similar but much larger circle over at Loch-a-nan-Ragh, which we saw only for a few minutes. Instead of going straight to the ferry, let us cross the moor to **Lochanabeich,** and see the deep basin, and then pass over to Loch-a-nan-Ragh. I shall read here an account I brought with me, and we may take this occasion to pay a second visit as we intended at the time. It is well to see how another man views it, and I should like to examine it more carefully— "When the Baron's Cairn was visited by us,[1] a place near it was noticed called *Cuairt a' Bharan,* the court of the baron. The court consists of the greater part of a circle, which has been made by throwing up the soil, at present about three feet high, thus making a ditch outside, now filling up with peat moss. In the middle of the circle nearly is an artificial and elongated mound. The circle is not complete to the north-west, and opposite this opening is a large mound nearly as large as the circle itself, and higher than its banks or walls. The wall forming the circle has no peat upon it, but only a little grass on the rough gravel. The mound inside the circle is entirely of peat 3 to 4 feet deep, or much more than the moss around. The inner mound has evidently been raised, that is, in contradistinction to being cut out, and the same may be said of the outer mound ; peat could not, so far as I know, grow to such a height above the level of the neighbourhood. I

[1] See p. 57.

imagined this to be the home of the baron whose cairn was near, and I therefore cut trenches in several directions in order to find traces of the homestead.   But within the circle the level part is only grass on a thin soil, the peat having been removed to make the mound, with a little gravel sufficient to indicate this.   There were really no remains of a house ; and it appeared much rather as if a Thing or Scandinavian court had been there.   And this I do not doubt.   The name and the appearance alike point to it.   The courts were not held close to towns.   The elongated mound in the centre was in all probability a platform of security, as well as of dignity, for the court.   The outer mound opposite the open part of the circle would suit well as a place for spectators.   Indeed, some such place was absolutely necessary, where outside the wall there was only a ditch.   This would account for all that we see. Extremely ancient, therefore, we cannot consider it ; we must look to the Scandinavian times first probably, and to the introduction after that of the more southern institutions, and the court of the baron.

" When examining this court, I was told of the other mentioned as about midway between Connel and Ledaig.   This was also examined by trenching, but nothing was found.   Towards the sea, on the north-west, there is, as at this court, a raised part.   It would hold few people certainly, but the circle was small also.   I suppose it was a very general thing, if not a rule, for these courts to be in secluded places.   Protection was required for the officers.   In the story of Burnt Njal, we see why that protection was required.   A difference of opinion on an important point in the trial ended in a battle, and the death of about thirty people.   Let us imagine a similar dispute to have taken place at the simple peat court on the shore of the small and shallow Loch-a-nan-Ragh on Ledaig Moss, and we can easily finish the quarrel by the death of the baron, and have him buried under the cairn now called the Baron's Cairn, standing near the Baron's Court. This is, of course, a mere conjecture, but it is one in accordance with a very probable event, as well as the facts of the case as they now stand connected with traditionary names."

However, I judge this cairn to be not from prehistoric times, but, in all probability, from a comparatively modern time. Of course, one may say that the name of the court may have been transferred to the cairn, and if a very great deal depended on the matter, greater care would be required before concluding ; but there is at present nothing hanging on the result, and I shall leave it with the belief that the traditionary name is correct until some positive reason, however small, shall be found to throw suspicion upon it. Tradition, we see, has much to boast of in this district, as the retention of ancient names shows.

It has been asked, why the courts were made round ? We may also say, why were circles made, instead of squares, &c. ? Is it not a mark of early work ? Children always build round at first: it is for want of a definite idea ; they hasten to make the lines meet. Dr. Livingstone could not prevent his Africans from making round walls. A straight line and an angle are exact ideas of later growth.

Loudoun.—No one has been able to explain the meaning of Loch nan Ragh, because they spelt it wrong. Let it be Radh, which is the same in sound and is Gaelic (whereas the other is not Gaelic, so far as I know), and we have at once the Loch of the Speeches or Decisions. See the use of a Thingvalla in that wonderful book, Burnt Njal. It quite agrees with all the rest, and is a beautiful piece of old history.

O'Keefe.—Why not Rath, the Loch of the Rath, and this *court* might have been a Rath as well as a court?

Loudoun.—True, it is possible, but Radh refers more to speaking, although more fanciful than Rath. We have also the Norse and German word *Rath, counsel,* for a derivation. It would not seem that this form for a court could be called Celtic, in which case it does not take us to very early times, and I must leave the exact relation to be found. But the baron seems to have been buried near to this, and I shall read an account of the place. We had our luncheon here once, and it is well to come again to renew our acquaintance. It certainly suggests difficulties. "The Baron's cairn" (see Plate) is not so large as some others, and nothing remarkable is seen about it—a dreary heap of stones in a moss. It is not chambered. An opening was made at the top in order to see, and without disturbing the sides in the slightest. Indeed it is too low to be chambered. It has been mentioned by several who have written of this district, and been sometimes spoken of alone as if it were important, but its only importance seems to consist in its having a name that speaks of times less distant than in other cases. No one can tell who was the baron.

Cameron.—As to the enclosure called the "Baron's Court," do you not think that it may have been the homestead as well as the court of the baron? This old garden, as I suppose it to have been, may have enclosed a house. One cannot mistake the changes that take place on turf near inhabited places. The site was chosen probably to be a little off the moss, and near the small lake. It is not mentioned in Sir John Sinclair's Notes, or in the Statistical Account. The choice of place may have arisen from the accessibility. The way from Loch Etive is less mossy if one keeps on the road near to the first little lake, and skirting it for a while, goes on to the second. It may, however, be that the frequent passage of feet has rendered this more solid. It may also be that the solid grass plots around houses near a moss are obtained in a great measure by the occasional tread of feet pressing and draining, as well as by the waste products nourishing a richer vegetation. At present it is interesting to connect a cairn with the old dwelling-place of its occupant. The "Baron's cairn" stands on the soil below the moss, and there is a depression round it as if the moss had been cut down to make abundant room for the cairn. It is not at all probable that a burial, which evidently took a good deal of trouble, would take place in the wet moss. I think this the proper explanation of the resting place of such a cairn, although the weight of stones might cause a depression; and water passing, along with air, continually through the cairn, would remove peat.

Loudoun.—By the side of the loch from Connel Ferry westward, we come to several cairns. One is very large, and the farm takes its name from it, Achnacarn. I will not at present pretend to characterize every one. All those along the road have been diminished in size, and some are scarcely distinguishable. That they should be found along, the roads speaks in favour of their being raised when the moss was difficult to traverse. It is true that these roads are new (forty years old); but consider that the line along which they go would even in remote times be passable; that towards the lake manifestly so, as the moss ends there, and that towards the hill would no doubt have been made passable from its convenience for those going from the extreme points of Benderloch. The latter must have been frequently traversed, even if the place were thinly inhabited, exactly as it is daily now passed by many persons as well as the postman. At any rate the cairns are near the roads, as a rule, and I think this shows the moss to be older than they. There are one or two towards the cottages of Loch-a-nan-Ragh, and three near Lochanabeich. These were not less than fifty feet in diameter; only the bases remain. Dr. Wilson is quite correct in saying that they stand in the soil below, but we need not consider them older than the moss, nor does he say that they are, although one might infer it. One at the house of Lochanabeich cost a great deal of trouble in digging, but nothing was found. It was large, and the houses and byres were built out of it. Who knows if it was not a mere collection of stones to clear the land, as we see so often in Deeside.

But we may now return to Oban, crossing the ferry again.

Cameron.—Let us watch : at about a mile from the ferry on the road to Oban, we find the house of Sir Donald Campbell of Dunstaffnage, somewhat retreating from the sea. Not far east of the entrance is a small plantation, it marks the spot of a stone circle which was destroyed long ago. Now Sir Donald preserves reverently the very site. One wonders at the usual destruction, as the people spend more strength upon it than would serve to put their garden walls in order, and to sow vegetables, or clean the cow-houses. A little nearer Oban, in the same valley and on the same level as the above, is the farm of Salmore. Inland from the house was a mound partly natural; an opening was made to obtain sand, I believe, in 1874, when a large stone kist was found. The men were below the level of it, and the whole fell down. The stones were built into the wall along the highroad next the house, and when I arrived a few days afterwards, no trace was left on the original spot except a hole in the earth. As this happened only three years ago, we see how memorials of the past leave us.

We shall soon now be in Oban, and as we look at that Castle of Dunstaffnage, we see that, if the situation is not so good for defence as Dun Uisnach, it is at least more convenient for men who sometimes wish to go farther inland.

Urn from a Cave under Dun Bhaile an Righ, (Valanree).

CHAPTER XV.

A WALK ABOUT KEILLS AND BARCALDINE.

CAMERON.—We can never finish Keills, there is so much interesting matter, but we can run over and go again into the Ledaig strawberry garden; if we walk high enough up and exactly under the great overhanging rock, we shall see a hollow part, scarcely a cave, it is so small. In this Mr. John Campbell found the urn[1] of which I showed you a drawing yesterday, but we can go into the house and see the urn itself.

Margaet.—I should be afraid to live under such a rock, beautiful as it is. I saw some sheep on the top; do they never fall over?

Shepherd.—Very seldom; one fell close beside me in the garden. It never moved, it was struck quite dead at once.

Margaet.—And can you go up to the top of the rock?

Ossianite.—Yes; and a beautiful walk it is. Let us go by the end of the house to the south, and up along the little wood and the small brook. You see the path steep, but look now what a beautiful sward is above, and what a view!

[1] See Figure.

One wonders in this weather if heaven can be finer.   I brought
with me a cup to drink out of this well of Fingal.

O'Keefe.—Oh, this is the well that is said to have communicated with the well in Dun Uisnach ; but you surely do not
believe it ?

Ossianite.—This hill, *Dun Bhaile an Righ,* is named by us
from tradition, the fort of the Town of the King ; and I do
not doubt that there were people enough to drink of the well.
I used to be told fine stories of this water—that it flowed down
in pipes to Dun Mac Uisnachan, and that it supplied the
heroes of Fingal with drink, and perhaps with this they made
the heather ale which they drank out of shells in Selma.
But I have learned to be satisfied with the romance, even
when the facts do not appear strong.   There is an old man
down there who tells you that he saw the pipes that led the
water along the fields between the two Duns, and these
pipes were made of lead.   Now this is too much even for
me.

Loudoun.—Yes ; it is too much.   The pipes spoken of by
some person last century were made of wood, and they are too
far back to have been seen by the man you speak of.   Besides,
we have no certainty that there were any pipes ; there were
hollow stems of trees, and although unbelievers are apt to
exaggerate difficulties, it is not the less true that the proofs
do not come to us sound, and we require very good proofs
for such a thing.   At any rate, it is clear that the water could
not have been led through this rock ; it must have been led
down the brow of the hill if led at all.

Ossianite.—Well, it may be so ; but the idea was that
it went down through a tunnel in the rock, and along the

chief Dun. I remember when it was very deep, and we used to throw stones down it. My father used to say it was deeper once, and he used to wait till he heard the stones touch the bottom, and the length of time showed that it was deep, but it has always been filling up.

Loudoun.—Well, let us go to Dun Uisnach, and let us set a man to dig the well till he comes to the bottom and we shall hear. This well which you see, supposed to correspond with that on Valanree, is on the side of Dun Uisnach, on a rather dangerous place. The sheep go there to drink, unconscious of the many mysteries which have long been connected with it. We need not go up until it is cleared, but will pursue our walk. It is probably not very deep, but it may take some days to clear it.

They did not return till the next day when they met the man who had undertaken to dig the well. So we may, for the sake of continuity, give the result here—

Donnachan —I have got to the bottom.

Loudoun.—What! a hundred and fifty feet deep?

Donnachan.—No; about three or four feet deep.

Loudoun.—Oh, Cameron! what has become of your stories? The well has been in books as a wonder for a hundred years; the story about pipes has made people look for a great civilization here, and the great depth of the well gave people an idea of skilful engineering, but it is an exaggeration to say even that it is five feet and a half deep, although by taking the upper side you may call it so. And we have a clean, hard clay slate all the way, with a few cracks through which water trickles from above—the drainage of the Dun.

Ossianite.—But suppose cracks to exist down to the bottom and up to the other hill. Is not this possible?

Loudoun.—Possible in the work of nature, but impossible for man to lead it through such compact rock, impenetrable for water; besides, there are no cracks, and the water comes from the upper side of the well, and the amount is no more than the surface above it could supply several times, if there were an outlet. No; the whole delusion is gone with the touch of a spade. Let us go to the other wonders.

Herd Boy.—I know a very wonderful place over there; if you stamp upon it, it shakes and sounds hollow. There must be great rooms below.

O'Keefe.—Now, here is another grand discovery; Aladdin's Cave over again! I can imagine six great chambers for the six great kings that were here, and these rooms filled with their treasures, received when they had messengers from Spain and the Indies, and lived in glory. It is, however, very strange. The ground sounds very hollow; we may make a beginning to-night. Dig here.

Donnachan.—The spade will not go down; there is rock within a few inches.

Loudoun.—Nonsense; it must be only on a small spot. Try there, and remove a good deal of the surface.

Donnachan.—It is certain. There is only a thin turf, and then rock. When the turf is gone there is no more shaking, and no sound of hollowness.

Loudoun.—Another delusion gone, and the sleeping kings

if they are there must be stoned up. This is a land of wonders.

O'Keefe.—For this hour at least it has proved one of delusions.

Cameron.—Down in the field, when ploughing, Stewart once struck on great flat stones, very large indeed, and as they must be near the surface, you might dig for them.

Mr. J. S.—These were sought for, and borings made all over the. spot indicated, and on still more ground, but there was no obstruction so near the surface and no indication could be found. (They are previously noticed.)

Cameron.—Let us move on and I will show you something curious in another way. Here on the road to Loch Creran and the New Barcaldine is a circle that only appears occasionally. That is, it comes out for a few weeks in the year and then disappears.

Loudoun.—I think you must be joking now. Is it the ghost of a circle or is it a delusion of your mind? I would rather believe in one of the mist ghosts of Ossian.

Cameron.—See it for yourself. There the stones of the circle are gathered together, and some are broken up and fill up a hole, but you see the circle clearly on the corn. When the corn is cut the circle disappears, and, indeed, in the ripening it does so.

Loudoun.—I suppose you see the reason. The soil where stones were is different from the rest, the corn grows higher and keeps longer green. The farmer has made little out of his desecration. I should have thought there had been many circles near this place.

Cameron.—I should think the same. There was a large

one near the Dun that we have left ; it was called " Clagh nan Druidhneach," or the burial place of the Druids. It was taken down to build that ugly two-storied house ; you saw that some of the stones came from the Dun also. A bard of the place, famous here and around for his cutting satires, wrote a severe poem on the act ; but he was hooted at by stronger men with less feeling. The bard was James Shaw—a native of Mull, and called the bard of Loch Nell ; his poem was against Finlay M'Kichen, who took down cairns and circles for his very poor buildings, unfitly called Selma. The poem alluded to is in Mackenzie's " Beauties of Gaelic Poetry," but it is not a remarkable production.

You must not suppose that you have seen all. As you go on you come to a slight elevation of ground, and not far from the road side, to the left, is a circle of stones very complete. There are also indications of another circle of which only two or three stones remain. The stones are not high, but they may be seen by attention from the road, half hidden among whins or gorse.

I must show you also two beautiful but small and double circles, although much in ruin. They are seen before we come to the first farm-house on the right, and you will know them at once by the drawing which you saw, and the pleasant view it gave you of the Appin hills.[1]

Margaet.—This is a magnificent position—surely chosen for its beauty.

Cameron.—Yes ; and at the house there you may see a tall stone that had fallen down, but was re-erected by the farmer. We must thank him.

[1] See Plate.

Remains of two double Circles at Barcaldine and outline of Appin hills.

Whilst we are here, nearly south of the old castle, we must look at the long rídgy rising gróund; it is almost artificial in appearance, but examination proves it natural. The people call it Tom Ossian or the mound of Ossian, and they will tell you that Ossian used to sit there and admire the scene whilst his father Fingal reigned in Selma on the Dun we have studied.

Loudoun.—They may fancy anything, but the smallest trace of authority is wanting.

O'Keefe.—I fear it is; I wish he could be imagined sitting here. In Ireland we hear of him sitting in sorrow lamenting former days, speaking evil of the clerics and the sound of bells, and admiring his own comrades, thus—

> " Didst thou see the fight and the noble banners,
>   Never wouldst thou think but of the glory of the Feinn ;"

and saying to the clerics—

> " Were my men all in life, I'd not bear thy howling,
>   And I'd make thee suffer in return for thy talk."
>
> *Dean of Lismore's Book.*

Cameron.—But that is not fair, these are only spurious Ossianic Irish poems.

O'Keefe.—Well, I promised not to begin a controversy, but you gave some specimens of your Ossian, and I thought I might introduce a line or two of ours, especially as it was preserved in the sixteenth century by the Dean of that very island we see before us, between us and Morven. The dispute with the cleric is very curious: Ossian trying to prove that his Fenians were grander than all the army of priests, and Finn himself more generous than heaven.

M

Loudoun.—The origin of these poems translated by Dr. M'Lauchlan is not known, but the writer had fully imbibed a spirit by no means Christian, and we see that at whatever time they were written the Finn spirit had not died out.

Cameron.—I believe there is a cat-stone over in the new Barcaldine direction, but as we are walking to-day, it is much too far, and we cannot leap like Cuchullin, or fly like Sweeny. I shall only tell you about it.

Margaet.—What is a cat-stone ?

Cameron.—*Cat* is a corruption of *Cath,* which in modern times is sounded Cāa (very long ā), and means a battle.   The field in which the stone is, the people know by the name of Achaw, which ought to be Achadh a Chath. The language, I must confess, is breaking down, and first the consonants go, and then intermediate vowels, and nothing will be left soon, as a friend said, but " pechs and sighs." [1] However you may at some other time go towards the farmhouse of Auchinreir, and you will see the pillar about three quarters of a mile from the spot where the private road leaves the main road.   There are no markings on it, and no indications of any remains in the neighbourhood have been noted.

Margaet.—Well, let us take a rest, and I propose that you give us an account of Sweeny's flying and Cuchullin's leaping, as I never heard of such things before.

Loudoun.—We'll sit down on Tom Ossian ; whilst we are eating lunch, Mr. O'Keefe will tell us how active the men were of old.   I dare say he will not be pleased if I laugh at some of the tales.

---

[1] " Pech " is Scotch for " panting."

LEAPING, FLYING, AND SPIRIT HUNTING.

O'Keefe.—Cuchullin is said to have made wonderful leaps —he leapt easily over a house. There was a great trial of skill and championship between Cuchullin, Conall Cearnach, and Laeghaire Buadhach, and it was at the Cathair or fortified mansion of Curoi MacDaire, King of West Munster, on the peninsula in Kerry, which separates the Bay of Tralee on the north from the Bay of Dingle or Castlemaine on the south. The house was to be attacked by men and monsters, and each one was to watch one night. Cuchullin watched on the third night, when the three green men were to come, and the three wandering herds, and the three sons of the musical Dornmar. It was also the night when the lake monster was to devour the inhabitants of the house. After killing the nine men, and other nine, and other nine, the monster came up, and thirty cubits were above the house, and the best of a king's house might enter his jaws. "Cuchullin then executed a leap called the *form-chleas,* and sprang up in the air, and, with the velocity of a twisting wheel, flew round the monster." To find the other two champions, he thought he must jump over the wall, as he fancied they had done. "He would fly from the ground till his face came plump against the Cathair; at another time he would leap up into the air till he could see all that was in the Cathair." "At last in one of his furious fits he flew over the Cathair from without and lighted on the Cathair within, at the door of the royal house." [1]

[1] *Manners and Customs of the Ancient Irish,* O'Sullivan, vol. III. p. 76 *seq.*

But perhaps the most wonderful account of leaping is
that of Sweeny's. I must read it over to you when we get
to Oban ; it is found in the battle of Magh Rath, as
translated by Dr. O'Donovan, and at p. 231 of the edition
of the Archæological Series. I have not seen it quoted
except once by myself. "With respect to Sweeny, the son
of Colmar, Cuar, the son of Cobhthach, King of Dal Araidh,
we shall treat of him for another while. Fits of giddiness
came over him at *the sight* of the horrors, grimness, and
rapidity of the Gaels ; at the looks, brilliancy, and irksome-
ness of the foreigners, at the rebounding furious shouts and
bellowings of the various embattled tribes on both sides,
rushing against and coming into collision with one another.
Huge, flickering, horrible, aerial phantoms rose up, so that they
were in cursed, commingled crowds tormenting him ; and in
dense, rustling, clamorous, left-turning hordes, without ceasing ;
and in dismal, regular, aerial, storm-shrieking, hovering, fiend-
like hosts constantly in motion, shrieking and howling as they
hovered about them (*i.e.* both armies) in every direction to
cow and dismay soft youths, but to invigorate and mightily
rouse champions and warriors ; so that from the uproar of
battle, the frantic pranks of the demons, and the clashing of
arms, the sound of the heavy blows reverberating on the
points of heroic spears, and keen edges of swords, and the
warlike borders of broad shields, the noble hero (Suihhne)
Sweeny was filled and intoxicated with heavy horror, panic,
dismay, fickleness, unsteadiness, fear, flightiness, giddiness,
terror, and imbecility ; so that there was not a joint of a
member of him from head to foot which was not converted
into a confused shaking mass, from the effect of fear and the

panic of dismay.   His feet trembled, as if incessantly shaken
by the force of a stream ; his arms and various edged
weapons fell from him, the power of his hands having been
enfeebled and relaxed around them, and rendered incapable
of holding them.   The inlets of hearing were expanded and
quickened by the horrors of lunacy ; the vigour of his brain in
the cavities of his head was destroyed by the clamour of the
conflict ; his heart shrunk within him with the panic of
dismay ; his speech became faltering from the giddiness of
imbecility ; his very soul fluttered from hallucination, and with
many and various phantasms, for that (*i.e. the soul*) was the root
and true basis of fear itself.   He might be compared on this
occasion to a salmon in a weir, or to a bird after being caught
in the straight prison of a crib.   But the person to whom
these horrid phantasms and dire symptoms of flight and
fleeing presented themselves, had never before been a coward,
or a lunatic void of valour ; but he was thus confounded
because he had been cursed by St. Ronan, and denounced by
the great saints of Erin, because he had violated their
guarantee, and slain an ecclesiastical student of their people
over the consecrated trench, that is, a pure clear-bottomed
spring over which the shrine and communion of the Lord
was placed, for the nobles and arch-chieftains of Erin, and
for all *the people* in general, before the commencement of
the battle."   When Sweeny "was seized with this frantic fit,
he made a supple, very light leap, and where he alighted was on
the boss of the shield of the hero next him ; and he made a
second leap and perched on the vertex of the helmet of the same
hero, who, however, did not feel him, though the chair on
which he rested was an uneasy one.   Wherefore he came to

an imbecile, irrational determination, namely to turn his back on mankind, and to herd with deer, run only with the showers, and flee with the birds, and to feast in wildernesses. Accordingly he made a third, active, very light leap, and perched on the top of the sacred tree which grew on the smooth surface of the plain, in which tree the inferior people and the debilitated of the men of Erin were seated looking on at the battle. These screamed at him from every direction as they saw him, to press and drive him into the same battle again; and he in consequence made three furious bounces to shun the battle, but it happened that, *instead of avoiding it,* he went back into the same field of conflict, through the giddiness and imbecility of his hallucination; but it was not the earth he reached, but alighted on the shoulders of men and the tops of their helmets."

"In this manner the attention and vigilance of all in general were fixed on Sweeny, so that the conversation of the heroes amongst each other was, 'Let not' said they, 'let not the man with the wonderful gold-embroidered tunic pass from you, without capture and revenge.' He had the tunic of the monarch, the grandson of Ainmire upon him that day, which had been presented by Domhnall to Congal, and by Congal to Sweeny, as Sweeny himself testifies in another place—

> ' It was the saying of every one
> Of the valiant beautiful host,
> Permit not to go from you to the dense shrubbery
> The man with the beautiful tunic.'

His giddiness and hallucination of imbecility became greater in consequence of all having thus recognized him, and he continued in this terrible confusion, until a hard quick shower

of hailstones—an omen of slaughter to the men of Erin—
began to fall, and with this shower he passed away like
every other bird of prey ; as Sweeny said in another place—

> ' This was my first run,
> Rapid was my flight,
> The shot of the javelin expired
> For me with the shower.'

And it was by lunacy and imbecility he determined his
counsels from that time as long as he lived."

In ecclesiastical and saintly records we have other accounts
very remarkable, and this curious peculiarity, especially in
Celtic literature, ought to be accounted for.

Loudoun.—I doubt if it is more than the Celtic method of
running ideas to a conclusion rapidly, and *light-headedness* is
taken in its fullest sense, so that the person is said to fly.
The same faculty makes the Irishman a wit ; he jumps over
several lines of reasoning in an instant, and as he does not
care to fit them exactly, they produce the ludicrous. If he
is carefully educated and connects the reasoning, it makes
him a mathematician able to leap over several formulæ,
which it is beyond the patience of human nature to go over
very coolly except with the hope of learning the methods.

I shall give an idea of the exaggeration : it is in a most interesting volume,[1] by Dr. Reeves, " The Life of St. Columba."
In a note, p. 289, we have an old account—"Brandubh was killed
on the morrow, and demons carried his soul into the air, and
Maedhog (a saint), Abbot of Ferns, heard the wail of his
soul as it was undergoing pain, while he was with the reapers,
and he went into the air and began to battle with the demons,

[1] Published by Edmonston & Douglas, Edinburgh.

and they passed over Hy (Iona); and Columbkille heard them while he was writing, and he struck the style into his cloak, and went to battle to the aid of Maedhog, in defence of Brandubh's soul. And the battle passed over Rome, and the style fell out of Columbkille's cloak, and dropped in front of Gregory, who took it in his hand. Columbkille followed the soul of Brandubh to heaven. When he reached it, the congregation of heaven were singing 'Te decet,' &c. Columbkille did the same as the people of heaven, and they brought Brandubh's soul back to his body again." This is, certainly, very wild, but it is decidedly led by the reasoning powers, it follows out the consequences of the power of flying, and it follows the power of flying farther than any previous idea of it, ignoring many physical conditions.

Margaet.—But are we not told of many saints who have been raised into the air in prayer?

Loudoun.—Yes; the number is considerable, and in a very interesting volume by Elihu Rich, entitled "Occult Science,"[1] you may read of them and many strange things.

Margaet.—But have they any truth?

Loudoun.—I never saw an act of levitation, but do not presume to decide. Why should a saint not cling to the ceiling, when half a hundredweight of iron may be made to hang to a magnet? There is a counter-agent to the power of gravitation for iron; may there not be one for man? No wide-minded scientific man rejects the idea as impossible, but it certainly is not proved. There does lurk in diamagnetics a little seed of thought, which may make it intelligible, and science which in its youth taught us that we could often use the word

---

[1] One of the volumes of the "Encyclopædia Metropolitana," Griffin.

impossible, is now teaching us that its use is more dangerous than before.

Cameron.—The world is full of wonders, but we only get a glimpse of a new one occasionally. At present we have a view of something more homely before us.

We must have a look at the old castle of Barcaldine now. The new house is much more beautiful, in its fine park rich with trees as if in the South of England, whilst its hills are of the wildest, and its garden and hothouses give tropical fruit; but the position is close, and I prefer that of the old one. The building is a ruin, and it scarcely belongs to history. We shall only go up the stair and wonder at the smallness—but don't wonder too much. These chieftains living in castles were certainly surrounded with numerous followers who had smaller houses, and there must have been more life and happiness than we can well imagine possible within these poor bare walls. Now let us go to Ach-na-Mona(dh).

Margaet.—What a beautiful name! *Ach,* a field, I suppose, and na-Mona—what is that?

Cameron.—Perhaps you will think it less beautiful when I tell you that it means the Field of the Peats. The house there we must look at, and from the people that dwell there learn the style of living.

Beyond is a very large cairn. I don't think it has ever been opened, but many stones have been taken from the top. I think there have been other cairns near. It is a wild burying place, perhaps used by the people of the great Dun, which was the predecessor of Barcaldine Castle.

Loudoun.—Let us not go on to Loch Creran; it is well to see how the lochs cut this part of the county, so that

between Loch Etive, Loch Creran, and the sea, it is almost
an island. It is called Benderloch or Ben-eider-da-Loch—
a hill between two lochs—Ledaig being the hill, and the
plains on each side being left for us to inhabit. We could go
back by the north road, and on to Ard-na-Mucknish, as people
call it, but we should lose the sight of the beautiful little loch
or mill pond, covered with water-lilies; besides, I think the
walk to Ardnamuic ought not to be hurried, and I want to
show you a peat-bog, in which is a stone kist. We turn in
here south of the little mill, and behind these low but rocky
picturesque mounds, and where they are cutting peats, we see
(Ach-a-Mhuilin) Achavuilin, the field of the mill. The cairn
was found lately here by trying with a stick simply, so as to
find the place where the deep peat was interrupted; a stone
was laid bare on digging, and a small stone kist, with a cairn
over it. It was rude, almost as rude as the baby's cairn
spoken of, and although larger, was not above four feet
across; the inside of the kist was square, and not above two
feet in diameter. No proof of burning was seen, and no
appearance of the place having been opened; but well burnt
bones are white, and are soluble to some extent. Nothing
was found within, and it is perhaps less difficult to account
for total disappearance in this case on account of the acid
of the peat which would probably dissolve burnt bones.
Still we can suppose the place to have been opened
and carefully closed again. This, however, must be said
that people mistake when they suppose that charcoal cannot
disappear. It can disappear in two ways, either by being
washed away in fine powder when there is very open
drainage, or by being oxidised when there is a current

of air.   It is not possible to let oxygen enter into charcoal
and to bring it all out as oxygen; it becomes carbonic acid.
This would occur in peat when wet, so far as I know, but
unquestionably this cairn was built before the moss grew.
The depth is of little consequence, as it will be shown elsewhere that peat in some situations grows rapidly.

Cameron.—Here at least is an ancient burial, of the time,
perhaps, when stone circles were made.   We can say no more ;
we must now walk home by the only road to Keills, and as
the water is smooth, and the tide, although coming in, is not
direct in our teeth, we shall row back to Dunolly and Oban.
As we go you can look at the shores on our right and the
tower on the highest part, where we may some day have
a view of sea and land for a good hundred miles I daresay.
And now we have a rest in the boat and go in fresh, and
even the rowers, finding the tide with them at Dunolly, run in
with ease and speed.   It is an unsafe spot at times, and the
current is hard to stem.

CHAPTER XVI.

BARDIC SATIRE.

MARGAET.—In the story of the sons of Uisnach a bard is mentioned as being important at Conor's court. Will you tell us what a bard is, and what he is known to do or to say?

O'Keefe.—This is not a place to give you a history of bards even if I could, and I shall not attempt it, but I may tell you some things about them and give you a specimen of their doings. It is part of our plan to picture to ourselves the life to which the sons of Uisnach were accustomed. The word *Bard* was early known. We find it alluded to in Greek and Roman writers, but I do not think it is claimed by any nation not of the Celtic race. It seems quite true that great chiefs kept a bard or bards to sing their praises, and to tell the famous deeds of their forefathers, also to tell anything interesting which they might know, so that they were closely connected with, and sometimes the same as the story-tellers. We have a not very flattering drawing of a bard in the Scoti-chronicon. Mr. Skene gives a facsimile of it in his little volume on the coronation chair. The bard is reciting the pedigree of Alexander the Third at his coronation at Scone in 1249. He is called by Fordun a certain Scotch mountaineer, and the drawing gives him a very scanty plaid as the only covering, besides shoes and stockings. But by this time the singers had probably lost their early high position.

The bards were united in some fashion, and, to some extent, acted in union. Some, of course, rose, by individual character, higher than others, and their power was high accordingly. They are said to have been taught by the Druids, and the functions of the two sometimes became mixed. I dare say you will laugh when I mention Druids, but it is easy to laugh at the absent, and you may laugh also when I tell you that a bard may rise to be an ollav, and that an ollav was a learned man, sometimes, if not always, a judge. Ollamh Foladh, for example, was a judge in Ireland 600 years before Christ. If you doubt this, you may read what Mr. Conwell has to say of it, and I leave you to settle it with him.

Bards were very numerous before St. Columba's time, and during his time they were becoming very troublesome and overbearing. The habit, if not the gift, of singing was heredi- tary, and as the bards did not run the same danger of being killed as the fighting men, they increased. They were expected to praise the great and the great were expected to feed them and make them presents. A song demanded a present, and the bard could ask whatever he wished. This right was extended so far as to be intolerable. I suppose the exaggerations are poetical, but the chiefs were afraid to refuse, because a song against them, or a satire, was attended with serious consequences. Satire kills men amongst us, some- times with long tortures, whilst unfeeling critics, we know, sometimes wreak their vengeance by writing unfairly, but it caused death, much more certainly in Ireland, and a bargain was made with heaven that the false satirist should die. Were it not for this kings would have ceased to have power. One poor king, that was the sport of a bard of a coarse nature, is mentioned as an extreme case, I suppose. A bard asked the king, who was already blind of one eye, to give him the other. The king did so; and the bard, to show still more his dignity, put it under his feet as a gift not worth having. Such, you see, was the power of an Irish bard, and I dare say it was the same in Alba.

Loudoun.—Would you not call this the result of the same spirit that invented the flight of saints; it is a rush to the very extremity of an idea: in this case it is the extremity of power that we can imagine any man to have over another.

O'Keefe.—It may be so. When the bards became insolent, the kings and saints of Ireland took the matter in hand, and there exists a curious story relating to their disputes. It is called, "Imtheacht na Tromdhaimhe," the Proceedings of the Great Bardic Association. I don't know the language critically enough, but I confess the latter word sounds very much as if taken from Troubadour. However I must tell you of this remarkable satire on the satirists themselves, and the no less famous results which came from it. You will see that in early days in Ireland we also had a literary association that went from place to place, and feasted as much as your associations do now, and had equal power. Its transactions have been translated by Prof. Connellan, and published by the Ossianic Society in Dublin. I cannot tell you every word, but will try to give you a good idea of it. It has also a connection of a peculiar kind with the sons of Uisnach, as I shall show. The Uisnach episode happened long before the time ascribed to the subject of the satire, but the great forgotten poem was partly the consequence of the Uisnach tragedy.

THE PROCEEDINGS OF THE BARDIC ASSOCIATION, OR A SATIRE ON THE SATIRISTS.

Hugh the fair, son of Duach the dark, was the King of Oirgiall,[1] and he had a shield called *Duv-gilla*, which made every one opposed to it weak and cowardly. And there was a King of Brefney,[2] who very much coveted the famous shield. At the same time there was the chief Professor of the Bards living with the latter king, and he agreed to obtain the shield from Hugh by means of his satires. Eohy, or Dallan, was living at Brefney with a great band of his bards, and "the quarter that he liked best was Brefney, for numerous were its flocks and cattle-herds."

The king flattered Dallan, and also reminded him of favours : "Thou hast great honour and privilege from me." "That is not to be wondered at," said Dallan, "for great is my honour in Alban, in Saxonland, in Britain, and in France, because I hold the chief professorship of all these countries."

Dallan was a proud man, but he condescended to go and extort the shield by the power of satire from Hugh, after being promised a great reward.

[1] Antrim and Down.
[2] Cavan, Leitrim, and part of Meath and Sligo.

Sheena.—One would think that with such a shield he would become a monarch himself.

O'Keefe.—True, but he went to the Dun of the King of Oirgiall with a following of three times nine professors, and the king met him on the lawn, and gave him three kisses. The other professors were welcomed in like manner. Dallan entered, but said that he would not stay until he knew his success, and he then requested the shield. The king said, "That is not the request of a truly learned man." Dallan said, "I have brought a poem for you—

> "A hero of fortune art thou, O Hugh,
> Thou daring, determined foe,
> Thy goodness as the great ocean,
> Thou canst not be subdued.
> Thou canst not be impeded,
> O Hugh, son of Duach the dark.
> Good and great is his substance,
> Without censure and without reproach.
> Thou sun after leaving its stars
> Which is awful to me ;
> Thou white chess board.
> We will return, O hero."

"That is a good poem," said the king, "if only we could understand it." Then Dallan says that the man who makes a poem ought to explain. This he does, and the king says that he will give money and cattle for it.

Then Dallan repeats another poem still fuller of praise and ends—

> "A surprising and beautiful shield
> Will be given to me by Hugh for praise."

The king says he will give gold, silver, jewels, and substance for it. Dallan tries again, and the king promises gold, silver, and a hundred of each flock for it, but not the shield. "I will satirize you," said Dallan. Then the king reminds him that when St. Columba and other saints made peace with the bards and kings, it was agreed that three blotches of reproach should fall on the bards if a satire was not true.

But Dallan said that it would not save him, and he uttered his satire—

> "O Hugh, son of Duach the dark,
> Thou pool not permanent,
> Thou pet of the mild cuckoos,
> Thou quick chafferer of the blackbird.
>
> Thou sour green berry,
> Swarms will suck the herbs,
> Thou green crop like fine clothes,
> A candlestick without light.
>
> Thou cold wooden boat,
> Thou bark that wilt give dissatisfaction,
> Thou disgusting black chafer,
> Thou art most disgusting, O Hugh."

The king said he did not know if this was better or worse, so Dallan had again to explain. You can suppose the explanation of this ribaldry. It is curious to learn that a "pet of a cuckoo" is the worst pet in a house, "because he ceases to sing, except a little, and will as soon do so in winter as at any other time."

The king dismissed him and said, "The might of God and the saints pursue you if you have satirized me wrongfully."

When Dallan went away, he said he never felt so well, although he had satirized the king wrongfully, and his

N

attending bards could not believe it. But he said that when
he came he had .the sight of only one eye, and now he
could see with both. But he was not sure, after all, if it
were good, because Columba had told him that something
wonderful would happen to him before his death, and he
went home and died in three days.

Such was the power of falsehood in old times. No need
for actions for slander. We have no saints now to make
such compacts with the powers of heaven and earth.

This event was a severe but just rebuke to bards, who were
greedy and false, and it was felt by the whole association.
After this Seanchan (pronounced Shenchan) delivered the
funeral oration over Dallan. This reminds one of admission
speeches in the French Academy. Seanchan's duty was to guide
the bards, so he decided to go to some king who had never been
annoyed by bards, " never been satirized, or reproached about
gold, &c.," and he chose Guaire, King of Connaught. The
proposal was received with great respect, and Guaire built
a house for the company ; it had eight sides to it and a door
between each two, and lavatories for the men and for the
women. Seanchan humbly said that he did not wish to bring
too many. He took only " three times fifty professors, three
times fifty students, thrice fifty hounds, thrice fifty male
attendants, thrice fifty female relatives, and thrice nine of each
class of artificers," and Guaire went to meet them, and said, "My
regards to you. My regards to you, nobles and humbles! I
have great welcome for you all, both professors and poets,
both scientific men and students, both sons and women, both
hounds and servants ; you are too numerous for a separate
welcome, although there are not too many of you. My

respects to you on all sides!" A welcome full of good feelings.

Guaire told them to ask anything they wanted. It was no easy matter to give each a separate bed, and meals apart, and it happened that every night some one had some fantastic wish, so that the "activity of all Ireland" was scarcely enough to satisfy them. The wish must be gratified within twenty-four hours.

The first extraordinary wish was on the first night. It occurred to Muireann, the foster-mother of the learned men ; she began by uttering a loud moan. Seanchan said, "What is the matter with you, chieftainess." "A desire has seized me, and unless it be procured I will not live." "What is that wish?" "A bowl of the ale of Tormentil, with the marrow of the ankle-bone of a wild hog ; a pet cuckoo on an ivy tree between the two Christmases (Christmas Day and Twelfth Day) ; and on the back a full load of a girdle of lard of an exceeding white boar, and to be mounted on a steed with a red mane, and its four legs exceeding white ; a garment of the spider's web around me, and humming a tune as I go to Durlus."

Both Seanchan and Guaire thought that this was not one wish, but a number of strange and bad wishes, and Guaire was in despair, and thought of running off to his enemies at once, that they might kill him, and so free him from the blame of inhospitality. Poor fellow! he must have kept people running about at a violent rate, feeding so many capricious people. There is a road at Durlus, still called the road of dishes,[1] it so astonished the residents. Poor

---

[1] Bothur-na-Mias.

Guaire prayed all night in great misery. Although we remember that this is a satire, and we cannot imagine anybody much troubled about these whims, we cannot help giving some pity to Guaire walking out early, and contriving methods to please his strange guests. When doing so some one saluted·him; this man was called Marvan; he was the chief prophet of heaven and earth, and lived as a swine-herd in woods and desert places; he was Guaire's nephew also, elsewhere called his brother, and took care of his pigs.

Pigs were very early connected with lofty ideas in Ireland, as we may find both in history and romance.

Marvan soon got over the difficulty which was too much for the king; he even had a pet cuckoo, which would coo in the lady's presence on an ivy tree., He had also a garment of spider's web, and of many colours; but when he heard of the yellow lard of a pure white boar, Marvan was angry—" My malediction on the person who desired that. Sure it is I who have the boar, and it is a hardship to kill him, for he is to me a herdsman, a physician, and a musician." " How does he perform all that?" said the king. " In this way: when I leave the swine at night, and the skin is torn off my feet by the briars of Glen-a-Scail, he comes to me and rubs his tongue over my feet, and though I should have all the surgeons and healing ointment in the world, his tongue would cure me soonest; in that manner he is physician to me. He is herd to me, for when the swine wander through Glen-a-Scail, and I am wearied, I give him a blow with my foot and he goes after the swine. There are nine passes into Glen-a-Scail, and there is no danger of any hog of them being carried off by a thief, vagrant, or wolf of the forest. He is musician to me, for when I am anxious to sleep, I give him a stroke with my foot, and he lies on his back and sings me a humming tune, and his music is more grateful to me than that of a sweet-toned harp in the hands of an accomplished minstrel."

Poor Marvan could not kill the white boar; some one must do it for him, but he promised to call on the great bardic association some day and have his revenge. Little did the lady think of this when she went with a full load on her back, humming a tune on the way to Durlus.

Seanchan, next evening, heard a heavy moan from his own daughter—"What ails thee, what is thy wish?" "That I might have the full of my skirt of my mantle of large black berries (this being January, you must know), and that when I abide in Durlus, the people may be all sick." Seanchan said that Guaire was their consoler and comforter, but she said she was like the nettle, and wished evil to no one so much as to her benefactor.

A new grief to Guaire; but his friend Marvan had always a wonderful story to account for his power of obtaining these strange things, and even the sickness he managed by praying that they might be all ill, and then all well again immediately. He was a saint, and his prayer brought all this to pass.

The next groaning came from Bridget, Seanchan's wife. " Unless it be obtained I will die," she said as they all did. " Say the wish." " To get my fill of the fat of a water-ouzle, and again my fill of a red-cared and purely white cow without a liver, but having tallow instead of a liver ; and my fill of red strawberries and purple berries and drink of the honey of the woodbine." We must suppose here another wonderful discovery of all this by Marvan. Hitherto all the groanings were amongst the ladies, and Seanchan had a good deal to bear, but now his time came, and he groaned in the usual way; his heart desired ale made from one grain of corn, and enough for the whole bardic association and the nobles of Connaught feasting together. Guaire was now at his wits' end, but the wonderful swineherd had actually this ready, for he had found a grain of corn under his foot as he returned from sowing, planted it, and kept its produce for planting, year after year, for eleven years, so that now he could make plenty of ale from it for all.

The great bardic association and the nobles feasted on this ale for three days and three nights, but when Seanchan saw so much food eaten, his heart softened towards the king, and he was ashamed of causing so much expense, so he said he would eat nothing until the nobles were sent away, and accordingly they were sent away to please him. Now we must attend to Seanchan, who became pettish after all at this great feast, and would not even now eat for other three days, even although the nobles went away. The king was sorry for him and sent a favourite servant with a goose on a long white hazel spit to tempt him. But Seanchan said, "Why have *you* been sent with it?" "As a person of mild manners and cleanliness selected by Guaire to bring you your food." But Seanchan was cross and dainty, and said, "We believe he could not find anywhere a more uncomely person than yourself. I knew your grandfather, and he was chip-nailed, and I shall not take food out of your hands."

The king then sent a young lady—his foster-child and a

favourite, who brought salmon roe and flour to bake in Seanchan's presence, but he said, "I am sure there is not a young girl in the place more unseemly than yourself. I saw your grandmother sitting on a rock pointing the way for lepers. How could I take food from your hands?"

The king was roused, and for the first time spoke in anger. He must have been patient to stand it so long.

He hoped that Seanchan would kiss a leper before he died, which, on the whole, was a gentle kind of revenge.

After another day and night Seanchan was obliged to yield a little, and inclined to eat some of the leavings that his wife wished to send, but the servant said that the mice had taken them.

Seanchan was very angry at the mice, and said he would satirize them, and when he had done this nine mice died in his presence. Then he began to think he had done wrong, and he ought to satirize the cats for not killing the mice, and he satirized the cats. The chief of the cats felt the power in his cave, and said that he would be revenged, and the cat's daughter hoped that Seanchan would be brought hither, that they might all have their revenge. The chief was called Irusan. He was not to be put down by satire; he was "blunt-snouted, rapacious, panting, smooth, and sharp-clawed, split-nosed, sharp and rough toothed, nimble, powerful, angry, vindictive, quick, purring, glare-eyed." He took Seanchan on his back and ran off with him, and the poor bard would have been scratched by the whole family, but when they came to Clonmacnois, they passed a forge where St. Kieran was forging iron. The saint saw the plight of the chief bard, and in a moment threw a red hot bar of iron at the cat so well

and violently that it not only hit, but went through to the
other side. One would have expected Seanchan to thank
the saint, but he only cursed the hand that killed the cat,
wishing rather that he himself had been killed in order that
the great bardic association might have an excuse for
satirizing Guaire the king. He went back sullen and replied
to no salutes.

That is very hard on the bards, and the object is to show
that no amount of kindness could prevent them from becoming very selfish, unreasonable, and exacting.

I think it very pleasant satire, some of it very witty, all
very cutting, despite its wonderful exaggeration.

But hear Marvan's revenge on the association.

Marvan, the wonderful swine-herd, had gone into the woods,
chiefly for his devotions. He was a prophet and a poet.
He had so much work that it is not easy to see what time he
had for the religious exercises of a hermit. But it turns out
that Marvan kept a prime house for general hospitality in
Glen-a-Scail. This sounds somewhat modern, but we are
told that such houses were kept by the government for the
learned and for travellers, and the sick and indigent; even
then, however, we cannot help being reminded of the great
amount of ale that this prophet happened to have in
his possession, and probably the writer is having a thrust at
the people who presided over these establishments, and who
were called *Biadhtach-s.*

This looks like the origin of the story of St. Patrick's keeping a shop, as the comic song has it.

Marvan now made his great visit of revenge. He went to
the great bardic association, and seeing one of the ladies, the

daughter of Seanchan, Meave Veitigh, at the fountain, he asked where the mansion was. Meave answered, "You must be a wandering seafarer that knows not the palace, its stories and music." "Herding swine is my business. I am told that every one obtains what music he wishes in the palace." "Not," said Meave, "unless he is connected with the arts and sciences." "I am connected with the arts," said Marvan, "through the grandmother of my servant's wife who was descended from poets." I abridge the speeches.

Marvan entered, and when asked what art he desired, he said, "I desire no better than as much *cronan* as I like." The performers came and wished to prepare the regular cronan, but Marvan insisted on the bass cronan because it was difficult, and he hoped they would "break their heads, feet, and necks," and be sooner exhausted. *Cronan* is a simple kind of singing. We have the word *crooning*.

When they stopped Marvan said, "Prepare for me as much cronan as I desire," insisting on the promise. Again they began, and when they stopped Marvan again insisted, but this was too much for the singers, and some one came to relieve them by a change of performance. A professor from Leinster came and endeavoured to puzzle him, but Marvan answered and humiliated him, and then insisted on more cronan.

Another learned professor from Thomond came, but Marvan showed him that he was ignorant, and again asked for cronan. Having puzzled every one, or made them ashamed of their presumption, he called for cronan three times and got none. It must be remembered that it was a disgraceful thing for any bard to be unable to give a song when required, and for any story-teller to be ignorant of the story demanded, and in this case it was a double disgrace, because at this chief establishment everything was supposed to be in readiness. The failure to give more cronan made Seanchan himself ashamed, and he said he would prepare it himself. The chief performed till he was strained so much that one of his eyes fell out of its place. Marvan put it back, for he could do everything, but still asked for more cronan, for he had his plans ready.

And now came the crowning piece. When a story-teller or bard could not tell the story or sing the song called for, he dared not stay in the same place two nights until he learned it. A person came and said, "Marvan, I will perform an art for thee." "Who art thou, and what is thy art?" "I am the best story-teller in the great bardic institution, or in all Ireland." "Well, then," said Marvan, "tell me the Cattle Raid of Cooley.[1]" But the Sgeulee or story-teller could not tell it. Nobody could tell it, and Marvan knew that. It had been quite lost. But Marvan took advantage of the letter of the law and said, "I put you under enchantment until you relate the Tain to me; and I put the whole bardic body under injunction that they should not remain two nights in the same house until they discover the story of the Tain. Henceforth you will not have the power of composing verses until you find the Tain; and were it not for Guaire, well would I revenge myself on you for the wild boar, you indolent, ignorant, bardic clan."

The bards were obliged to get up immediately. All men

[1] Tain Bo Cuailgne.

must follow *geasa* or spells. The king kindly took care of the company of attendants when the professors went forth, they alone being under the ban. These wandered over Ireland, and spent a year in Scotland, but never found the Tain, and were obliged, after many humiliations, and being unable to make a poem all the time, to come back to Marvan again, for they found that he, after all, was the only one that knew how to obtain the story.

So thoroughly was the tale lost that it could only be had by wakening up the author, and he had been dead for centuries. Even this difficulty was overcome by the prayers of the saints of Ireland, of whom Columba is first on the list. Fergus rose from the grave, and gave out again the whole poem, and thus the great epic of Ireland was recovered. St. Caillin, Marvan's brother, managed as secretary to the listeners. Seanchan had now learnt humility; he made a vow to Marvan that none of the great bardic institution should seek "a wish" from any person in the world from henceforth to the day of judgment. Another account says that the association was dispersed, and all went to their own homes. But all agree that from this time the tyranny of the bards ceased, and it probably marks a historic period when a step was made in freedom of thought.

CHAPTER XVII.

TAIN BO CUAILGNE.

" Much I loved the jocund chase,
  Much the horse and chariot race,
  Much I loved the deep carouse,
  Quaffing in the Red Branch house."
  Songs of the Western Gael, by Sir Sam. Ferguson.

THE CATTLE FORAY OF COOLEY.

MARGAET.—And now that we have heard of this wonderful raid of Cooley, so wonderful that a dispute about it was considered one of the best occasions for cutting up actually, as well as by satire, "the great association of the bards," what was it really ?

O'Keefe.—We must not go too far from Loch Etive ; but this great event was pretty closely connected with the occurrences at Dun Uisnachan and the revenge of our heroes, the sons of Uisnach. We must not claim too much lest we imitate Marvan, entering the bard's palace. You will remember that Conor sent Fergus to bring back the sons of Uisnach from Loch Etive. Fergus had given up the kingship of Ulster to Conor, and was a man of a light heart but strictly honourable, and one to whom has been attributed this greatest ancient poem of Ireland. The verse heading this chapter is supposed to represent his character. O'Curry says, " Fergus mac Roigh was a great Ulster prince, who had gone into voluntary exile, into Connaught, through feelings of dislike and hostility to Conor mac Nessa, the King of Ulster, for his treacherously putting to death the sons of Uisnach, for whose safety Fergus had pledged his faith according to the knightly customs of the time. And afterwards, when the Tain bo Cuailgne occurred, Fergus was the great guide and director of the expedition on the side of the Connaught men, against that of Conor mac Nessa, and, as it would appear, he was himself the historian of the war."[1]

You see, then, the connection of this famous poem with Loch Etive and the sons of Uisnach. The appearance of Fergus on the scene gave a new motive to the battle ; had it not been for him, and his desire to revenge the murders, the raid would have probably been a commonplace affair. As it was, it not only gave him exercise for his arms, but must have taken the leisure of the rest of his life, by causing him to write the history. And so we shall suppose it.

The beginning of the fight was on the side of Meave, who had been married to Conor, but had quarrelled and left him ; when her father and brothers were killed, she was made Queen of Connaught and married Aillil. She seems to have been happy, but nevertheless disputed with her husband, a son of the King of Leinster, about their property. Female rights were far advanced in Ireland. Meave and her husband compared their property, and brought out all their wooden

---

[1] *Lectures on the MS. Materials of Ancient Irish History*, p. 30.

vessels and metal vessels, which were equal. Then they brought out their finger rings, clasps, bracelets, thumb rings, diadems, and gorgets of gold, and they were equal. Then they brought their garments of crimson, blue, black, and green, yellow and mottled, and white and streaked, and they were equal. Then they brought their horses and cattle from woods and glens and remote solitudes, and all were equal, except one bull, which was better in Aillil's flock. Now it really was Meave's property, but the bull himself had gone to Aillil, as he did not think it honourable to be under the control of a woman. Meave heard of a better, and sent to say she would like to have it for a time, but the messenger carried threats instead of friendly speeches, and a struggle ultimately ensued between the south and north, Fergus and his followers taking the lead against their own countrymen. With a rush Meave entered Ulster, the country at that time being feeble and spellbound. Meave came with all her princes and chiefs, her husband Aillil, and her daughter Finnavair, the fair-browed, and met the forces of the Ulster men, who were prevented from meeting their opponents for a long time by a state of enchantment into which they had been thrown. We shall not inquire into this. It is probably a mode of accounting for a want of readiness in the people of Ulster. It is most pleasant to read in O'Curry's lectures and Dr. Sullivan's continuation, the description of all the nobles as they are collected on both sides, and there is a richness and fulness which to me surpasses anything of the kind which I have seen. | " The march and array of these troops, including Cuchullin, the distinguishing description of their horses and chariots, arms, ornaments, and vesture—even their size and complexion and the colour of their hair—are described with great vividness and power."[1] Fergus mac Roigh knows all the chiefs and tells the names to Meave and Aillil, but the messenger Mac Roth describes them. Here is a specimen of Mac Roth's careful details.

"Then came another company. No champion could be more beautiful than he who leads them. His hair is of a deep red yellow, and bushy; his forehead broad, and his face tapering; he has sparkling, blue, laughing eyes; a man regularly formed, tall and tapering; thin red lips; pearly, shining teeth; a white, smooth body. A red and white cloak flutters about him; a golden brooch in that cloak at his breast; a shirt of white, kingly linen, with gold embroidery at his skin; a white shield, with gold fastenings at his shoulders; a gold-hilted, long sword at his left side; a long, sharp, dark green spear, together with a short, sharp spear, with a rich band and carved silver rivets in his hand. 'Who is he, O Fergus?' said Aillil. 'The man who has come there is in himself half a battle, the valour of combat, the fury of the slaughter hound. He is Reochaid mac Fatheman from Rachlinn.'"

It would be long to tell you of all the glorious men and women, and beautiful garments and armour; it would even be long to tell you of the combats of Cuchullin, who offered to fight any one of the opponents, and who was supplied with knights on whom he might show his prowess, Queen Meave persuading one after another to attack this formidable chief of Dundalk.

It would be too long to tell you of Cuchullin, who put on

[1] From O'Curry's *Lectures*, First Series, p. 37.

him twenty-seven shirts, cased and smooth, and braced up
with strings and pins, "so that his fury may not exceed his
reason." Nor can I tell you enough of his charioteer who had
"a raven black cloak which Simon Magus had made for the
King of the Romans, who gave it to Conor mac Nessa, King
of Ulster." You must read it for yourselves.

Willie.—You have never given us a battle after all, although
I quite expected one when they were fighting for the bull.

O'Keefe.—I might tell you of one, but it is very long ; it is
the single combat between **Ferdiaidh**[1] and **Cuchullin**. They
were taught together as boys, and, without any cause for
enmity, they were made to fight in the great cattle conflict
in single combat. They began with knightly formality and
courtliness, chose weapons, which, on the first day, were
missiles, darts, and spears, and ivory-hilted small swords, but
neither could do fatal injury to the other, and they stopped.
" Each of them went towards the other and threw his arms
around his neck and embraced him three times." Then
there came professors of healing to cure them. " Every
herb and every salve that was applied to the sores, cuts, and
many wounds of **Cuchullin**, he sent share of the same over
to Ferdiaidh, in order that the men of Erin should not have to
say, if Ferdiaidh fell by him, it was in consequence of an
inequality in the healing."

" Next day they began the fight again, and now with heavy
thrusting spears. Each began to pierce, to perforate, and to
lacerate the other, from the dawn of each morning to the close
of the evening. If it had been the custom of flying birds to
pass through human bodies, they might have passed through

[1] Pronounce Ferdiai.

their bodies on that day, and carried off lumps of gore and flesh from their cuts and wounds into the surrounding clouds and air."

Next day they had swords, and cut off flesh as large as the head of an infant a month old.

Then came a fierce, bloody, and cruel struggle, when all courtliness was gone, and real rage and brutality entered—a good image of war. Ferdiaidh was killed. The spot at which the battle took place was called Ath Ferdiaidh, the Ford of Ferdiaidh, which is now contracted into Ardee. It is in Louth.

If you want to know much more about the Tain, I fear you must learn Gaelic. O'Curry thinks there is some foundation also for the tale which I have called a satire, and many a wild story has a good foundation. He thinks the poem may have been lost or carried away, and after a long time recovered. This may be. We do not know the original words, and we can readily imagine a good story swelling in the course of centuries; poetry and prose mingled as in this case. The famous bull frightened all Connaught, and attacked his chief opponent there, carried him on his horns, dashed him to pieces, and left bits here and there, and returned home to Ulster quite mad. The people of the town ran away, and he attacked a rock, which he took for an enemy, and dashed himself to pieces.

Sheena.—That is something thorough ; and now may we hear about Seanchan. Was he a real man ?

O'Keefe.—Yes; I suppose he was—about the time of Columba—long after the Cooley battle of course, because that took place about A.D. 30 or 40 it is said.

O

Margaet.—And had the Irish people·all those beautiful ornaments and dresses so early ?

O'Keefe.—Fine gold ornaments they had very early, and the Danes robbed the tombs of them when they came in the ninth century. What other proofs of wealth they had who can tell, at the time when Tacitus said that merchants knew Ireland better than Britain. My own inclination is to believe that in Ireland there were, in very early times, one or more tribes or aristocracies of a very advanced character, far beyond the nation generally. If we hold that we get over several difficulties.

Loudoun.—But that would not show that the tale was written so soon as is supposed, since Simon Magus could not have been in Ireland, and he is mentioned in Dr. Sullivan's book.[1]

O'Keefe.—You are right there. No one ever does suppose, so far as I know, that the tale is as it was at first. But I say that we do not know when was made the first of the rich gold ornaments found in Ireland, and on some points we are driven very far back, how far is a question gradually clearing itself, but still too slowly ; too few people study it, and too many people speak with confidence.

Margaet.—This little interruption with battles is pleasant enough, but before we go far I want to hear the end of the bardish story. I want to hear about Seanchan. He was humbled very deeply, and the whole association suffered with him. Was he ever restored to his position as poet ?

O'Keefe.—Yes, he was. There are various ways of telling the story of the restoration of the Tain. At the intercession of the saints of Erin, Fergus Mac Roy rose from his grave

---

[1] See *Manners and Customs of the Irish*, vol. II., p. 300.

and repeated the Tain, which Kiaran wrote down, whilst
Seanchan sang it with his first full recovery of powers after
his somewhat magical loss, which was the consequence of the
spell put upon him by Marvan, and which prevented him or
the association from making any poems, so that these proud
men became common, inert and ridiculous. The moment of
recovery is painted in a most spirited poem by Sir Samuel
Ferguson, who supposes the bard to have been inspired with
the Tain-quest before King Guary and a great company at a
feast. He says in the "Lays of the Western Gael" :—

> " Set the harp ; no prelude wanted, Sanchan struck the master key,
> And as bursts the brimful river all at once from caves of song,
> Forth at once and once for ever leapt the torrent of the song.
>
> Vision chasing splendid vision, Sanchan rolled the mystic scene ;
> They that mocked in rude derision now at gaze with wondering mien,
> Sate, and as the glorying master swayed the tightening reins of song,
> Felt emotion's pulses fasten—fancies faster bound along." [1]

  .   .   .   .

During the excitement, Fergus, the long-buried king,
appeared, whilst Seanchan,[2] after his repentance and punish-
ment, stands out with double honour.

Margact.—And is the poem so grand ?

O'Keefc.—Few men can read it in the original, and it is not
all translated ; it is in the Leabhar na h-uidhri. It contains
many things that are extremely interesting, but like most of
the Irish literature it is too much confined to description of
individuals, and the feelings when described are more remarkable by exaggeration than insight. It fails to rise up to the

---

[1] *Lays of the Western Gael.* By Dr. now Sir Samuel Ferguson.
[2] Or Sanchan.

universal or to the plane of general human interest.   There
is gold and silver, but there is not the refined sculpture of
Homer.   There is neither the parental nor conjugal love
shown by both Hector and Andromache, nor is there the
delicate and simple but princely Nausicaa.   The outer life is
too much for the development of the inner.   At least I gather
so much, but I do not pretend to have read it.

Margaet.—Does it contain ancient, really ancient thought?

O'Keefe.—I certainly inclined to say of this tale as
of the others of which we have spoken that there is very
little of the thought which is essentially after Christianity in
its character.   The groundwork and most of the superstructure
is purely heathen, and it would seem to me that the current of
heathen thought and feeling ran with little mixture into the
ocean of life which Christianity had covered with its saints
and martyrs.   Let those who make this a life study learn to
say more.   We desire more students of Irish Gaelic, and
more publications of the originals and translations.

CHAPTER XVIII.

THE CAIRN OF ACHNACREE.

CAMERON.—I wish to take a walk round the moss, and we may begin at the ferry. There is a little mound here called the yellow mound of Connel; it may be old, and it may contain something interesting.

Loudoun.—Here at least is something certainly old, the deeply cut bed of the river below. It must have taken long to cut through that rock.

Cameron.—Can water do such a thing?

Loudoun.—Water may do it in time, or in the ages that look to us like eternity, but we do not rely on it wholly. It brings down stones from the hills and they grind rapidly. It is rock against rock, and you know sand or small stones are now used as a means of boring and of polishing.

Willie.—At any rate it has left the banks capital for rabbits, and these gipsies live here and probably feed to a great extent upon them.

Cameron.—Yes, these are *Ceardan*, or, as we should say, tinkers. In Scotland they are not called gipsies often. I suppose that before the gipsies came the tinkers went about

much as they do now, doing metal work for the people.
They can make, or at least they could make, silver brooches
with very simple tools, and we know that in other countries,
in Persia, for example, there are similar wanderers, but far
more skilful, who make those beautiful and elaborate bronze
vessels of open lacework with figures numerous, fantastic, and
mythical, some indicating serpent-worship, ideas received
probably from neighbouring states or Indian nagas.   I mean
that either the art, or the idea, or both, came from elsewhere.

Margaet.—Can it be that these men live out of doors with
no covering but a slight tent, and some with only a covering
for the head?   These women, too, seem no more robust than
ourselves, and they are poorly clothed.   How can they live?

Loudoun.—By ceasing to think, it would appear that a good
deal of the vigour goes into the body, and these people are
very idle in body and mind.

Margaet.—But I thought that exercise kept us warm, and
if these people were idle they would starve.

Loudoun.—Exercise does make us warm, but great exercise
needs rest, and we must be strong indeed if we do not
cool too far after it.   I think it probable that these people,
not being of the strongest, would need more shelter if they
were very active.   They would convert into energy that which
they now have in warmth, and lose much heat also in evapora-
tion.   They do not usually stand the winter well, they go
into towns as a rule; but there are some who keep out, and it
is only lately that one died in a tent on the snow near
Forres, the rest of the tribe lying around him.   He had
never since youth lived under a roof.

Margaet.—But surely vigorous men can stand cold best.

Loudoun.—Certainly ; but cold brings down even their activity, and if very much exposed they cease to be powerful. I don't like these people ; they are lazy and beggarly whether real gipsies or not.

Cameron.—This is a great moss at our left. And the road seems to be on an embankment around it. Cairns are on the roadside as if the moss were very old. This cairn at Lochanabeich has a large base, indeed only the base remains, as the barns were built out of it. There is nothing in it above the original surface, but no one has gone lower and it may conceal something interesting. Some people say it was only a collection of stones to clear the land, and there is some land cleared here for the farm.

O'Keefe.—Here to the right is another collection of stones ; do you think people would put them in such a picturesque place if they were only collected from the road? These look down on the loch and ornament the fine bank.

Cameron.—Yes, it is a fine bank, a bank of whin and gorse, and lively with rabbits black and white. Who would have thought a few years ago that the telegraph poles would have run along the top and the wires crossed the loch, and that a dyer would be building works opposite, and the school board interfering with the lonely shore.

We progress, as you from the South say, but I do not like the people better. I like the old people in these cottages, with their little crofts behind, and I know they enjoy walking out in that wood and round the great curve of the road which opens up the wide part of the loch and shows us Ardchattan, the churches and the priory, as well as the great hills and the openings into their dark recesses.

Down there is a piece of an old ruin near the sea-shore. I do not know what it was, but it is near the houses of decent men whom I know, and I admire the view on which they feed daily when standing at their own doors and looking up to Ardchattan over the broad part of Loch Etive. Those who do not fear running down the hill may run and look, those who prefer to keep to our principal object will walk along. Here we come to the peat moss out of which we got the spear head. We shall follow the road as it leads round the great bend of the loch, widening like a sea, and turn round to the left until we come to the clump of trees and the great cairn.

Sheena.—I think I must be showwoman here as I took so much interest in this cairn. You perceive that the enclosure is great although the traces of the ditch are small, and of the large stone circle around it there remain only some fragments. The height appeared greater before opening, although there was only a little taken off—the change is more observable in the shape. If you go to the top you see a wide opening. The stones taken out were thrown to the side, and the original appearance is best understood from the drawing. It took two men eight or nine days to make that opening. The plan was to go down from the top, but as the stones were continually rolling in, it was quite necessary to make a broad opening above, and in order not to diminish the height, if possible, we kept a little to the west side. After sinking about eight feet we came to a flat stone which broke readily in pieces— some of the slate of the country. This really had an Aladdin's cave appearance, and we were all anxiety.

We had come to the extreme edge of a number of flat granite stones, which were found afterwards to form a roof.

Great Cairn at Achnacridhe, (Achnacree.)

had been filled up with slatey material, and it was this opening which served for all the exploration. Fortunately we had struck upon the spot which, of all others, was most suitable for entering without destruction of material, since the avenue forming the true original entrance was found to have collapsed, and had we seen it at first we might have been tempted to remove the stones from their position in order to make way, thus destroying the form to a considerable extent. And now every stone of the building is exactly as we found it.

It was a weird thing entering that cairn that had been so long closed, and it was a cheerful thing to come out and see the people that had gathered, even from this lone district, as soon as they heard that there was really a building and chambers found in the cairn. It was curious, also, to listen to the superstitions that came out. One woman who lived here, and might therefore be considered an authority, said that she used to see lights upon it in the dark nights. That you may explain as you please ; distances are not easily judged of in the dark. One man, who also lived near, and who certainly was intelligent, said he would not enter for the whole estate of Lochnell.

We have often inquired the name of the cairn.

The cairn really has had no definite name. Some people have called it Carn Ban or White Cairn, but that is evidently confusing it with the other cairn which we saw over the moss, and which is really whiter. Some people have called it Ossian's Cairn, but that is not an old name, and even if it had been, we know that it is a common thing to attach this name to anything old. We call it Achnacree Cairn, from the name of the farm on which it stands. It was a pleasant day for us and all around to find an interest so human and natural arising out of things deep in the ground in this secluded place, and it makes one wonder whether there be not, in every part of the world, something that might interest us all if we only knew how to look at it. But I shall not describe the structure of this cairn, leaving you rather to read what has already been said on the subject, which is as follows :—

DESCRIPTION OF THE CAIRN OF ACHNACREE.

It was desired not to disturb the actual top, so as to diminish the height, but it is to be feared that the care has not been sufficient. After the men had worked for seven days, a granite slab was found sixteen inches thick. After three more days the boulders of the cairn were taken down in quantity sufficient to render the slope safe enough to allow of an entrance. The great danger in these cases comes from the rolling of stones easily moved by a touch, and falling down to the bottom, so that they require to be lifted up at least as high as the side entrance. The intended entrance was then sought for. Two stones that seemed to us to have been portions of a stone circle round the cairn, now showed themselves rather as gateposts, since the chamber seemed to point in that direction. An opening was therefore made between them, and a narrow passage found. This passage was made of brittle slate pieces of about three feet in height, and, in many instances, less than a foot broad, forming the sides, and covering the way. These were not in good order, the weight of the cairn had evidently caused a tendency to collapse. The way was also nearly filled up with stones, put there with intention to make the entrance difficult, as it would seem. When working at this narrow entrance, an old man from the neighbourhood, who had been engaged to assist the others, said that he had found an opening there forty years ago, when removing stones for building. When General Campbell, who was then proprietor, saw this, he prevented further disturbance. There was no entrance made, but the opinion continued that the cairn was hollow. Evidently no one had entered it at that time. There was a story of some bones having been found, but I do not know at what spot; probably in a cist outside the cairn.

The apparent dimensions of the cairn were 75 feet in diameter, and 15 feet high. It is now somewhat lower. If the pillar stones at the entrance made a continuous circle at the same distance from the centre, the diameter would be less; at present the boulders of the cairn pass even that limit. Possibly an outer circle was meant to support the sides of the cairn, but I incline to think not. Many of the stones have been removed on the side, so that one might doubt the shape of the original; but I think, from the remaining part, that the whole was one great circle. On the side farthest from the road is a ditch, forming part of an outer ring of 135 feet in diameter. On the edge of that, again, there are some stones which appeared, when I first saw them, to be the remains of a stone cist rudely built, but so much displaced by

dozen feet from it, a circle of standing stones. Of this I can
find only one stone remaining ; but it is so like a standing
stone for the purpose, that it seems to have no other duty.
I received this idea from those circles round the cairns at
Clava, for example. An embankment is not uncommon ; one
is seen on a gigantic scale at the Giant's Ring, near Belfast,
where several acres are enclosed by a high earth wall ; in the
centre of the circle is a cromlech, with two covering stones,
like one of those described at Ach-na-Cree-beag ; one has
fallen down on one side. Some of the supporting stones have
been removed.

We must suppose the cairn itself to have been at first
much smoother and more regular than now, even if not
supported all round by a wall of standing stones, like those
now forming the entrance.

Before entering the cairn, I had the pleasure of a visit
from the Rev. R. J. Mapleton of Duntroon, who kindly came
with his great experience. This relieved me, as I was then
inexperienced and was unwilling to venture on touching
ancient monuments, and I began with the full hope of finding
help. Mr. Mapleton has aided me in the description.

Fig. 1, Plate showing the sections, gives the size and height
according to the measurement of Mr. Ritchie Rogers, who
kindly undertook to survey the whole, both within and
without. From him the originals of the drawings of this
cairn have been obtained on a scale, and they are now
enlarged to be shown.

The inner circle shown on the diagram is that of the cairn
itself. The dotted line is the original passage, now a good
deal obstructed with loose stones, and not passable. The

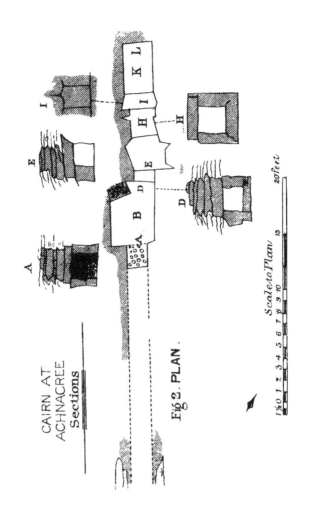

CAIRN AT
ACHNACREE
Sections

Fig. 2. PLAN.

Scale to Plan

20 feet

outer circle is that of the fosse. A supposed third circle would be between these two.[1]

A (Fig. 2) is the entrance, as seen from the chamber B, C chamber not marked. The point A is to the S.S.E., and may be called the southern point. In reality, however, we entered at L, where a few of the loose stones at the top of the wall were removed. It was needful to go feet foremost, and to allow ourselves to drop gently to the floor.

In the diagram shown at the Society's meeting, there was also a view of the side walls of the chamber and passages on the east and west.

Fig. 2 gives plan and elevation of passages. Going from L we first meet passage I next to H, then E and D, with the stones of the wall over them always becoming smaller. We then come to A, where the proper entrance is; the plans of the openings are placed in the plate opposite to their positions.

In a corner of chamber B is a large boulder, probably put there from its having been ready at hand; at present it forms a part of the wall, although by jutting out it becomes an irregularity.

Having then entered feet foremost at L, the first thing that struck the eye was a row of quartz pebbles, larger than a walnut; these were arranged on the ledge of the lower granite block of the east side, with two on the west. When we looked into the dark chamber from the outside they shone as if illuminated, showing how clean they had remained. They are rounded and not broken. The total length of the chambers is nearly 20 feet, not including the long passage, and it may

[1] This diagram is not engraved.

be said to be tripartite, although the centre part might be held to be merely a passage. The southern part, B, was intended to be entered first, and is the largest, 6 feet long and 4 wide, the height 7 feet, but diminished by an accumulation of 8 or 10 inches of soil. The entrance at A was capped by a large and roundish block of granite resting on two slabs, and leaving the doorway to be only 2 feet 2 inches high and the same wide. On the stones forming the passage no markings could be expected; they were rough and brittle and slatey; no markings could be seen even on the granite, although there were places convenient enough for the purpose. The walls were formed of two blocks or rather slabs of stone, supplemented only by a rough walling, as seen in fig. 4. The slabs are placed on edge and lying end to end. On both sides where two large stones met was a kind of triangular space filled in with loose open walling, so that the hand could be inserted between the stones. On thrusting the hand in, the place around seemed to be so open that Mr. Mapleton was inclined to think that a recess might be behind. The roof was very interesting; the stones of the rough walling rose from the rocks below, and gradually approached each other, until the space was only 3 feet 4 inches by 1 foot 10 inches. This was covered over by one stone, as depicted. The chamber was therefore roughly domed, in this respect resembling many buildings of later times. The soil was loose to the depth of 10 inches, chiefly fine gravel, with some larger pebbles. When Mr. Mapleton lifted it up with a small trowel it was passed through the fingers; after bringing it to the light, many dark specks were found, appearing at first to be charcoal, but on examination they were found very soft, and might have been from decaying vegetable matter. It rained whilst we were in the cairn, and heavy drops came down into the domed room where the centre slab did not cover.

There was nothing found indicating a burial except the urns; in the large chamber was one, or rather part of one. There was no instrument of stone or of metal. We dug down to the natural surface, or some inches lower. However, the urn was not below the natural surface, but on it, and under the looser soil, lying on its side close to the mid part of the eastern wall. The position seems to have been its original one, the parts missing have probably decayed from being less completely burnt. The loose parts came out as if from their proper places, although detached. Another explanation is possible. The form is seen at Fig. 1, small neatly raised portions forming incipient handles. The urn is round below, and consequently could not stand by itself. Earth and stones were the only contents. A pebble of the same size and quality as the white ones mentioned was inside, and had become brown like the earth around.

The markings on the urn have a neat appearance, although done by simply drawing a point down the side. See Plate as before, Fig. 1.

The exit from this chamber leading to the middle compartment has two large slabs, supporting the roof or cover on the east side, resting on a wall of small stones, and on the west are the more solid blocks. The walling ran half way across the passage, which became narrowed to about 2 feet. This doorway E was filled up with stones built firmly in after the chamber had been completed, and not supporting the structure. They had no appearance of having been placed there recently,

although they were lighter in colour than those forming the
upper part of the wall. Those in the passage had the same
light colour, and were still of the original building. I understand that the apparently premeditated filling up of a passage
is not uncommon.

The middle part H, which may be only a passage itself, is
6 feet 6 inches long, and 2 feet 4 inches wide at the south end,
and 2 feet 1 inch at the north. It is 5 feet 4 inches high.
Both sides were very similar, each formed of two blocks, and
above them 3 feet of firm dry walling. A stone was found
lying across the compartment nearly hidden in the loose soil.
This gave the idea of sub-compartments, such as had been
found by Mr. Mapleton at Kilmartin, but on examination it
was seen to have been placed there only for strength, being
large and irregular, and occupying a great part of the floor,
although well fitted for keeping the sides from approaching.

The floor of the whole was strewed disorderly with boulder
stones, but this I understand is common ; to me it suggested
entrance and robbing, whilst some careful hand closed all up.
This, however, must have itself been early. The cover of this
middle compartment was a large slab, the edges of which
could not be seen.

The doorway, I, into the north division, is 2 feet 9 inches.
A long stone lay across, perhaps to tie the two sides, perhaps
to support the ends of the covering slabs, or both. We suppose there were two slabs to this and the middle division, but
we could not see the junction. This north compartment is 4
feet 6 inches long, 3 feet wide, and 4 feet 8 inches high, if we
do not remove the loose soil, otherwise 5 feet 5 inches. This
north end is formed by a slab, supplemented as elsewhere by

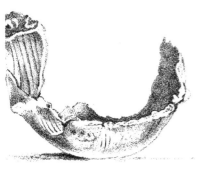

m S. Chamber of Cairn Achnacree.   Urn from N. Chamber of Cairn Achnacree.

Cross at Cleinamacry.

rough walling. The east side was formed of two long slabs set on edge, the upper one resting on the lower. The space above has rough walling 1 foot 6 inches high. The west side was similar, except that the upper slab rather bent down and left a wider ledge. The lower slab was 1 foot 4 inches thick, and 1 foot 9 inches high.

About the middle of the ledge, on the east side, were placed six white pebbles of quartz—four in one part and two a little separate. On the west side were two white pebbles; others of the same kind, but discoloured, were found in the soil. Three pebbles were found in the urn on the east side, and one in the others, so far as the broken state allowed us to judge. One urn nearly entire was found on the west side, and above the ground on the east side were fragments of two which appeared to have crumbled to decay, although the appearance could be explained by their having been broken and parts removed. We may ask, why should people have removed portions? The most complete was found exactly below the greatest number of quartz stones.

Fig. 2 shows the best preserved urn; it accompanied the fragments of two others. All of them had been quite round below, and they had no feet; this is true of two of those in the north certainly, and of the one in the south. Those in the north had no handles, not even incipient.

There was no injury done to any part of the structure, unless we except a crack in the tie-stone between the north chamber and the passage. This crack was old, and seems to have been the result of weight only.

The quartz pebbles have been often noticed. Mr. Mapleton has found them often in urns and cists in this county, and in

P

one case near Lochnell and far from quartz rock. He
thinks they are generally associated with cows' teeth. He
found three angular pieces of quartz firmly imbedded in a deep
cup made in the rock, and surrounded by rings or circle markings, in the Kilmartin district lately. These markings were
covered over with about 15 inches of soil, in which no quartz
occurred. Dr. Wilson mentions twenty-five urns having been
found on the Cathkin hills, each with its face downwards,
and a quartz stone under it. Mr. Mapleton inclines to dwell
on the idea that the quartz pebbles were symbols of acquittal,
according to the custom of the Greeks of using white stones,
shells, or beans, and refers to the second chapter and 17th
verse of " Revelation." There certainly we have the word used,
psephos, a pebble, from which *psephizomai*, I vote, is taken ;
votes were put into urns, or in Rome into kists. In Egypt
stone tablets were put with the dead, but these were written on.
We know that the Egyptians measured out the good deeds of
the person who died. These ideas are interesting to keep in
mind, but do not bring absolute proof. We might, indeed, say
that quartz pebbles, from their remarkable whiteness, were
selected as ornaments out of the brown material generally
forming the rocks or soil. Children are very fond of collecting
them, and most families at the sea-shore have some. They
are even seen in rows on window sills, and along garden walks
and at rockeries. The same idea of beauty might take hold
of the national mind of an early age ; this would explain to us
why the peebles are found in so many positions, whether in
Asia or with us. They are known to form smaller circles
within the large stone circles and elsewhere. Still this does not
contradict the idea of their being symbols, it may even assist it.

It is not easy to tell the age of this cairn—some will say the Neolithic, but we have found no instruments or manufactured articles besides the urns to prove it, and their forms are not conclusive. The lack of metal leads us to think of iron which is readily rusted. Still we found the spear-head at the bottom of the peat over there, and it was good bronze, and you may imagine the warrior who used it to be buried in this great memorial, for it was great, and its surrounding ditch and rings made it ornamental. Bronze was used at a very late age in Celtland of the north, and old habits would keep with it. Burial also in chambers allowing of a sitting posture was used up to the twelfth century among the Scandinavians. However, I know no such cairns of that age in this country. We read in "Burnt Njal" of one, a chambered tomb having, for honour, been given to the fine hero Gunnar; but had this been of his age, arms would certainly have been found here.

Sheena.—But there were urns. The people must have been burnt.

Loudoun.—No. The vessels may have been drinking vessels; no body was found, and it is fair to argue that high and chambered tombs could not have been intended merely for urns, and it is probable that they were meant for bodies in the sitting posture originally, although used afterwards for the lying posture. The proper, and probably original receptacle of the urn of burnt ashes is a stone kist; later it descended to be a niche only.[1]

---

[1] See "*Notes on the Survival of Pagan Customs*," by Joseph Anderson, Esq., Proc. Soc. of Antiq. of Scotland, vol. XL, part ii., p. 363. 1876.

CHAPTER XIX.

CONNEL MOSS—LAKE DWELLING.

IAN.—This time I think it would be better to walk over the moss and learn to jump over the wet places : it is a weary thing to wander along a straight smooth road, but on a moss we leap from tuft to tuft, and it keeps up our spirits and gives us a springy step.

Margaet.—And wet feet. I must dance like a young girl to get along ; you are much older, but you Highlanders keep up your vitality.

Ian.—Of course ; by walking over mosses. Well, I will show you something wonderful. I will lift that grass and dig black peat from below, and near the peat I will show a wooden foundation. We shall see ashes and bones, with proof enough that these wild looking places were not wildernesses in all times.

That hollow is a watercourse for a small stream : it once held a greater supply, but the water was sent down the other way, namely by Achnacree, about a hundred and twenty years ago. You see that where the water flows most rapidly there is green grass ; where it is most stagnant there is moss, and where there is little or no water there is heather.

Margaet.—But that is quite flat. Surely it never contained a stream.

Ian.—The broad flat part was a little lake from which the stream flowed, and the name was and is Loch-an-Tawail by sound, which may be Loch-an-t'Samhuil or Loch-an-t'Shomhairle, the Loch of Samuel or the Loch of Somerled. It is sometimes flooded now, and was more so when I was a boy, and I used to wade into that green place in the middle, which now is difficult to distinguish from the rest.

Sheena.—Yes, yes; it is all nothing. Willie and I walked over it and there are only a few holes and a few stones. Like so many things we come to see, they are all gone before we come. I expect the hills soon to disappear; indeed I should not be surprised if they are gone when we waken to-morrow, these antiquities produce so many illusions.

Cameron.—If a mist comes over the hills or over your eyes you will not see much, and a thick mist of peat covers that which you will see here. The best part is not on the surface. In this hole, into which you looked carelessly, are seen beams or rather young birch trunks lying horizontally heaped over each other like pig-iron. This extends to the bottom. I am not sure of the deepest, but some are about five layers deep, perhaps usually four, and others may be more. There is a nearly oval figure formed by a slight raising of the turf, and in the middle is a still higher part. This oval is about 50 feet long and 28 broad; it evidently marks the dwelling, but the tree foundation goes beyond this to the breadth of 60 feet. And now I will leave you to ask questions, or to read a description which I have taken out of a book. The book itself is new, as the discovery was made but lately.

No piles were seen. There were many leaves, half rotten, and a few branches. The young trees had been felled with sharp axes; there was none of the clumsiness of the stone age. The encircling mounds were but a few inches high, but they showed organic matter decaying and turned into peat. It seemed as if a double wall of wattles had existed, it might have been peat or grassy turf. I saw no proof of clay to fill up the chinks: the Highlanders do not object to chinks even now.

The wood was birch. It is near the "Lake of the birches."

There are few trees that can give it that name now, but we can imagine a time when there were many birches. Many scores of the same class must have been laid under this spot. At the east end of the oval was an elongation not surrounded by the turf mound. I believe the foundation extends along it, and I suppose this to have been a platform before the door, a place for the inhabitants to sun themselves, and a landing and disembarking spot. (This platform was afterwards found to extend all round.)

In the middle nearly, but a little to the westerly end, of the oval house was the fire-place. It is higher than the rest of the space. It is here that the bones were found, with shells and nuts. Under a few inches of a white powder is the hearth. It consists of four flattish stones; under the stones is also to be found more peat ash and some few remnants, but very few, of the substances connected with food. There were no implements, but we did not look into the most promising spot. They, if at all, will be found farther from the fire. Under the ashes is a floor of clay about six inches thick. This is laid as flat as our wooden floors are.

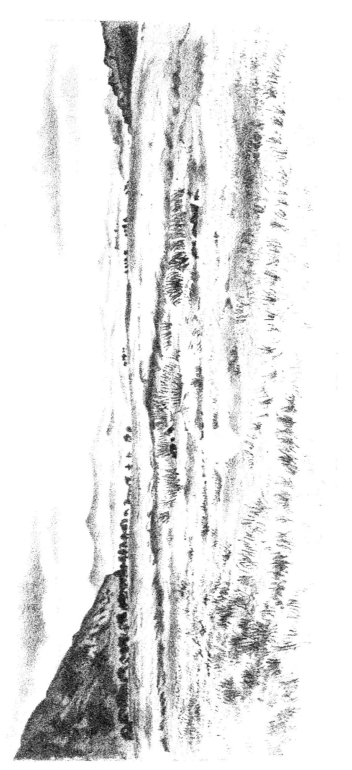

Lake Dwelling at Ledaig.
Connel Ferry.

At the east end, at an opening or door apparently, to judge from the failure of the encircling mound, was another smaller and ruder fire-place. The stones supporting it were found, with abundance of peat ash, bones and nuts. But the finest fire-place was at the west.. The end was that of an oval, and a large fire-place was at the extremity, with bushels of ashes. The fire-place was rudely made by a bank of flattish stones raised above the floor. On each side was a raised seat, made also of flattish stones, and quite broad enough to serve for two or even three persons. These seats were the chimney corners of the chief inhabitants, and fine fires they seem to have had. The seats might have been covered, and in any case I do not doubt that they were comfortable. There were then three fire-places in the length of fifty feet, increasing in importance until the west was reached.

On the outside of the enclosure, a large amount of nutshells was found as if thrown over into the "yard" in a slovenly way.

There is a full account of lake dwellings in Switzerland by Professor Keller; this comes nearest to that at Wauwyl. There are no piles.

There were found several wooden pegs, and a piece of a knife not larger than a large pocket one, a hook such as might have been used to hang a pot, several pieces of skin soles, and a slipper of thin skin rather neatly made, not in the Icelandic fashion. There was also the side of a wooden basin well turned. The wooden articles dried up, shrivelled, and completely changed their shape in the open air; but a comb was preserved by being kept in a box filled with peat, which was allowed to dry slowly for two years. It was made of wood, one side having smaller teeth than the other.

This dwelling was larger than single rooms in the Highlands now are. It may, like Deirdre's, have contained three apartments. The people need not have been lower in civilization than some we see now, if houses are to be the criterion. The bones found were split up in the recognised prehistoric

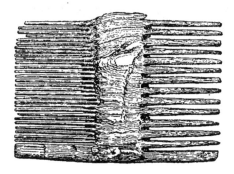

Wooden Comb found in Lake Dwelling.

method. This is supposed to indicate a scarcity of food : it may also indicate an idle way of spending time and lounging over the meals, as well as a liking for marrow, in which we succeed them. When thinking whether it was possible to judge from this as to the age of the remains, I asked some friends who had been brought up in the Highlands, whether any peculiar attention was ever given to the marrow of bones generally, independent of the admired " marrow bones."

I heard of nothing like splitting bones among the inhabitants, but it is known in Iceland even now. A lady from near Loch Broom said that her father had a peculiar knack by which he could break a bone, and he occasionally performed it as a feat before his sons and guests, using a leg of a sheep. The lady did not know if it was done by strength or by skill, but thinks it required both. Her brothers, who were strong men, often tried, but could not accomplish it. This is an evident relic of early times. As many of the prehistoric are also contemporaneous habits, it would be interesting to trace out that of bone splitting more fully.

And now as to the age of this dwelling. The peaty turf over it was soft and full of fibre. I see no reason for arguing great age from this. Even allowing a very long term for its growth—a foot in a century—we have only three hundred years, and, as until 1740 there was a greater supply of water to it, the growth may have been more rapid. On the other hand, the stream, in former times, went through here, and it may have washed off the surface of the moss or prevented the increase. The trees, however, are quite rotten, and although in every respect looking fresh, even preserving the perfect appearance of the bark, the spade goes through them with ease. Birch does not keep well under water; still, although easily crumbled by the fingers or cut by the spade when wet, it became actually hard and strong when dried. It seems as if the water united with the woody fibre, and made a soft compound or hydrate. This compound was easily decomposed by driving off the water. It is analogous to the soft gelatinous hydrate of alumina or iron which becomes hard by drying.

The circumstances are a little contradictory. The size and independent position of the house might point to a person of some local village importance: do the split bones and the poor hearth take us far back, if so how far? We do not require to go out of this century in Scotland to find men having only two apartments and still giving judgment as magistrates or so-called bailies to the neighbourhood for miles, and keeping the peace better than more learned lawyers have been able to do. In the Highlands I have myself seen men living in hovels, dark and inexpressibly low in material civilization, whilst the inmates had really as much good feeling and general wisdom in their speech as many men who gave much better dwellings to their cows, and incomparably better to their horses.

The dwelling does not show the civilization of the occupant correctly, neither does the food. In the dwellings mentioned, the food seems to have been far inferior in variety and elegance to that used in the lake dwellings of Switzerland among men who are said to have worshipped the water and the moon.

If the dwelling does not show the condition in civilization of the individual, neither does it of the race. We have dwellings from London to Caithness and Kerry in abundance, as uncomfortable as those of many savages, but out of some of the worst some of our best minds have emerged.

According to Scott, many of the Highlanders of the last century were savage, but a sudden peace brought an almost instant civilization. The talent for rising was there ; where was it prepared ? Such a change is not made among negroes except in rare individuals. The theory of development forbids us to believe this sudden step to be taken by any nation never previously affected by civilization. This, I believe, is a very important point. Such a step proves the organization to have been previously developed. The organization of a nation cannot be supposed to develop at once, not even that of an individual. I do not therefore expect to find savage traits among such people, except so far as the necessity for struggling produced savage habits, just as we see that it produces them in war in our own times.

In order to see if a wild race has a developed organization, it would be needful to bring up some of the infants to civilized ways. If they showed an incapacity, we might presume, if the numbers were sufficient for a good experiment, that they were really savage. If they showed a capacity, we could not imagine them to be properly savage. The power may lie dormant, but cannot far precede, we may suppose, its first exercise. This is said without objecting to the supernatural.

As there is no reason to suppose that, however inferior as architects, the men were savage, let us now look for the inhabitants. Who were the people that cracked nuts at that hearthstone? Did the "mighty Somerled" live in this lake dwelling?—or perhaps some of the relatives? We are told that he had possessions both on the mainland and the Western islands. His power went to the second son, whose descendants are Macdougalls of Lorn, and live within six miles of this place.

Did not Somerled, who died in the twelfth century, live in a stone castle? It is most probable. One of the family may have done otherwise. It is only certain that he was closely connected with this neighbourhood. We do not depend wholly on traditions concerning him, as the family and this loch have kept the family name.[1]

A piece of wood with a cross burnt on it caused a good

entered. It is, however, an old form also in Iceland, which greatly weakens all this speculation, already shown by Dr. Stuart to be incorrect. Indeed, we may see almost exactly the same forms in his great work, " The Sculptured Stones of Scotland."

As the present Icelandic forms are identical with the cross found, so may the purpose be ; but we know that religious forms sometimes degenerate into such things as witchcraft and charms. Mr. Hjaltalin tells me that they make in Iceland exactly the same cross, but without the circle, on a piece of paper, as a charm when going to wrestle. It is put in the shoe with these words :

> " Ginfaxi under the toe,
> Gependi under the heel,
> Help me the Devil,
> For I am in a strait."

These words at the beginning may be very old, the meaning not being clear I am told. Mr. Hjaltalin also refers to " Travels, by Umbra," for several varieties of crosses like these.[1]

It may be repeated that I do not consider the lake-dwelling to be very old.

---

[1] A cross with different lines upon it is given by Jón Arnason in his " Islenskar Þjodsögur og Aefintyri," vol. I., p. 446, and *Ginfaxi* under it. The charm is given a little different on p. 452.

WILLIE.—It is very early, and I should like to go farther. Sheena and I could run up the hill.

Ian.—I dare say we could all go up ; it is not far. We must go to the next farm house ; here you see is a precipice. They say, and it seems true, that it was produced by the washing of the waves at the foot of the rock, at a time when these very waves nearly levelled all that ground which is now moss.

Willie.—There is no sea now, so let us run ; you can follow.

Loudoun.—We who are calmer can go up behind the house, and a fine walk it is to the well. You see near this well a few bushes, and on the bushes there used to be a few **trifles**— pieces of cloth, or string, or buttons, or needles ; these latter were also put into the well.

O'Keefe.—That is a relic of very old times, when perhaps they worshipped wells.

Loudoun.—I do not think that they ever worshipped wells ; but spiritual beings are often connected with them in history and tradition. I think this a good proof of an Eastern origin of the fancy. Wells are valuable there; they are of little consequence here.

It is a steep road up this hill, and even these youngsters must creep.

Margaet.—But, oh! how glorious on the top. Lismore is below, Loch Linnhe all in our view, and Kerrera is near; even Mull comes close, and these distant islands are scarcely far away in this fair weather; I mean Colonsay and Oronsay.

Loudoun.—The view is grand; but it will not allow us to look at it long. It is cold up here; at first we walk about thinking that we should like to live on such an Olympus always; whilst in ten minutes we lose the warmth got by climbing, or we become hungry. Sometimes the mist comes and we lose our way, and if we go straight down there we shall come to the precipice. Indeed it is a hill of abundant danger, and we must keep to the road by the well.

Cameron.—I hope you will all stay a little; we cannot often see so far, and this is like a map of the world. Our vision is multiplied by ten, and our spirits rise in proportion. The passage down is pleasant and not too far to weary us; there we have some interesting things to see that were passed over when we went along the moss looking at the cairn and the lake dwelling.

CROMLECHS.

Loudoun.—Be it so. We have to go by the road, and as it turns near the joining of the way to Achnaba, there is a short walk to a very interesting spot. We pass down to the stream, and cross it either at the little cottage on its steep bank, or below where it is lower, and among some bushes and

deep grass and nettles we come upon two cromlechs, megalithic or big-stone structures, standing not so high as those
before seen, but clear and distinct. The largest and most
easterly has a great granite table on ten boulders; the
smaller has only five boulders for supporting the top stone.
The arrangement is as if for a grave. Around both there is
the evident remains of a cairn, and I doubt not that each was
heaped over with the smaller boulders of the district exactly
as the large cairn spoken of was. These two stand close to
each other; the two circles of the cairns must have met, and
now these stand in a romantic spot, hidden, however, from the
view of all passers on the roads. One wonders why the cairns
have been laid low, but the boulders were small whilst the
cromlechs are formed of great masses. Is the ring a symbol
of honour around the great heroes, or was it only left because
some one found it convenient to take the stones to build a
little house near the cairn as a home for old Duncan Stewart,
who used to live there, or some one before him? That is
most probable. (See Fig.)

Some have denied cromlechs to be in Scotland. These
are two cromlechs—certainly not one stone on two, but one
stone on a few. I prefer the word cromlech, which seems to
have been made so long ago that we have lost the certainty
of its meaning, to any name such as dolmen, foreign to our
country, but more applicable to the structures of Brittany with
galleries such as we have not.

Margaet.—What is a cromlech?

Willie.—If you put two stones up and one across, that
is a cromlech, just as we have in graveyards now, only at
present they are cut smooth and thin and don't last at all.

Crom is *bent* and *leach* a *stone;* but why these words are so united who knows? The stones are not bent.

Loudoun.—It is true they are not; but the Welsh word *cromen* is a dome or cupola according to the dictionary, and here we have a stone, if not bending, one may say leaning over from one stone to another and making a covering. These were called in Ireland Leaba Diarmaid agus Grainne (*i.e.,* beds of D. and G.), which shows again that they were capable of being used as coverings. But it is believed that these stones were in the centre of mounds or cairns, of which the tops have been removed. It is probable that there were earth mounds over them in some cases; but stones are more apt to be removed than earth. If they were covered the name must have been given them after they were uncovered.

O'Keefe.—But do not the French call these dolmens and the standing stones cromlechs?

Loudoun.—A good deal of confusion arises here; it would be well for us to keep our native names until we know their origin. Dolmen may be good; it is a table stone, or a hole stone; there are good authorities for both. Here uncertainty arises; but the meaning "table stone" suits well those large broad masses in Brittany.

Margaet.—I think I have heard them connected with religion.

Loudoun.—Certainly they have been; and it connected with worship we should expect the word to apply to standing stones also, which seem at times to have been used for pur-poses| much greater than the ornament of a tomb, although such ornamentation has called forth great architectural efforts. There is a great desire to reduce all our knowledge to some small facts, and the eminent antiquary, Dr. John Stuart, led the way to prove that even the largest circles were mere tombs; but we know that man is very low indeed, when an idea of worship does not animate him in connection with death.

O'Keefe.—Crom Cruach was a great idol of the Milesian branch of the Irish. It stood in Magh Slecht, in Cavan, and was ornamented with gold and silver, surrounded also by twelve other idols ornamented with brass. St. Patrick visited the place along with King Laeghaire or Lire and struck at the idol with his crozier; but although the crozier did not reach the image it made a mark in its side. The earth swallowed up the other twelve idols, and O'Curry thinks that the circumstance is so carefully recounted that one may probably find them still there. It seems to be indicated that the chief idol was swallowed more deeply than the mere earth would answer for. The story is a most probable one so far as the destruction of the idols by St. Patrick is concerned, and as the name has no meaning at all clear it is not likely to have been manufactured; but people make great difficulties about believing nowadays; they are afraid to believe in the worship of horrid idols or human sacrifices or anything they dislike. To me the more horrible the more probable. Man has emerged from a lower state than even the worship of Crom Cruach.

Loudoun.—But does not *crom* in Irish mean a maggot? And is it not the maggot stone—the stone of corruption?

O'Keefe.—This is a new derivation, and it seems true. It has been called the bending stone, or the stone of worship, but it does not appear as if these smaller or common ones at least were other than places of burial.

Sheena.—If crom is a maggot, why is it the name of an idol, and what is cruach ?

O'Keefe.—Cruach may be held to have its common meaning of red, or gory or deadly, in which case the Crom Cruach would be a power to be appeased. The people were afraid of it, and were afraid of dying until St. Patrick had sent this demon to Tophet. The word *crom* is in another place the name of a pestilence : for example *Crom Chonnaill* in Ulster, in the sixth century. It was killed by fire from heaven at the prayer of Mac Creiché, and it was reduced to dust and ashes in the presence of the people.[1] It is spoken of as if it were an animal destroying the people : it is not an unusual thing for men to personify a pestilence. In Squier's *Peru* we find that a man seeking shelter after having lost his clothes when bathing, was taken for the impersonation of a plague. " The word *connall* signifies the yellow stubble of corn." O'Curry says, " It is a remarkable fact that the name of the celebrated idol of the ancient Pagan *Gaedhil* was *Crom Cruach*, which would literally signify the 'bloody maggot,' whilst another idol, or imaginary deity, in the western parts of Connacht was called '*Crom Dubh*,' the black maggot, a name still connected with the first Sunday of August in Munster and Connacht."

" The word Buidhe chonnaill or 'yellow stubble' would appear to be a particular disease of the jaundice kind, but not produced by the presence of any animal like a maggot or fly."

Still here we have a rude connection of disease in animal and vegetable.

Another connection is less rude ; crom or crum may be the

[1] O'Curry. Appendix, CLI.

same as worm or wurm, and this brings us to the serpent
form of power for good or evil, or serpent-worship. In France
the standing stones and circles are called cromlechs. This
removes all idea of crookedness and bending; indeed, it is
not easy to connect the idea with any form which we have,
and the old object of worship, Crom, seems to me by far the
most probable source. This is not fashionable, however,
but that is not against it. The stones set up for Crom and
the other gods destroyed by St. Patrick suit the account of
the temple given in the Kjalnesinga Saga remarkably well,
and point to early communication unknown to us. But this
Crom theory is against the burial theory apparently, and is
therefore disliked. There need be no opposition; it is but
natural to devote the dead, when loved, to the gods, or to
appease these when feared. At any rate you have seen two
cromlechs of a great size, and you have heard several opinions
curious to me at least, and consistent with the wild nature
out of which we seem to have sprung.

Cameron.—It seems to me that we have done enough, and I
have asked the men to bring the boat to the kirk at Achnaba.
It is, as you say, not beautiful, but I like it. The building belongs to the kirk of my fathers and it is one which is associated
with many early days; let us sit for awhile in the churchyard,
and look at the beautiful loch, thinking of the monks on the
island opposite, and even of the Druids on the shore by the
great stone circle that once stood there, and of **Kilmaronaig**
and the saint that left his name near the point a little to the
right of it. I cannot forbear alluding to the places more
than once, or whenever we come near; if we do so, we
remember better.

When we have seen these long enough we shall row to Acha-Leamhan, near Connel, and find the coach which will take us rapidly to Oban, as I fear the falls will not allow us to pass, and the men must wait there for two hours before they can begin to row home.

O'Keefe.—Meantime I shall give you a part from the Saga spoken of. " Thorgrimr Godi was a great worshipper, and built a temple on his farm (in Iceland) a hundred feet long and sixty feet broad. All the people were to pay a tax towards it. Thorr was most worshipped there. It was made round within like a skull-cap. It was hung with tapestry, and there were windows in it. Thorr was standing in the middle, and the other gods on both sides. In front of Thorr stood an altar finely made, and covered on the top with iron. There was to be the fire which should never go out; we call that consecrated fire. On that altar a large ring made of silver was lying. The temple priest wore it on his hand at all public meetings. By it all people were to swear in giving evidence. On that altar there stood a large bowl of copper, into which the blood of cattle or men sacrificed to Thorr was to be poured. This they called Hlautbolli (bloodbowl). From this bowl men and cattle which were sacrificed and feasted on were to be besprinkled when there were sacrificing feasts. But the men who were sacrificed were thrown down into a pool close to the door." [1]

---

[1] That is, the cattle were eaten and the men thrown into a pool. Human remains do not always prove honest death and burial. The above was kindly translated from the Icelandic by Mr. Hjaltalin.

CHAPTER XXI.

LOCHNELL AND GLEN LONAIN.

Αἰάζω τὸν Ἄδωνιν· ἀπώλετο καλὸς Ἄδωνις·
Ὤλετο καλὸς Ἄδωνις, ἐπαιάζουσιν Ἔρωτες.—*Bion.*

AS the conversation was not well remembered on this excursion, one of the party was requested to write an account of a day at Lochnell and its neighbourhood. They had all heard of Lochiel, but who of Lochnell? Even the guide-books connect the name with the wrong place, namely, the land over near Keills, beyond Connel Ferry, instead of with its own region, surrounded by its own hills, draining its own fields, and sending its own river Feochan down to the sea at Loch Feochan. It is a very small lake, not a sea loch, for we may make the distinction, which, however, is not made in Gælic, or even by the English, between lake and loch. The name is poetic, *Loch-a-ncala*, the lake of the swans; there may have been many such birds here once, but they are gone. Still there is left a pleasant memory of airy life, and the low land where the stream falls out of the lake is called Dalineun [1]—the valley of birds. Here is the report of the excursion.

[1] *Eun, eu* sounded as *e* in *there* long (Dalinyēne).

The road from Oban to the loch itself is steep, but it is good, and only about four miles long. To go by land to the other side of the loch would make four or five more round, so that it needs a good walker to traverse in a day all the ground to be visited. Glen Lonain itself needs some ten miles of walking to and fro if it is all to be visited. We preferred, therefore, to have a conveyance to take us to the ground, and to help us at need. As the party drove out of the glen leading from Oban south-east, the rugged heights showed themselves more than on the other side, and the strange shapes of the hills seemed more and more the playthings of numberless streams and violent submarine currents. But soon we came to a not extensive moor, and saw before us the isolated but warm-looking, because wooded valley, with its couple of good country-seats and the manse of Kilmore. The valley goes to the right, and below is Loch Feochan, the entrance of the sea; but we went to the left, and immediately came to a house or two, poor enough looking, and with a desolate kind of name, *Cleigh*. This name signifies a burying-place, and one of the younger of us naturally asked, " Why do you take us to burying-grounds? We never visit such at home, unless it be to see the tomb of a relative." The answer was easy: " We are here to see the memorials of the people who have long passed; history is among the dead; at home we live among the active men. Besides, here are our distant forgotten relatives." And here, certainly, there are few and scattered dwellings to see, but the name seems to indicate that many persons, living or dead, were brought here, if they did not live and die here. It is not hard to imagine all this pleasant valley filled with houses, small of course ; there is much good grass, and there is still some corn. People pass the road and see nothing, but Cameron stopped us at the little farm-house of Molee before arriving at Lochnell, and, walking to a field on the left, we saw the remains of a great cairn sixty feet in diameter. Now, it must have been an important person who had such a burying-place. Who of the men of this century, has such a great space to rest in ? Such cairns are at first a dozen feet. high or more, and yet the stones are gone, probably to build the neighbouring house and byres. The stones had been gathered from the fields, probably old rounded boulders, and thus the land was cleared ages ago, doing good to the living by remembering the dead. And now we have the benefit, because these fields show a good crop of oats. The people, probably, were not very irreverent when demolishing the heap in later years to form habitations for the living. Tradition has no knowledge of the inmate of this cairn, but an inmate there was, and, as soon as the stone kist was seen, no more theft was perpetrated there ; the nearly square box remains in the centre, formed of the best of the stones. The body had been burnt, and the urn containing the ashes had been removed and given to a lady living for the time in the valley lower down. It will go to make up some unknown collection, and people will say, " It was probably a Celtic urn." Who knows if the body was not bent up and buried, dissolved long ago, whilst the urn was only a water or food vessel, deposited by the friends, according to some ancient custom, and alone remaining undecayed. The kist or cist is small for this mode of burial.

There has been only one burial in this great monument of the Cleigh, and it makes us dream and express feelings that never can be old and commonplace to man who is so short-lived. The builders mourned over their friends, even if they were not so wise as men are now. They had feelings even more intense than ours, since they laboured so long to perpetuate the memory of one whom they loved or admired. It has become common not to mourn much for the dead ; this is a beautiful feeling when it arises from the hope of a glorious resurrection, but we can only call it brutalizing when it arises from an intense love of the present, and a removal of the lost from our minds as mere matter, the memory of which is an inconvenient interruption to the business or pleasures of life. In this sense these great cairns are a proof of a higher life than is led by the men who forget the graves, and rejoice in the heritage left them by the dead.

Bronze dagger found in a cist at Cleigh, Lochnell—length, 5 in. —now in Museum of Antiquaries, Edinburgh.

The party were pleased when they had only to walk a little farther from the road, and, near the rising ground, to see the base of another large cairn. This had been certainly surrounded by a ring of heavier stones, as probably the other also was. The boulders forming the cairn had been removed here also, and the stone kist remained; it was elongated, not square, like the former. This too had been opened not very long ago, but imperfectly, and on finishing the examination of the kist, some five or six years ago, a very fine bronze dagger was obtained, one of a class very rare. It is deposited in the Museum of the Society of Antiquaries in Edinburgh.

It is only of late that these things have been cared for, and we wonder that Scotland has been so little known. It is only now being discovered. The men in the glen did not know that such remains were not everywhere, and had no idea that these were interesting memories to all men, if not now foundation of legends for themselves, and usually visitors did not go over the ground, but stood at one end of a valley and, if they cared at all, only admired or wondered. Loudoun had been saying this, but Cameron objected, as he said that it was all well known in the Highlands once, but books made people lose their memories, so that this district just behind Oban, like many others, is a new region to tourists.

Our company had not far to go to meet another surprise. When on our way to the lake, a little north of the shortest line, was seen a double cairn. It seems at least to have been a cairn, and the circle is clearly defined, but the covering boulders are here also removed, and two stone kists were found, the greatest being in the centre, each with a megalithic covering. These are almost like the cromlech, as usually named, but being low, they are more like stone graves. The larger stone is the more remarkable. The great granite covering has been broken, and a part removed to form a millstone some time in this century. The burying-place is a fine one, both for strength and position, and the stones must have lasted for centuries, how long, as in other cases, we cannot say. The cairns just spoken of, made with the smaller stones, were from the bronze age; this grave being megalithic speaks of a ruder age, perhaps the polished stone, but every-thing buried had been removed. The spot is a pleasant knoll evidently chosen for effect, and looking over the lake, as well as over the fine vale of Feochan, whilst it may be a cheerful spot on which to sit and hear the music in this "valley of birds." The men who chose it not only knew what had a fine effect, but they had a love of nature that is not exceeded now if we may judge from this. This grave is called the tomb of the giants, and of the Finn; and people, wish-ing to be more exact, add the name of the individual, and even give it that of Cuchullin; but it is to be feared that this will not stand, and will not even find a faint reason for its continuance. See drawing.

There is here a fine proof that the great stone structures which stand out were once covered with earth or smaller stones; when we look also on the monuments at Achnacree, where the debris of the cairn and its circumference are clearly seen, the same opinion is formed in the mind of even a-care-less observer. Still it is not a final proof; the circle may have been an enclosing ring.

It may be that those cairns which were seen are only the few remaining monuments of a great cemetery, and we can readily imagine many small ones to have long disappeared. Moving a little to the north, on ground a few feet higher, is again a cairn. In this case care had been taken to seek a separate elevation, and nature had assisted in the search. It is not, however, so easily observed as the lower, since it is at the end of a long ridge. This cairn has of late been opened, and a few **trifles** have been found in **it**—a piece of mica and a piece of flint were remarkable objects.

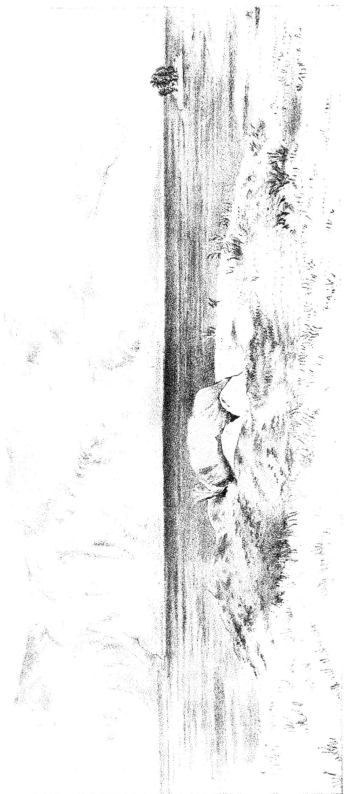

Tomb of the Finn.
Lochnell.

Both must have come from a distance, the flint from a great distance; both inserted as precious things. It had been opened by Mr. Phené, and apparently also at a previous time. The small boulders have not been removed, an opening only having been made down to the centre, which contained the square and small stone kist. This mound seems to be an eskar—a Celtic name for a small hill, and applied by geologists to a heap which ice or water has left in a forlorn and desolate way, and in very remote times, at the foot of hills or even in plains. They are very various in shape, and sometimes very irregular, winding often as streams wind, and this specimen has been supposed to resemble a saurian, and even to be a relic of serpent worship. As we do not know anything of saurian worship here, it is a fancy that we cannot accept, and in Glen Lonain there are other eskars far more curved than this. It is true that the serpent is among the Celts a very interesting animal, and stories of enormous ones, both on sea and land, exist among them as well as the Norse. They are found in carvings on stone and on metal. It was in Lorn, not far from this, where a man saw an eel passing by as he was fishing in the morning, and it passed all the time he was there, and when he returned in the evening there it was still passing, so that it must have been a very long sea-monster. (See J. F. Campbell's *Popular Tales of the West Highlands.*) Campbell thinks the serpent stories were brought from the East, and this seems almost—I should say altogether— certain. This country could furnish nothing interesting about them. People are very much afraid to bring any traditions from the East to Scotland, although the very language has come thence. I would not even say that serpent worship has never existed here, but we have no proofs, and the stories have the appearance of having been old myths before they left their native Asia.

In relation to this I must give the substance of a letter from India by Dr. Mapleton, which would seem, at first sight, to justify some of the ideas connected with this place.

Copy of a letter from Dr. Mapleton, 1876 :

" Close to the camp of **Deolati** is a Hindoo temple on a hill; the entrance faces the east ; in front of the entrance is a stone column, about 8 feet high and octagonal in form, with one or two raised rings around it. It stands on a pedestal of four diminishing steps, on the second from the bottom of which are a number of pits.

"At the eastern side are several (about 8) very superficial pits, arranged in no order. At the northern aspect are only 3 or 4 pits, two being very distinctly jointed by a groove. There is no other mark on the whole thing. Thirty yards to the west is the temple, in a square court of burnt brick. This is about 25 yards square and has an entrance at the eastern side. Within the walls are the temple, a Buddha, a half Buddha, and also two small dome-topped houses, like dog kennels.

" I went round the outside of the temple and took a general look at it. I then went westward along the continuation of the hill, and noticed far away to the west an arrangement of peaks like this. (The lines are not reproduced.) I thought of Phené and the Glen Feochan snake, and really there was the same serpentine form of the hill. It made four curls, and ended on a hill on which the temple stood. I drew the attention of a friend to it. He said, with a hasty exclamation, " It does look like a snake too !" The hill is a hard sandy clay ridge, running E. and W. nearly. It is to one side of a small river, and is completely detached from all other hills.

" The snake is apparently from 10 to 30 feet above the'level of the plain, and has evidently not been fashioned. There may be a backbone, but this I was unable to determine. I saw the three peaks before I saw the serpentine form of the mound. There are several hillocks of the same nature in the neighbourhood, but no other ' megatheriums.' "

This letter has an interest in itself, but the accident of a curved eskar in view of a hill has no particular interest, neither has a cairn any special interest because of being here, unless we can show a serpent. When this was said to be a saurian or a dragon at Lochnell, we preferred to call it a fancy ; we are disinclined even to say a word about it, since people may imagine there is a something, whereas there is nothing to reason upon. The spine was said to be indicated by a row of stones as vertebrae, but this was sought immediately on the supposed discovery being made, and the conclusion drawn was that such a line was entirely imaginary. Still dragon myths abound in the East and in Greece, although we have looked in vain for this mode of embodiment out of America. The serpents carved on stones in Scotland are not saurians or dragons, they |are more like eels.

Having seen these cairns, we crossed over to the islands, of which there are two in Lochnell. One of these is very little and near the outlet of the loch, with two small trees upon it. No one would think it to have been inhabited. It is nearly round, not much larger than a good-sized cottage. It is surrounded by stones large enough to be difficult to lift, and in some places showing themselves to have been put together by art. It would appear as if there had been a pretty firm wall all round—very firm it could not be without mortar or heavier stones. Three or four feet within the range of stones is a raised turf mound, as if this had been the wall of the house; the centre of the space was rather higher than the rest, and there we expected a fire-place to be found. By digging about three feet and a half, the ashes of peat were obtained, bones, charcoal, and nuts. A very small hole was made, as we had not then received liberty to dig. We were satisfied that this had been a lake-dwelling, and that it had been defended by a wall. Advantage seems to have been taken of a shallow place, and stones must have been carried to it. It may turn out that there is a wooden foundation. It is not easy to see by what means the covering of earth now over the floor was so much raised. The water of the lake forms little or no deposit in summer; art rather than natural circumstances may have raised the soil. The bones here were split as at the lake-dwelling in the moss.

As it is probable that these lake-dwellings existed till a very late date, we may find some clue to the inhabitants of this lower one, as we supposed ourselves to have done in the case of Somerled's Loch.

Stories had been told us of a buried city which was submerged by the floods that made the lake, and of which parts could be seen on a clear day. It was also said that there, on the larger of the islands of this loch, the Campbells of Lochnell lived in former times. Their estate has the name of Lochnell, and from it they take their present territorial name always used in the Highlands. This island is at the upper end of the lake, and cannot be approached without a boat. The number and size of the stones upon it show that some building had been there, but there is no surface proof that a large well-constructed house existed. There are trees upon it. The stones must have been carried to the island and they are all too similar to be natural. However, there was a natural island there or a shallow place, as the depth and distance from the shore prevent us thinking of such a great undertaking as the manufacture of one from the average lake bottom upwards, whilst some of the rocks seem *in situ.*

There is no boat to be hired on the loch, but as we were fortunate enough to get the use of the private one, a visit was made to this old haunt of the Campbells, on the way to Glen Lonain, instead of going round by the road, which involves a very steep climb and a very deep descent. Passing from the island we crossed to the upper end of the lake, and landed upon a very flat piece of ground, which rises gradually among knolls of a shape peculiar to the Oban district.

Legends of Diarmid.—As the weather and season favoured we came amongst pleasant corn fields on the farm of Sron-t-Soillear. One might expect romance in this upper end of Lochnell, as it was abundant at the lower, and there we saw a tall pillar—one of the finest in Scotland. But our party preferred to go straight on to the farm-house to ask questions and to learn the way. It was melancholy to think that no native guide was to be had ; all the inhabitants around were strangers lately come ; not a soul was found to belong to the land. Before coming to the house a great circle was seen made of boulder stones, as all those of this district are. The stones are doubled irregularly on the west side. In

Aberdeen and Kincardine the custom is to lay a great stone on the southerly side. There are said to have been other circles destroyed here, and indeed this isolated valley of Lochnell is the very place for men to have enjoyed peace when commotions existed on the shores, when the "black Danes" harried the land or the fair Norse came for plunder. Every mound here has an artificial look, and one almost expects to find history at every step. This circle, which remains entire, is 60 feet in diameter, a very favourite size, and one that seems to have been chosen for a reason. We saw it lonely among hay, itself enough to give interest to the whole valley even had the sun been absent. (See drawing.)

A couple of fields off, after passing along graceful mounds and good grass, was seen Diarmid's pillar (Clach Dhiarmaid or Carrach Dhiarmaid). And now we were in the very midst of a land of legends. No story is more persistently told than the story of Diarmid ; no story has the places connected with every transaction more minutely given ; but, unfortunately, some half dozen places claim the originals. The story itself is told in Irish literature, and some old MSS. give it at great length, but the writing is modern compared with the events which go back to Finn or Fingal, a little before the arrival of St. Patrick in Ireland.

Grainne was the daughter of Cormac MacArt, the splendid king, the judge, warrior, and philosopher, who reigned at Tara, and who was the grandson of Conn of the hundred battles, and in whose time the world was all goodness, the land fat and fruitful, the sea productive—no killings, no plunderings — everywhere peace and happiness. Grainne was espoused to Fingal, but compelled Diarmid to run

Stone circle at Lochnell.

away with her; this seems to have been according to ·
usage in Old Ireland; Deirdre, the great beauty, did the
same. Fingal pursued them, and the adventures make a long
story; however, when they met, it was agreed to have a boar
hunt on Ben Gulbain, as if the offence had not been deadly.
Here Fingal sought some new cause of quarrel. Diarmid
killed the boar, and was asked to measure it; he did so
from snout to tail, but he was desired to measure it from tail
to snout; he did so, and the bristles went into the vulnerable
part in his heel and poisoned him. Some say the bristles
were poisoned; but the longer account mentions Diarmid as
having leapt up on the boar and sat upon it looking backwards, whilst the beast ran down the hill, jumping over
streams rapidly, and trying to throw him off, putting the
hero in a not very dignified position. It then turned up Ben
Gulbain again, and at last succeeded in tossing and also
wounding Diarmid, whilst soon he killed it. And now he
was dying of his wound and nothing but fresh water could
help him. Fingal pretended to bring some, but always
spilt it, and Diarmid died.

The account we got at Lochnell was that the magic water
must be brought in the hands of the most beautiful women,
to make the cure certain; but the ladies could not manage
to bring any—the way was long and rough and the day
was hot, so that before they arrived their hands were empty.

It is said in Ireland that Diarmid was buried on the Boyne.
The Irish account does not say that he came to Scotland: the
publication of the Ossianic Society chiefly is alluded to.
Here at Lochnell is a pillar called after him and a grave
beside it. The pillar is about 12 feet high, rough, and

R

seems as if squared artificially. The grave or small stone circle has twelve stones—boulders. None of the farmers cared much for Diarmid, since all were strangers; but when some persons lately were looking for a stone kist in this place which is called his grave, a poor woman going by said, in great anxiety, "Oh, oh, they are lifting Diarmid." He is not forgotten yet. (See Fig.)

There are many names here connected with the great boar hunt. The parish itself has been called Muckairn, as if meaning the Boar's Cairn, but Mr. Duncan Clerk tells me that it really was Magh Chuirn—the field of cairns—from the great number that were at the eastern part of it, not far from Taynuilt. The farm next the pillar is Tor an Tuirc—the boar's hill. A shepherd coming down the hill and asking for sheep was told in our hearing to take them up Ben Gulbain; so here is the classic name in common use. Up this hill is a well called *Tobair nam bas toll*—the well of the empty palms. This is a memory of the hands coming down dry to poor Diarmid. On the slope is *Gleann nam Fuath*—the glen of spirits. Fuath, in the singular, also means hate or spite, and Gleann na Fuath would be the glen of spite, referring to Finn's conduct here: his proverbial nobleness did not shine at the death of Diarmid.

We were troubled about the name Glenlonain. One of us wished it to mean the meadow of blackbirds—is not *lon* a blackbird? and this fits beautifully in with the vale of birds; another of us laughed at this, because the plural could not be *lonan*, and laughed for the same reason at *lonn*, which means anger; rejecting the word *lonan*—a prattler, and giving *loinain*—a passage for cattle. This is probably correct. But,

To face page 258.

Clach Dhiarmaid — Lochnell.

says a third, here is the farm *Sron-t-Soillear*—the nose of light, just at the opening of the glen, which is narrow at first, and might once have been dark with woods, from which the travellers emerging would better see the light of day. This led to another opinion—viz., that as the Dun beyond Cleinamacree had a beacon or light upon it, and Dun Tanachan had fires upon it, as the name would indicate, the *nose of light* would be the first point of seeing the former, whilst the valley itself would be called Gleann Lonnain—the vale of brightness—a word in the Irish dictionaries, if left out of the Scottish. The vale is not so very bright now, but the mystic fires might brighten it to the heart. If any one sneers, let him better explain these concurring names, said our comrade thoughtfully.

Loinean means also a little meadow. The glen opens into the plain by a narrow passage little wider than the stream that rushes through. *Drum na Sheilg*—the height of the hunt, is, we suppose, a part of Ben Gulbain, and Allt-ath-Cormaic reminds us that Cormac mac Airt was the father of Grainne, concerning whom the dispute was. But we may be met again by some one saying that there was a St. Cormac in Argyll. Even with this fact, the proximity makes the name telling.

With all these names we might say, "surely this was the real spot of the hunt." Can so many coincidences be possible when it is not the actual place? And yet we go to Lochgilphead and we are shown a hill with a claim of a very decided kind ; we go also to Glenshee in Perthshire and find another Ben Gulbain and stones of Diarmid ; and Ireland has at least one claim—Ben Boolban in Sligo. So what are we to say? We can only say that we cannot account for so many places claiming to have been the scene of the boar hunt; but it may be that, like children at play, inhabitants of several places chose representative spots for the names.   Nothing is more probable than a quarrel at a boar hunt.

J. F. Campbell, of Isla, would lead us to think of an Aryan myth, and we, remembering one of our early favourites, think of that beautiful lamentation of Bion—

" I lament, I lament for Adonis, the beautiful Adonis is dead—
   The beautiful Adonis is dead, and the Loves call, Ai, ai."

These words are a more refined expression of sorrow than we have in our story; but why go so far for a hunt when boars were as common here as in Greece?   And yet there are coincidences—the extreme beauty of Diarmid, for example, and the only spot where he could be wounded being on the heel where the bristle entered, suggest ideas which might be originally importations from Greek.   But even these ideas might rise in thousands of minds.   Still there is another curious fact: Diarmid is called O'Duibhne, said to be after his father, but this word is pronounced Odoonye by some, and it is very like Adonis.

Nevertheless, with all these possibilities, there is no reason to doubt the existence of a Celtic Diarmid, simply because all the incidents are human, and most of them occur very frequently.   When two somewhat similar stories are told, the circumstances of one are apt to become mixed with those of the other, a very common occurrence in daily life.   This would readily account for Greek ideas being added to the Celtic story, which has become much more complex.   There is also found a warning to those who too easily indulge in the theory of the single origin of ideas, since man's constitution and the phenomena of nature produce of necessity the elements of many tales in repetition in a continuous stream.

The Campbells are said to have descended from Diarmid. They are called the race of Diarmid, whose sons are rather mysteriously disposed of in the story. The Campbells are by others said to be named from "Campo bello"; but this Italian origin is less probable than a French one would be. It is certainly curious that whilst their name means, as sounded in Gaelic, *crooked mouth, Cam beul*, their neighbours should be *Camerons, cam (s)hron* (the *s* is not sounded), crooked nose. These look like two nicknames of rivals given by some contemptuous enemies. The coincidence is remarkable, and tells strongly, but not decisively, against the Italian origin.

The Campbells have a boar's head with a stone in the mouth as crest. A writer in *The Highlander*, of December 1st, 1877, by nom de plume *Coire na Sith*, says that it arose from an incident in the life of Donnachadh-an-aigh, Duncan the happy, a son of Campbell of Lochow, in the time of James the Second. This man chose as a hiding place a cave near Lochlomond : not far from him the road became impassable because of a wild boar which troubled so many people that the king offered a pardon to the man who would kill it. Campbell threw a stone into its mouth and then stabbed it. This procured his pardon, and along with the lady with whom he had eloped, and with whom he was hiding, he went as ambassador to Rome. He never returned, but he founded an abbey at Kilmun in honour of St. Mun, and for the soul's health of the donor and his family. At Kilmun is the burying place of the chiefs of the Campbells, the Dukes of Argyle.

The most romantic and interesting explanation of the origin of the crest with the boar's head is certainly that connected with Diarmid O'Duibhne.

Campbell says (p. 54, vol. III. of *West Highland Tales*), " I am inclined to believe that there was a real Diarmid, in whose honour poems have been composed by many bards, and sung by generations of Scottish Highlanders, and that to him the attributes of some mythic Celtic Diarmid have been attributed." This seems a reasonable conclusion, after careful weighing of all the evidence. Perhaps it would be better to say that every story becomes mythic when the fancies or reasonings of men are applied to it long, and the mythic quality is no proof of non-reality, but only proves age and the play of tradition.

It was thought well to walk up from the more interesting pillar of Diarmid to a knoll on the side of the hill, a place called Cleidh-na-h-annait. It is an old burying-ground, walled round, and remarkable for having two small cairns in it, as if it were a meeting of heathen and Christian habits, that is to say, if cairns were always heathen. The proverb of " adding a stone to his cairn " shows the custom to have come down to the later times ; and the habit really does exist, we are assured, in the west of Ireland now. It is not certain that it has gone out of Scotland. A man now living told one of us that when a boy he used to throw a stone on a cairn, by his father's wish. *Annoit,* in O'Reilly's Irish Dictionary, is explained to be " one's parish church." Mr. Duncan Clerk, of Oban, says the word is always connected with sacred places.

Mr. Skene (vol. II., *History of Ancient Alban*, p. 70) says, " The
Annoit is the parent church or monastery, which is presided
over by the patron saint, or which contains his relics." Perhaps there was a church here, and these memorials would
point to a very early one. Indeed, we may be sure that
there was one, and we were sorry that we could not find
any special name. If we go up the narrow mouth of Glen
Lonain we come to a small knoll with a stone, on one side
of which is a cross, on the other a floral ornament, with an
elongation below not very definitely seen. This suggests
mixed Christian times. The late Dr. Charlton (Newcastle-
on-Tyne), to whom a drawing was shown, thought it of the
eleventh century at the earliest. The mound is called
Cnoc-na-Croise—knoll of the cross. (See Fig. facing p. 225.)

Going farther on we come to a mound on the right, which
is called *Cnoc-an-t-sagairt*, or knoll of the priest, and beside
it there is one called *Cnoc-an-t-seomar*, or knoll of the
chamber; why so we could not tell, it seemed to contain a
rock in its natural position instead of a chamber. These
three mounds are nearly opposite Cleigh-na-mac-Righ
(Cleinamacry) farmhouse.

Glen Lonain grows grass and corn and peat, and Lochnell
may be said to be the lower part, or rather the middle, since
we must follow it along the Feochan before we reach the
sea. It was once full of little houses, but now it has only
a couple of farms and one cottar, an old woman. The old
inhabitants have been the victims of improvement. Cameron
said that if Maghcarn or Chuirn—meaning the field of cairns
—is not the origin of the name of the parish, and if it is
not called from the muc or boar which Diarmid slew, this

similarity of sound may be only one of the curious coincidences of which we have so many in the strangely supple
Gaelic tongue. (The old woman is now dead.)

Although the *muc* was a famous animal among the Celts,
eaten, and it is said worshipped as well as hunted, its use as
food went out of fashion in Scotland, probably in Puritan
times, for reasons derived from the Old Testament, and with
it also went the eating of " things strangled and of blood."

Passing the house of Cleinamacry we come to an elongated
rectangular enclosure with signs of a circular mound having
been round it 60 feet in diameter. The rectangle is about 30
feet long and 10 wide ; little more than an outline remains.
The rectangular form may denote a certain advance in
building. It is said that the king's children from Dunstaffnage were buried there. Cleinamacry means the burial
place of the king's children. But referring to Mr. Skene we
read of no kings at that place. Still, *king* was a word that
was used more readily in earlier times, and there might be
many chiefs who would like the spot. I do not know if the
chiefs of the Macdougalls were ever called Righ.

We decided not to go down Glen Feochan this year, even
to see Dun Mac Raoul on the shore of Loch Feochan South,
just as it begins to join the sea, or to see Dun Eidin, which
must be mentioned as a very curious part of a name, in a
district by no means connected with Saxons, and yet having
the same name in it as Edinburgh. Is this a memorial of
Aidan the Dalriad, whilst Edinburgh is of Aeduin the
Northumbrian king ?

Stone Cist at (Avile) Athbhile.—At Athbhile, about a mile
above Cleinamacry in Glen Lonain, there is a bridge over the

stream; as the name shows, there was a ford there. A short distance from the bridge, and in a field higher up the stream, is a 'mound which appears to be natural. We were shown a flat stone there; it was discovered not long ago by Donald Sinclair, who, as his son avers, took good care not to disturb it. Here was an opportunity, then, of seeing a place opened up for the very first time. It goes by the name of Kist a-Chlachan. The slab was raised with great difficulty by the strength of at least three pairs of strong arms, but the hole was found nearly filled with earth, in which were the skeletons of several rabbits. There was a small hole in the side under the slab affording entrance. The kist was 36 inches long, 20 broad, and 25 deep. There were a few small pieces of bone mingled with the earth, but merely such as weighed only a few grains. The mound was probably an eskar to begin with, a deposit caused by earth and floods. Double burials, one over another, are not found in these regions, to account for the height. Although nothing artificial was found within the kist, it was large and important looking, and the spot itself interesting.

We may go up Glen *Lonain*. We may pass Duntanachan, and up to Lairg and down again to Taynuilt, from which we may, if we wish, return to Oban; or we may turn back past Diarmid's pillar, and onward till we reach the strait road to Connel Ferry; this we did and enjoyed a pleasant and varied scene, neither very rich nor wild, but one that certainly was once richer in man and joyful life. The curse of wealth has come over the country, the little crops have been despised as trifles, and the men who fed upon them have not been considered. One civilization refuses to tolerate another; and ours is slightly Roman, we make a desert to produce refinement. These men would have suffered less had they been expelled in fighting, but they were often smoothly turned away from their own; they were betrayed with a kiss.

Mr. Clerk, of Oban, mentions that there are several names in the upper part of Glen Lonain connected with the hero Gaul or rather Guill. We did not follow the fortunes of the Fingalian heroes; their story is difficult to disentangle, and we have no history of them except from Ireland; but we must look, by Mr. Clerk's desire, at a very beautiful poem given in *Galic Antiquities* by Dr. Smith, of Campbelton, in which Gaul's death is described. It is curiously entitled in Gaelic, *Tiomnadh Ghuill*, the testament of Gaul, but it is generally called the *Death of Gaul*. At the top of Glen Lonain is a wooded height called Bar Ghuil, or the height of Gaul, or Barguillan, *an* for river being added. A little to the north is another wooded height, which is called Barran-a-chuil, between them is Tomghuil called Tom-na-Guille. These latter two have the same meaning as the former. Mr. Clerk puts Gaul's first battle at Ichrachan, between the Awe and the Nant, outside of Glen Lonain, but not far off, and mentions the numerous cairns that used to be there before they were levelled by the "iron" company from England. These are the cairns alluded to as having given the parish its name. Morni is said to have been Gaul's father, and Mr. Clerk considers that his dwelling was at Strumonadh at the top of Glen Lonain. This word, meaning *a mountain stream*, is not very precise.

The valley in the poem keeps up its character for birds;

and birds to a farm, or part of the valley, if not to the valley itself; and in the " Death of Gaul " it is beautifully said : " The birds of summer from their distant land shall first perch on Strumon's oak ; far away they shall behold its green beauty. The ghost of Gaul shall hear in his cloud their song, and the virgins of the race to come shall praise Evirchoma."

Many would be glad to fight and risk their lives like Gaul if they had the hope of receiving the land which contains the valley of birds, the lake of swans, and the glen of "the summer fowl from the distant land."

The bards thought more of Gaul than their successors have helped us to do. The poem finishes thus : " When thou, O stone, shalt crumble into dust, and thou, O tree, shalt moulder with age away; when thou, mighty stream, shalt cease to run, and the mountain spring shall no more supply thy course ; when your songs, oh bards, in the dark flood of time shall be lost, and the memory of yourselves, with those you sing, in its vast current be swept away and forgotten ; then perhaps may cease to be heard the fame of Gaul ; and the stranger may ask, 'Who was Morni's son, and who was Strumon's chief?'"

CHAPTER XXII.

CHRISTIAN MEMORIES.

"Thy saints take pleasure in her stones,
Her very dust to them is dear."

LOUDOUN.—We shall go again to Keills; I never can weary contemplating that old burying ground, and the small remnant of the chapel hidden in the long grass. The men who built it are forgotten, but the place has remained sacred. The chapel must have been very small, showing that the attendants were few; but the church-yard was comparatively large, strikingly reminding us that "the many" are laid there. The sanctity of the place is shown by the growth of the burial ground, which, even after the church was forgotten, was used until it reached the shingles on the beach and the rocks which the higher waves wash. When the present road was made, not very long ago, remains were found in great numbers. There never could in Christian times have been a great population here, although it may have been, and probably was, much greater than it is now; and as this is the only way to pass from the south of Benderloch to the north without going far round; a road, or at least a path, must be supposed to have always existed. But a road for carriages would not be required, and we know that men and horses can do with a very narrow one, such as would scarcely desecrate a burial ground. If even in old times it was necessary to bring a body of men somewhat closer than in single file, there would be abundance of room before the church-yard was made, and there would be no hindrance to mountaineers even after it was held sacred. In later times the road went behind, and nearer the rocks.

I have sometimes asked myself if this were not a sacred place before the introduction of Christianity; but as we know nothing certainly, we can only imagine what may have been. It is true that the place itself under the shadow of the great rock inspires awe and is, as it were, sacred by nature, and it is also true that a greater reverence is due to it from the long period during which it has received the remains of many inhabitants; the little chapel also suggests the struggle of a very small band in a place only in the process of Christianizing, and we may add that the people would be only in the process of civilizing. But was there another period when the instincts of men ruled and nature awed them more than now; when its worship in times of danger caused them to seek the rocks for shelter, and when they chose this spot for meeting together to communicate their fears, as sheep would do, or to hide from the spirits of the hill that had inspired awe, and finally to pray to them or to the manes of the dead? Modern reasoning would lead us to say this simply because the church was there and probably built on an old sacred spot; but then the nature of the place, and its convenience for meeting the inhabitants of both sides of the hill would themselves give consequence. Then the urn found in the cave is another proof of a very ancient attachment, whilst the great collection of urns found at the entrance to the garden of the hexagon school-house shows that a burial place existed before Christian times. I view the place, therefore, with the belief that it was probably sacred at a very early period; certainly a part of the ground under the rock was devoted to the dead in pre-Christian as in Christian days. Then there was another importance belonging to it. It is evident that the kings lived near. This rock is called *the Dun of the King's town* as we found, and what is meant by a town? It really means a house; it is a Baile, a Bally, a Vaille in the aspirated case, or a villa; the origin being the same. At any rate we know that the name is given even to single residences (perhaps with outhouses); but people forget to be careful in these cases. However, if a chief of an outpost or small king lived here, it is probable that there would be several houses around his. It is a remarkably safe place; it is more easily defended than the chief Dun. With his men on either side the chief could be well looked after, and he could readily guard the narrow pass and also have an outlet by the shore, whilst from the height above he could see farther than from the vitrified fort, which, however, would hold a much larger garrison and would be much more convenient; it would be resorted to by men not driven to extremities. In those days the lower ground would be safer than now, because there was the small lake which has been said to have existed at the south end of the hexagonal school-house and on to Tir-na-birlinn, acting as frontier.

This presence of a chief generally indicates the nearness of sacerdotal dignities and rights, whether of the higher or of the more savage kind. There is an alliance of the power of the growing soul and the rude body, and their representatives, priest and king; and religious rites, I cannot doubt, were performed under this hill. It is here, we may believe, where a king, however small, ruled; and where priests, however ignorant, performed solemn acts in memory of the dead. It is a place where for ages the love of power inspired a ruler, and the dark thoughts and bright hopes of the future inspired a people, headed, as they must have been, by some who thought more of these things than the commonalty. And who were these quasi-priests, we may ask? Modern inquiries incline to throw greater darkness than ever upon them; but I can readily believe in a long train of worshippers from the lowest to the highest—from the most distant to the latest times. The highest class I have seen in two positions: one in the wood leading up the little gully behind the school-house; the congregation sat on the slopes, and were sheltered by the trees, and the minister's voice resounded over the waters; another instance was in the little rock chamber below and looking on the shingles, when the voice of children's hymns came up as through a subterranean opening into the pleasant little garden.

You may imagine the lowest. Indeed I have seen a remnant of these up the Ledaig hill, on the slopes of which and over Achnacree there is the well we saw with some superstitious memories, and on the side of which people leave little presents—a remnant of fairy worship or Fetishism of some kind. There was, however, a worse, with scenes of blood, as we may fairly be sure of.

As we began amongst Christians to-day we shall keep to

their society, and take a rapid drive up the loch as far as Ardchattan.

Willie.—Look at that little island, only a collection of pebbles, and it seems to have a great black swan on it. Let us shout and throw a stone. It is off. What is it?

Cameron.—That is too far for you to throw; the bird is a cormorant or scart; we see them here occasionally. They are good fishers, indeed I believe they are used for fishing in China, and as soon as they catch a fish the fishermen squeeze the neck to prevent swallowing, or they keep a ring round the neck for the same purpose. It is rarer than the heron in this place, and so more interesting but not so graceful.

Loudoun.—This is a day for churches; we shall pass Achnaha, which we have already seen, and go through the grounds of the Priory, and behind through the picturesque field on the side of the hill, and up to the old ruin that was a church, long probably before Ardchattan, and dedicated to St. Modan. Very little stands. Perhaps it was a ruin when King Robert Bruce met his friends at Ardchattan, and even when the founder of the Priory admired the site; but the reason for admiring would be different in old times. There could have been no good road by the side of the loch then, and probably there was much wood; whilst here on the pleasant slopes there were perhaps both pasture and dwellings with protection.

It is not at all needful to believe that the church was built in the time of St. Modan. It is more probable that it was called after him when he was dead; but as he came here he would have a place for worship—a predecessor to this, most likely. Some people call this St. Bede's Church, because the aspirate of B and of M are both sounded as V ; but Bede had nothing to do here, and the vowels and consonants differ. Modan was a great saint, known from Dumbarton and Roseneath in a large semicircle. (Maodan, in the genitive case, is pronounced very nearly like Mödan, using the German spelling, or it is like the word "maiden" spoken with the mouth rounded when sounding *ai;* aspirated it is Mhaodan, pronounced Vaidan.)

We do.not know much of St. Modan's life, but it is just possible that he may have lived a good deal here. The place is called Baile Mhaodan, the town of Modan. We have seen that Baile may be applied to a very few houses or even to one house. The place is not called after the church of Modan ; the church is ignored, not a common thing, and we have here no word for Saint, but that omission may be too common to teach us anything. We may have some idea from the name, that the Saint did his work from this point at times. When ruling the church at Dumbarton, he is said to have gone often for long periods among the mountains, spending his life in solitude and in prayer. Most probably he did not give all this time to his own improvement, but devoted it to the education of others, and we can at any rate imagine the hills around Loch Lomond reflecting his labours, and we may look even farther, and, with sufficient reason, think of him wandering towards Loch Awe and Loch Etive. We must remember, however, that saints do not dedicate churches to themselves, and not only is it probable that the church was not built by him, but it is nearly certain. The church affords of itself no proof that St. Modan came quite so far, but it is believed that he did come, and his reputed labours are in this direction.

Cameron.—We visited Ardchattan before, and now we may return to Oban. I was sorry when we passed Ledaig hill that I could tell you nothing of a burial place up above those precipices that stand behind Achnacree, but nearer to Bhalanree. The place seems to be Christian, but I know nothing of any chapel there, and have heard of no traditions. Was the moss too wet? and if so, why did the people leave Keills of which we have spoken? Very likely there was a chapel on the hill, and if so this district would be visited more by men who met to worship, than it has been in known historic times, until very lately, when the two Free Churches have been built, one at Barcaldine and one at Ardchattan, and the little cave room below the post-office has been occupied.

In any case it is interesting to see the various traces of deep devotion and love to man and to God, that churchyards and churches show, whether by the rude burials or other memorials of the darker times, or tiny chapels of early Christians, or the simple but practical and comfortable churches of to-day. We love to look at them all, and grieve with poor man in his troubles, struggling to make a more decided connection between this world of sorrows and the future of calm, and to us this whole region seems peopled with many generations of dreams and hopes, so that even the winds and storms of winter cannot remove them. Every ruin seems to show how rich the place was in sorrow and in love.

Since the above was written, St. Modan's life has been looked up by Dr. Story, and published in a most interesting little volume. He gives the latest opinion—viz., that the saint was an Irish missionary who came to the shores of Loch Etive, and went to Appin and Morven, then passed by Loch Awe to

Strachur on Loch Fyne, and on to Loch Riddan (called also Loch Ruel), Kyles of Bute, where is a Kilmodan. He then passed to Roseneath, and from that centre went to the Loch Lomond district, and by the Campsie hills, as far as Falkirk, going back to Roseneath, where he died. He was buried on the spot where the parish church now stands. It was then called Rosneve, the promontory of the sanctuary.[1]

Skene finds the name Modan also at Kingarth in Bute, and looks on the saint as a companion of St. Ronan. Both in Lennox and in Lorn the name Kilmaronaig is near the church of St. Modan.

St. Modan must have passed over wild ground, but we do not know that the people were wild; a man cannot leave a fine memory among men who have no sympathy with him; his name is everywhere in the district remembered in some form, less at Roseneath because of its destructive nearness to modern activity. One instance of his power may be given in an interesting letter of the Rev. Dr. Clerk's (of Kilmally) quoted by Dr. Story in a note. The Saint's Well was resorted to by the sick within the last sixty years, and many offerings were left beside it (very trifling ones, not above a halfpenny). There was a bell called—to quote from Dr. Story's book—"Clag Buidhe Bhaile Mhoadain, the yellow bell of Baile Mhoadan, which was held in higher veneration for its curative powers than even the well. As a matter of very special favour it was sometimes allowed to be carried to the sick in other parishes; and, if, after accomplishing its benevolent errand, it was not immediately carried back, it

[1] See Bishop Forbes' *Scottish Kalendar*, where Dr. Reeves is quoted.

would take the matter into its own hands and fly through the air to its home, all the while ringing out the most melodious music ever heard by mortal ear. I remember conversing with old people who believed as firmly as possible that the boatmen on Loch Etive often heard the Clag Buidhe singing its saintly hymns in the sky above them as it returned to its home. I never heard what became of the tuneful yellow bell."

I have never seen *Suidhe Mhaodain,* or Modan's Seat, which was up in Glen Salach, through which you pass when going from Barcaldine to Bunawe. We learn from Dr. Story that it was hewn into pieces a few years ago for building purposes, and this in a land of good granite stones. I fear the saints of the time had no comfortable houses—they chose high and windy places to sit in, but it may have been from pure love of nature.

I know you want to cross to the Abbot's island, but I have not landed there, and cannot tell you what to see; I understand the remains do not seem to indicate important buildings. They are said to have belonged to the monks of Inchaffray, near Crieff, and if so they are a memorial of connecting links between the Eastern and the Western churches of Scotland. The establishment may have been used to give a change of air to the monks of Inchaffray, or a place of shelter in times of fear, or a corner from which to issue to civilize the district. I may remind you of the stone circle on the mainland opposite, now destroyed, but indicating that a native population was interested in pre-historic times in Ach-na-Cloich. There is no church exactly here, no public institution, no church land I believe; the next church foundation is not far down the loch—namely, over there at Kilmaron*aig*, or Kilmaron*ag*.

Ronan is supposed to have gone with Modan in evangelizing, since their churches are sometimes together. Poor St. Ronan is a good deal neglected ; he is left out of the Roman calendar. Skene says, " He has left his trace in Iona, where one of the harbours is Port Ronan. That church, afterwards the parish church, was dedicated to him, and is called ' **Teampull Ronaig**,' and its burying ground **Cladh Ronan**. Then we find him at Rona in the **Sound** of Skye, and at another Rona off the coast of Lewis; and finally his death is recorded in 737 as Ronan, Abbot of **Cinngaradh** or Kingarth, in Bute."[1] We may be glad to find him in a peaceful bay in Bute ; he went there soon after St. Cathan, who used to enjoy the place, sitting upon the little hill of Kilchattan bay called after him, and making it so much a habit that the hill is called his seat—Mount Sui (or **Suidhe) Chattan**. Ronan had difficult work in the Western Isles, and when he was very much troubled with rough people in **Eorrapidh**, a whale came and took him on its back to the island now called **Ronag**. This island was then inhabited by hardy creatures who went into the sea, leaving deep scratches on the rocks. There is now upon it the remains of an interesting little chapel called **Teampull Ronaig**, and the account is very pleasantly given, in a handsome volume full of interesting matter, by Mr. Muir, of Edinburgh. This work was published anonymously, and I do not know the full name. We like to know the name of one who does such good and loving work. The labour to obtain the information was not trifling ; he visited all

[1] *Ancient Alban*, vol. II., p. 282.

the little islands of Scotland, and even nearly bare rocks, and I know that it is not always easy to get through the seas that surround Ronag, which is some sixty miles from Lewis.

When these two saints, Modan and Ronan, became old they gave up their Highland adventures and settled down in Roseneath and Kingarth, very much as their successors do now; and we may believe that they met with that respect which the devotion of all their best days to the good of their fellow-men well deserved. This is seen in the name Moronog, a word of affection, as Mr. Skene shows, meaning my little or dear Ronan, a similar phrase not being unusual among the names of saints. Did I say "poor Ronan"? Ronan was called "the kingly bishop."

This name is found at the spot where was the nearest mainland church to Abbot's Isle, and where little else remains —Kilmaronaig. We can imagine the two friends, Ronan and Modan, working on each side of the loch, and occasionally meeting to speak of their labours and their plans. They would have friends among the people, or they would not so frequently have returned as it is supposed ; these men would act as assistants probably, and by degrees centres of faith would grow. The monks of Inchaffray came to a place already prepared, and they came perhaps with a certain fear and sought an island for shelter at a time when lake dwellings were by no means uncommon.

In looking over our Scottish history we certainly find terrible accounts of battle and murder, and we are glad to think of any quiet spots in which some men had the privilege of finding shelter. In the lower lands there was more wealth and more temptation to display, and among the early Celts there was always much attention to the rights of the Church and to the ideal. With the Scandinavian element came heathen opposition, and the great preponderance of that race has hitherto prevented the Church from ever attaining that influence which it has kept in Ireland among a more purely Celtic people.

We must again return to our hotel, after a peaceful, pleasant day.

Cameron.—Thanks for telling us so much; but I must tell you as we are going what became of the Clag Buidhe (pronounced bui), quoting Dr. Story. The bell was taken to Scone, and one night the people of Baile Mhaodan (pronounced Bailyivaidan) heard a noise and jingle in the air, when lo! the tuneful bell was flying home, but instead of its own grave sweet melody it was clanging out harsh sounds like "An rud nach buin dhuit na buin dha"—"Don't meddle with what meddles not with you."

Sheena.—I hope that was not his bell that was lost "in a forgotten mere on the tumbled fragments of the hills," and that it was not the same that was called "Maidie's bell," which was sold this century as a bit of old iron.[1]

Cameron.—It was taken again to Scone, and never returned to Loch Etive. Some say it was lost in a mere; but why should it go there? We may find it again some day, as we have found St. Fillan's bell and crozier, which are now safely deposited in the Museum of Antiquaries of Edinburgh. It is better to leave it with hope, and after all we do not know the end.

[1] Dr. Story's *Saint Modan.*

CHAPTER XXIII.

DRUIDS.

MARGAET.—You have mentioned Druids once or twice, what were they really? They were said to have brought magical charms to the struggle of Conor with the sons of Uisnach.

O'Keefe.—Your question brings up long disputes. There are some that speak as if there never were Druids, as if they were a class conjured up by the imagination of a few men to whose reveries Cæsar gave heed, adding his own. Nobody uses quite this language, but there is in England an inclination to depreciate Druids, and men have run to extremes. It is a wave of commonplace to which there is a desire to reduce all ages. You have great difficulty in causing ignorant or loutish persons to believe anything, they always know so much better than a well-taught man, who is, of course, wider in knowledge, sympathy, and receptive power, and sees the possible more easily. The most common of all scepticism is narrowness of view. All must, on serious thought, allow Druids to have existed somewhere. We cannot contradict Cæsar when, after careful inquiries, he fixes their principal seat, or, at least, an important seat, in Britain. He may make mistakes, but he cannot be altogether wrong on the whole question. The difficulty, however, is great when we attempt to connect the Druids with modern times and visible remains. Some authors have decided on seeing remains of temples; they say, and reasonably, that such an important body would have buildings. It is difficult to contradict this, but what buildings there were is a point on which we have simply no information. There were men who wished to make every cromlech, dolmen, cat-stone, or stone circle, a Druidical remnant, and perhaps some still remain, and the idea has, to a great extent, gone into the language, but we know for a certainty that memorials of burials are the chief object of the first one, and of nearly all the only object apparently. The cat-stone means a battle stone, and the stone circle surrounds the dead. Are there any cases of exception such as Stonehenge or Callernish? I am quite disposed to think that, for the larger, there must have been more intentions in the mind of the builders than commemoration of the dead : the worship of stones was simply the worship of images before artistic talent was developed. A child puts down a stone and calls it a house, and idols do not require Greek art. The story of Crom Cruach and the circle of gods in the Kjalnesinga Saga have been mentioned, besides many facts known to rude authentic story, but notwithstanding probability and this amount of tradition or folk-saws, we must keep to the point that we are not authoritatively informed of any existing building, or even of one solitary existing stone, connected with Druidism. We are told, but only by later writers, that sacrifices were offered on the cromlech or flat dolmens. There seems no proof of any such being made on tombs, although abundant proof that they were made at the death of important individuals, and perhaps on the stones. The habit remains in the world. The Suttee is scarcely extinguished, and in Central Africa worse habits are by no means worn out, whilst the blood stone is mentioned in Icelandic Sagas, and sacrifices entail burials as matter of course. Still we know of no Druids in Iceland, and we are unable to connect the blood stones with remains in this country and with the Druids.

It is quite certain that this country has not been free from the sacrificial phase of thought, and it is unlikely that the inhabitants have always been so tender-hearted as to confine the act of sacrifice to the lower animals, and I am quite willing to connect Druids and bloody rites as Cæsar has connected them. The early inhabitants of this island were never gentle—carelessness of life causing slaughter and cruelty, along with a wild enthusiasm and romance, growing into poetry, is the view in the distance, and in some parts it has come as far as the memory of early tradition. I never reject anything because it seems too foolish or too horrible for man to do or to think, but as I reject the idea that Britain was ever the land to which spirits invisible, but heavy enough to weigh down a vessel, were conveyed from the Continent, so I am unwilling to believe in the great advancement of the Druids of Britain in science or in thought generally. Still there may have been a band of men with a peculiar advance in a certain civilization, men different from the ¡ordinary inhabitants, and capable of ruling to some extent, by their mysterious habits and greater knowledge. Such a band is rarely wanting in the most savage country.

The system of the Druids has been so often talked of by later writers that we all have heard something about the opinions, and many references exist in early authors to confirm the belief in a widely spread band of this peculiar people.

But we are making a Highland holiday, and we shall not go for knowledge to Greece, to Rome, or to ancient Gaul, and we shall only try to obtain the idea of Druidism as it existed in traditions decidedly Gaelic, and these are chiefly from Ireland.

Loudoun.—It is said that there never were Druids in Scotland. The word is common enough, but we find no certain organized system of Druidism in Ireland or Scotland, and no proof of great advance in knowledge amongst the individuals. We learn, however, that the Druids frequently rose to great power, and their authority seems to have wavered along with that of the bards, probably according to the character of the professing Druid or consulting or maintaining chief.

O'Keefe.—It is certainly an old tract that speaks of Cathbar the Druid giving instructions in Druidism in Emania, and is good evidence, even if not before the first century. Dathi, a king, is said to have lived in the fifth century, and to have consulted Doghra, the chief of the Druids, as to his destiny for a year. By appointment, the king and nine nobles met the Druid at Rath Archaill, "where the Druid's altars and idols were," says O'Curry. So I suppose it is in the original. At the rising of the sun in the morning, the Druid repaired to the King's bedroom and said, "Art thou asleep, O King of Erinn and Albain?" "I am not asleep," said the King; "but why have you made an addition to my titles? for although I have taken the sovereignty of Erinn I have not yet obtained that of Albain." " Thou shalt not be long so, for I have consulted the clouds of the men of Erinn," &c.   Here Doghra speaks as a prophet, or rather a fortune-teller, since the prophecy does not rise high, and was not even correct ; and it is to be remarked that the Druid takes also the position of a priest, and it is also as a priest that he is met by St. Patrick. This account of the king is from the Book of Leinster. (See O'Curry's Lectures, p. 284.)

Cormac Mac Airt, when fighting with the King of Munster, consulted his Druids, and they thought the best way to conquer was to deprive the enemy of water, and by their spells and incantations they dried up or· concealed all the rivers, lakes, and springs of the district, so that both men and cattle were dying of thirst all around them.   The King of Munster sent to Dairbré, now called Valencia, to Mogh Ruith, the most famous Druid of the time, and he promised relief for a great reward in land.   On the promise being made he shot an arrow into the air, telling the men of Munster that water would arise wherever the arrow should fall.   This occurred, and the well is called *Ceann Moir*, or the great head. (O'Curry, p. 272.)   One of the verses describing a great house having Druids in it has already been quoted (p. 91).

A mound of the Druids is spoken of as at Tara.

I have already told you of Aoife who changed the children of Lir into swans by a metamorphosing Druidical wand.   In the absurd tale " The Fate of the Children of Tuireann " we find men transformed into hawks in order to enable them to steal apples from the garden of the Hesperides.   The king's three daughters turned themselves into ospreys and pursued the hawks into the sea, and also scorched them with lightning, but Brian struck himself and his two brothers with a Druidical wand and became swans and went into the sea, and the ospreys went off.

The Druids are said to have fought hard against St. Patrick, and brought on an intense darkness for three days and three nights. This was a favourite mode of attack.

An old life of Columba mentions that a Druid was his first teacher.

There was an ancient Irish Druid, said to have lived 600 years B.C., who pronounced incantations on a wisp of straw or hay, and threw it into the face of anyone, causing him to dance, run, jump, or flutter about in a lunatic manner. This mode of performance seems to have been externally very simple.

We are told of a very innocent man, Comgan, who became suspected by a Druid, who forthwith struck him with the grass, over which he had made incantations, and Comgan was at once covered with blotches, his hair fell off, his intellect decayed, and he soon became a bald, senseless, and wandering idiot.

Eithne, Queen of Cashel, was desirous of obtaining the friendship of the Druid Dill, who was an enemy to her people the Deisi, and she sent her maid, who was a daughter of Dill, to offer him presents. " Is it true," said he, " that you are attached to that hateful Queen Eithne." " It is true, but I am come to offer you wealth." " I will not accept it. They are a bad swarm who have planted themselves on the borders of Cashel, but they shall depart to-morrow. I am preparing incantations, the *Inncoin* (a town) shall be burnt to-morrow. I shall be on the west side of the hill and shall see the smoke ; a hornless red cow shall be sent past them to the west; they shall raise a universal shout, after which they will fly away, and they shall never occupy the land again." ". Good," said the daughter, "sleep now when you please." The daughter stole the enchanted straw and gave it to the queen, who now wanted only a hornless red cow to turn the destruction on the plotter. One of the Druidesses said that she would turn into such a cow and be slain, if her children were made free. This was done; the fire was lighted, the cow passed from the east and was killed, and the Deisi (Decies or Deasys) were victorious. Their enemies, the descendants of *Bresel Belach*, were called Ossorians (ossairghe, from os, a wild deer). The word Ossory comes from this (see as before). We can scarcely imagine a wilder story.

Illumination by the palms of the hands was an old ceremony performed by a Druid or bard. He chewed a bit of red flesh of a pig, a dog, or a cat, and retired with it to bed behind the door, where he pronounced an oration upon it and offered it to his idols. He was expected to receive illumination in this state, and if not he placed his two hands on his two cheeks and fell asleep. He was watched so as not to be interrupted, and revelation came in two or three days. (O'Curry and Sullivan, vol. II., p. 208.)

Brindsley the engineer went to bed when he had a difficulty.

The power of satire we have already seen when speaking of the bards. I could tell you of many more enchantments.

I have told you some of the doings of the Druids among the Irish, being very ignorant of the customs of the Scottish, but I suppose they were both the same. And now what shall we conclude? 1st, We cannot prove well that the Druids in Ireland formed a priesthood. 2nd, The words of the old writers refer to an old worship and idols ; there certainly was a religion. 3rd, The probability is that either the religion or Druidical system of Britain and Gaul had either been dimly represented in the outskirts of the Celtic nation as in Ireland, or that it had decayed before we hear of it from Irish sources. 4th, That in its decay it had become a species of wilful deception, fortune-telling, and witchcraft, with a variety of tricks and coercion of mind by mysterious words. 5th, That this had engendered a great variety of superstitions in the people. 6th, That these have been the foundation of many wild and romantic tales. Druidheachd means enchantment.

The power of the Druids in Ireland seems to have arisen partly from the talent of the individual, partly from the influence of the class. Some were poor, some rich. Some kings gave heed to the Druids, some not. We do not see the power of a hierarchy clearly expressed, although there are traces of it. The result has been that magic is equal to Druidism ; the Druids are sometimes called Magi, and some are said to have learned their art in the east.

Now comes the question. During the Roman domination did any breakdown of the Celtic centres further the introduction of these ideas from Britain or Gaul? The Romans themselves heard of them as from afar ; they could introduce nothing ; but Ireland is so easily approached from Wales that we require no other reason either in peace or war. A certain organization of Druids we must allow in Britain : did it come less organized to Ireland? The question as to the time of introduction even of the slight waves is left to conjecture. It is probable that the Druids passed very early, and would find in Ireland an excitable people ready to receive impressions, but not to organize, either from difference of character or because the amount of knowledge that passed over was insufficient for a profound impression. If we do allow a regular organization, we cannot believe that an *esprit de corps* could be wanting.

Loudoun.—If we examine the literature of Ireland and of Wales we find a remarkable difference. It is probable that the earliest books of both countries are of nearly equal age, and yet it is impossible to avoid observing that each proceeds from quite independent portions of the mind ; the initial object is different, and the mode of carrying out the ideas is different, notwithstanding many points of similarity. To one not familiar with the originals of either Welsh or Irish it is still easy to judge of style of thought. The Welsh is sentimental, often melancholy, metaphysical, and religious. There is great mysticism, which shows itself in the indefinite descriptions, so that one does not know the places referred to, one can scarcely understand what is meant to be described, and the similes also are often beyond comprehension. The Irish writings are very clear; they treat of events and are full of rapid action, minute description of persons, and very exact accounts of houses. There is little sentiment, little religion, and no metaphysics or mysticism, although there is an unbounded exaggeration and tendency to turn the most common events into romance. This exaggeration would require a long lecture to explain, so I will not attempt it. The fundamental feeling that one meets is not Christian, devoted as the Irish churchmen were ; we see a perfectly independent, or, as one may say, a perfectly heathen character of thought and motive of action. This is speaking outside of the avowedly ecclesiastical literature, and where we might have expected to see more than we do of the influence of clerical and Christian thought. The activity of the Irish did, however, show itself among those who entered the Church to such an extent that they can speak of their labours over that continent itself which sent them missionaries, and no more earnest men have been found in the world than the preachers and saints of Ireland. The severance of the usual literature from the Church literature is, however, remarkable, and makes me believe that the great body of the people were ruled by traditions and habits of life begun before Christianity entered the island, and that the devotees and preachers were a class very much separated in life as well as in feeling—perhaps a different tribe, race, or mixture. It is marvellous how different from us may be the men who live next us ; and savages exist still in England, how much more readily in a country difficult of access. I knew a small cottage, three miles from one of the greatest cities in England, where a man and his wife had lived till they were seventy years old, and they had only twice been in the town.

O'Keefe.—You seem to be defending the idea that Druidical learning may have long existed, and pre-Christian ideas have ruled the Gaelic literature of Ireland.

Loudoun.—Not learning, so far as I know, but ideas. If in Ireland how much more in Wales, a seat of Druidism. It seems to have tinctured the Welsh mind, and one probably sees it in the Welsh character still, being as peculiar as the fine bodily activity and liveliness of spirit in Ireland. The present people are like the ancient, and the groundwork of their minds is the same. The Welsh boys at Holyhead, a port of entrance, are still afraid, or were lately, of the Gwyddel or Irish, being a remembrance of differences in olden time.

O'Keefe.—But surely Christianity had driven out all the previous religion long before the existence of most of the writings, even the oldest, of our country.

Loudoun.—This is fancy. Our lowest superstitions refuse to be driven out for generations, and we keep them now in the most learned society. The only way to drive the effects of Druidism out of England was to drive out the population. This has been done greatly, and even there some of its fancies remain. No wonder greater than this exists in Wales where the strange Neo-Druidism has arisen. In its attempts at restoration I fear the fragments of Druidism were found too broken to lead to any success, and the earliest writings we have may contain as little of the really ancient Druidical ideas as the present, all three, however, having a similar psychological character. If the moderns had allowed us to seek the remnants as chance left them, we should have had more promising results, but when new ideas attach to the old a restoration becomes hopeless. We may expect only to see some pieces as of broken statues found among broken bricks, and cemented together to make a modern wall, as in Rome. I do not, therefore, draw any of my inferences from anything said by the professed modern Druids further than this, that the literature shows a mind allied to that which produced the earliest Welsh remains and probably early Druidism.

We may as well remark also that this difference in the Briton and the Gael shows how different people may be who are still called Celts. The difference is in body and mind, and clearly explains the hopelessness of the attempt, so fashionable of late, to make all the Celts to be the same ; much less hopeful is the effort of that school that makes the same people of Celts and Germans.

Well, men may laugh or rave about Druids, but I conclude that their history has not been written, and if you read Frickius'[1] and the Irish writings, you may leave out almost all the rest.

The word Druid and its compounds occur abundantly in Gaelic; and the Druidical ideas as held by the Gael, if the witchcraft alluded to is worthy of the name of ideas, tincture all their superstitions.

---

[1] Johannis Georgii Frickii, Johannis Fil., τοῦ μακαρίτου, *Commentatio de Druidis.* Ulmae, 1744.

CHAPTER XXIV.

OBAN AND DALMALLY.

LOUDOUN.—To-day we have a long ride before us, we must go to King's House ; we need not stay on the road.

Cameron.—You will fatigue us I fear. I should like to stay at Dalmally and see some friends.

Sheena.—And I want to go slowly on the road and feel happy as we go along.

Loudoun.—Then we give up the public coach and hire a carriage ; we can have a waggonette. It will give us an hour longer before starting, and I can also again look down on Dunstaffnage and beyond to the fort of the sons of Uisnach, and up Loch Linnhe ; I know few scenes so fine.

O'Keefe.—There is Dunstaffnage. The little hill here is called Dunbeg. I have not seen it well ; some people say it is vitrified. However, I may tell you a story here about a true Celtic hero, Colkitto ; he was a prisoner of the Lord of Argyll's, and Campbell of Dunstaffnage had him in charge. It was an easy prison, for although the prisoner was expected to be in view, Campbell had good feelings towards him and let him move about as he pleased, if he only promised to return when wanted. This was not pleasant to his enemies, and they complained to Argyle, who was a marquis at that time. This complaint, made at Inveraray, was answered by sending a messenger to find what Colkitto was doing at the time of arrival. The messenger went rapidly, but a friend was off a little sooner, and as he came, perhaps to the ground near the neck of land, he saw Colkitto amusing himself by helping the shearers. He shouted in Gaelic, "Col in irons! Col in irons!" Colkitto ran as fast as he could and had his irons put on by the time the messenger got into Dunstaffnage.

Cameron.—This refers to Colla Kittoch Gillespick or Macdonell, afterwards killed at Dunstaffnage. In a similar way the Macpherson of Cluny who went with Prince Charles was saved when a band of redcoats came to take him. There is a rapid turn of the road about five miles north of Cluny Castle, and on a mound there, one of the soldiers fell down and roared as in agony on the grass. He was left to get better, but as soon as the soldiers disappeared he was off by the short cut, whilst they went round the bend, and he had barely time to warn Cluny off to a long expatriation. This faithful friend was on the mound again when the soldiers returned.

We pass the ferry, but do not cross, and we see the falls of Connel again; a little beyond it there is now the Board school building. Education is becoming easier and commoner, but I am not sure if deep thought or wisdom is. It may be often said that science is very valuable for teaching you to obtain riches out of land called poor, and rocks that never gave wealth, and that it gives you even a knowledge of the laws of nature, so searching that with the commonest things, fire and water, you can do the greatest wonders. It is bringing a demon out of poor matter which we thought to be dead, and I should not wonder to find that our peat bogs gave out food and our hills yielded gold. This science makes us wonder, but it seems also to increase our greediness and destroy the simplicity of our natures ; it is an improved quality of industry.

But here we pass Lusragain, the *sedgy river :* the sedges are not down here but up nearer the sources. Above to the right is Luachragain, the *river of rushes,* rising at Deechoid, and Lundragan, the *sluggish river,* rising at Barguillein.

We pass Ach-na-Cloich ; it is a small place ; up the hill to the right they have built a good modern house in which the owner of all this district sometimes lives. They have translated the Gaelic into *Stonefield,* as I told you before.

But on we must go, although I am saddened at the desolation and the ruins of two ancient civilizations seen in the stone circle and in the ruined abbey. I am not sure but in this wood we have a third. We come to young birches grown for timber, cut every twenty-four years and made into charcoal for that unsatisfied furnace at Bunawe. It may have been a wood since the days of Naisi ; at any rate it is a wood now, and as it is called by his name when he is forgotten here, it must have been called so long ago. We may let the waggonette stay here, and I shall give you a walk, very beautiful, through a forest with occasional openings, and smooth but with occasional romantic depths, so that you may imagine great variety visible in it, and especially when you look towards Cruachan Ben from this centre, and the beautiful undulations between us and its feet.

Sheena.—Why do you say so often Cruachan Ben instead of Ben Cruachan ?

Cameron.—It is the usual name. I think it means that the hill is a *Cruach* or heap *nam Beinn*—of mountains—as piled on each other till they arrived at a point.

In this wood of Naisi I become sad and think of the many dead, and I fear for the many changes of the country, of which I am a native. Still I am connected with the past, and I sometimes think that the future may connect itself with me.

O'Keefe.—We must not have melancholy sentiment. They were Irishmen who gave the name to the wood, and it is I who may lament most; but I shall leave unwillingly this park or paradise and its varied undulations, with its memory of Naisi, and I must confess that I go forward with a certain hope and pleasure, as I want to see the fishing stream, which is said to be the finest in the Highlands—the Awe. What a rush, what a noble stream! not an Amazon, but a gigantic trout stream and a living place for salmon ; and what a gorge cut by violence out of a hard rock, first by nature and widened by man ; it is rather terrifying, and I do not wonder at any stories of wild cats up in the woods, or of wild Highlanders on the hills.

Cameron.—Observe! it was up on the left there, at a steep place where it is said Macdougall and Robert Bruce fought, and of Bruce it is said that in struggling with Macdougall he lost his brooch just on that rock above the stream.

You have heard of the brooch of Lorn.

Loudoun.—I have heard of another place where it was lost, much farther inland. I confess myself mystified about that brooch : it is said to have been lost in a fire at the Macdougall's, and also to have been presented to the Queen, and to be still in the possession of the old Somerled family—which version is true ? The brooch is an interesting piece of work as represented in engravings. We rush along and here is Loch Awe. After all I like to get out of a pass, and to see the open sea or land, and I like to look at these islets and to think of that island of the Druids. I suppose that is the meaning of the name. I could stay here long.

Cameron.—I call Innis Draighneach island of Druids, but everybody does not do so. I hope you will like to stay a while at Dalmally. Here take notice of the sides of Cruachan, or rather of the hill next to it, forming a base although called by another name. You look up Glen Strae and you see at the top the hills that form part of the Black Mount, and over which is Inveroran.

Loudoun.—I remember that glen long ago, it has not changed, there is not even a new cot in it, I believe. When you look round from it you see the great corry of Cruachan, where snow remains till after mid-summer, and sometimes until it meets the snow of the new season.

But of all changes, that of the village is greatest, this long village of Stronmialchoin, long and broken, no two houses together, each separate and having a croft, and each on some rising ground, a veritable village of little mounds, looking pleasantly on the great mountain, the old castle of Kilchurn, and the beautiful lake. It is no crowded lane, it never was, but it was pleasantly and fully inhabited, and the ground socially occupied ; now indeed it is only a few scattered houses along a road for about a mile and a half. The flat ground below grew the fuel, it used to be well covered with pits, the crofts grew and still grow potatoes and oats, and the hill behind grew sheep and cattle. It is one of the half-cleared places which is now likely to change again and to increase its inhabitants. One wonders that men can dare to thrust so many out merely that they may have more room. Murder is bad, and when many are turned out of house and home, some must die in the trial. Surely if repentance is pleasant, we shall call them back as we are doing in some places. But will they come? I remember when many left, but I daresay it was good on the whole for the young. I allude to a long time ago.

Cameron.—It is a new thing to me to come to a town, a place with a railway station. True, to you Dalmally is only an inn and a few houses; to me it is a connection with the active world out of which I am shut by nature and habit. We have time to eat and have a pleasant walk and another feast on the landscape before sleeping.

Margaet.—We shall look at the mouldy old church, damp looking and little used, and we shall go down past the roaring Orchy and seek out a boat. Mr. Hamerton has some poems on the isles of Loch Awe, and one about Kilchurn Castle ; we can listen if any one will tell of them.

Cameron.—Yes, and I hope you will continue rightly as you do to call it " Kilhuirn," and not " tchurn " as some people do.

Margaet.—There is a story of a knight who went from this to fight, I do not know where; his wife was thrifty, saved money and built the castle for him, but he was seven years away and she was persuaded to agree to marry a Macquorkadale. The knight, Sir Colin Campbell, came like Ulysses in the guise of a beggar to the marriage feast, but he had not such a struggle for the restoration of his position as the old Greek. He was a Breadalbane Campbell, and the land is still in their hands. Do you think it is true ? He was recognized by shewing a ring.

Loudoun.—As to this particular story being true or not I have no opinion, but as to the probability it is of the very highest kind. I do not doubt that in early times, when travelling was difficult, such things were very common. They occur abundantly even now; people are so afraid of believing romance, that the length of the absence of Ulysses has been held wonderful. It is the telling and the adventures that have made it so. I have heard of a woman that has kept her husband's apartment unaltered for forty years expecting his return, and her mind is apparently sound. I know another who has waited more than twenty. I know one who waited as long expecting her son, how much longer I do not know.

Margaet.—It is an inconvenience to have such a distance to walk to the boat, but it is beautiful when we are on the smooth mouth of the river.

O'Keefe.—It occurs to me that I do not remember seeing a sail on Loch Awe; it is a very gusty loch; people ought to have oars or steam.

Loudoun.—I have seen a sail, but it was not held wise to use it.

The stories of Kilchurn are not numerous; there is more historic romance connected with the Argyll Campbells, whose house was at Ardchonnel some ten miles below; there was Dugald Dalgetty when he took in his formidable provision for three days, and before he went to Inveraray. But not the less this Kilchurn castle has been painted oftener. The situation is fine, and we look from the cultivated to the wild, so that the natives, as well as people from the cities are attracted by this contrast; if not rich, it is not a desolate wilderness, but one that actively engages the eye and the thought in whatever direction we look. A waste is also a contrast with the city, but it leaves little to love and only uniformity to hate.

Margaet.—What do I see? a monument; is there something here to be remembered?

Cameron.—Yes, much; we have had our remarkable men here. You may be tired of the sons of Uisnach, even although they hunted here, but you will wonder at Duncan MacIntyre, or Donnachadh Ban, white Donald, who was born in this glen at Druimliaghart. He died about 1812, an old man, who had spent much of the latter part of his life as one of the city guard or police of Edinburgh. There he made his poems. He had in his strongest days been forester in Còire Cheathaich and on Ben Dorain, and also on Buachail Eite. We shall see these places, and I will give you a specimen of his poetry. Many people love the name of MacIntyre, and I like to give away copies of his poems. We ought here to have Professor Blackie to translate the poem on Glenorchy, but as he has not done it I will tell you in prose a part of what it says :—

GLENORCHY.

. . . . . .
. . . . . .

"A glen, warm sheltered,
Where very well grows the cornfood green,
Where there are the fields—
And where the corn is planted.

(Rich) branchy corn will grow there,
As soft and white as curds,
Strong, nourishing, and juicy,
Heavy, fruitful, full and thick.

We were happy there in winter,
At the wedding we had our sport,
Of the flowing pipe the music would not let us tire;

And the stirring music of the fiddlers
Playing the whirling reels;
The maidens with their own songs,
With their sweet and clear voices.

We found salmon going up every stream,
And grouse in plenty,
And thousands of black cocks.
The little scraping roe,
The little kid and goat ;
O glen, where the deer forests are,
And the many huntsmen ! "

Loudoun.—These simple thoughts make a pleasant poem.
I suppose we must leave it to the guidebooks to tell of
all the wondrous places, and to describe the castle ; we are
searching rather after that which is older than history, but
young compared with man, not to speak of nature. We shall
get the novelist and the poet to help us with meditations. But
we cannot be wholly in the past ; we must fill our souls with
the impression caused by this collection of scenes, for it is a
picture on every side. It needs a song, a lyric poem—to my
mind the finest kind of poem.

Margaet.—Then if the finest, why are there more fine lyric
poems by far than dramatic or epic poems.

Loudoun.—The reason is clear. The soul bursts out into
its highest feelings only for a short time ; why is the brightest
lightning only a flash ; no man has ever through a whole epic
spoken in the full glow of his power. It is usually a series of
links for the fits of inspiration. The dramatic quality may keep
up coherence : it is a long continued instinct, leading clearly
to an end. But when the mind is fatigued the dramatic force
weakens, and no reasoning has been able to retain it, although

the industrious poet goes on to finish his work. The epic is intellectual, and so far less poetic than the lyric.

Margaet.—Did not the "Highland widow" live about here ?

Cameron.—She lived at the foot of Cruachan Ben, Scott tells us, where a wild brook ran into the wild Awe, and where there are fine trees. We passed the place after leaving Bun-Awe two or three miles. You remember the account of the old oak where Elspat sat; her memory is a monument to this place; even nature is less interesting when man or his fate is quite absent. Every corry is more dreadful when man suffered there, and every hill more beautiful when man triumphed there. For this reason I like the monument to Wallace on the Abbey Craig at Stirling. Some people speak evil of it, but I say it lightens up the most interesting of the plains of Scotland, for which Pict and Scot and Saxon have in their turn fought and now occupy together.

Willie.—You forget the Romans—but they are gone.

Loudoun.—Yes, you are right and fresh from history ; Agricola's Valium would give of itself a pleasant tour, and so would the battle-fields of Arthur, but we shall keep to our Gaels for this season.

Margaet.—Did Druids really live on that island pointed out to us over there and which you named ?

Cameron.—I do not know any exact history of the place ; but, perhaps, we have had enough of the Druids said to have been here. When I was young we preferred to run after the salmon ; and many a time have I gone up Glen Strae with a spear and a lantern, and sought for the shining princes of the stream. We were often frightened by people coming after us, but we darkened our lantern and hid among the bushes, and luckily there were no blood-hounds to hunt us down.

Margaet.—But was not that wicked ? Do you not think you were stealing ?

Cameron.—From whom did I steal ? These salmon came from the ocean to the land of my fathers, a gift of heaven to us men, and a joy to young hearts and vigorous bodies.

Margaet.—But could you not say that of everything that nature gives, or at least something near it. The grass grows on these hills and no one helps it.

Cameron.—Yes, the grass grows, but the sheep need care. I obey the laws of my country ; but in early times, even in my recollection, it was scarcely required to protect salmon on all the rivers ; on some it certainly was. The time comes when so many parties are interested that to give liberty of fishing to all would be to destroy all the salmon, and indeed that time did come to many places and made laws necessary. New habits cannot enter rapidly into a country.

I remember that not far off there lived a Highland woman and three sons ; they were a very lawless family, the well-taught offspring of those who resented Saxon laws. It was not easy to get rid of these people. Perhaps they fed on the mutton of the hills, having but a small croft and the right to feed only a few sheep of their own ; they, I dare say, ate good salmon, but they refused to work. Strong men the sons were, and the mother would not hesitate to beg, and, when refused, to speak evil with a most alarming tongue. They were bad neighbours, but they would not leave. The cottage was deprived of windows by the farmers ; that was not enough ; the door was taken, but they still remained ; the roof was some of the walls at last sent them away. I wonder what became of them. There was here at least an apology for driving away people.

Margaet.—But why were the people bad? Perhaps they were starved.

Cameron.—Their field of labour was too small, and they fought against powers too great for them; with better chance of success they might have been better men; but powerless wrath is a melancholy sight, and the old woman and her curses haunt me, and therefore I spoke. Curses give a bad effect to language, and people who use them are lowered in their own eyes and in the eyes of others, not because they are always worse, but because it is a habit taken up by the ignorant, weak, and bad, on account of its being an easy mode of apparent revenge, whilst the curses themselves are often the production of cultivated minds. On the other hand, we sometimes find the worst persons refuse to curse in words; they even bless, because they know the effect of appearance, and hypocrisy is a power.

Loudoun.—There is little doubt that the Saxon people altered the character of the Gaelic population and kept it from its natural development for centuries. I at least believe it. It is the character of revolutions to destroy the past, and the new requires long building. Men who fight become rough; they lose homes, leisure, and culture. For this reason the living world moves forward by a succession of ups and downs like our own hills and glens. Sometimes it remains longer at one place than at another.

Even this spot changes. It used to be very difficult to come to Dalmally, and still more so to go to Oban.   It was a natural difficulty.   The Pass of Awe forms a long road and a hungry one, and there are no resting places.   Even the rats found it hard ; more than forty years ago our now common rats had reached Dalmally, but had not got the length of Loch Etive in 1835.   There was no inducement to cross Cruachan or its spurs.   They are across now, but I do not know the road they took.   Mountain chains interrupt armies both of men and rats.

Margaet.—Now we return.   Photographs will scarcely remind me of this place.   I hope I may obtain a memorial in a good painting ; if not, I must come now and then and renew the impressions which the greatness of nature and the violence required to struggle with it leave on the spirit, when these great old rocks look down upon us.

CHAPTER XXV.

TO GLEN ETIVE.

CAMERON.—I think we might go to Tyndrum by train. It will be pleasantly strange to rush up such a waste as Glen *Laogh*[1] in such a bird-like fashion. Once I went up by coach, but the horses grieved me, and I could not see the river as it rushed down its gorge. True, I saw the wilderness, and it pressed upon my mind. Surely the Sahara can scarcely be more desert, but it is different; Sahara has not even the winds, or they are rare as well as dusty, and even the demons of the stones have deserted the place. Here they rage on the hills, and Cailleach Bheir moves from mountain to mountain.

Margaet.—How dreadful to skim over the precipitous banks of this stream. No human being could see it in its natural state before this railway began to play upon its precipices, and here we take the way of the crows. They used to tell me that it was a terrible pass, only few people could climb it in winter, and none of the farmers could go up and down in a day with their carts unless these were empty. But here we are flying up and we shall alight in half an hour. The fables of childhood become silly, and its wonders turn to nothing even to the young.

[1] Called Glen Lochy (West). I imagine it to be *Laogh* (a calf) as in *Ben Laogh.*

U

Loudoun—It is not quite so. The fables of childhood do not become silly ; they never have been so important as now ; we neglected them, and now men of learning treasure them and learn philosophy and history from them. Let us learn the same from this road. In the memory of man it was a difficult passage for any one, and very hard for a horse with a burden. For a generation the road has been fair, but steep. I remember when it was a hard journey to Tyndrum, except for a good hill walker.

Cameron.—It is a strange valley this. You see it is a collection of heaps which exist in thousands, masses as if left by melting ice ; but they might have been made by local shower-water. The old poem which was before quoted about the sons of Uisnach calls it the glen of straight ridges—

Glen Urchain ! O Glen Urchain ! (or Glenorchy ! O Glenorchy !)
It was the straight glen of smooth ridges ;
Not more joyful was a man of his age
Than Naoise in Glen Urchain.—*Skene's translation.*

This at the upper part is not properly Glenorchy, which is more strictly the branch to the north ; but the stream from here runs into the Orchay or Urchaidh, and Glenorchy is the wider name that runs down along the side of Loch Awe. There is no manageable road up through the real Glenorchy.

This is one of the reasons why I brought you to Dalmally. You see one of the hunting places of the Uisnachs, and you learn that it is still as it was of old, leaving out the road and railway, if you can manage to think of it so.

We are at Tyndrum, Tigh'n druim, the house on the ridge. A dreary house it was once ; now there is a fine hotel. Even manufactures have tried to settle here, and in that little hole up on the side of the hill it is said that the last Marquis of Breadalbane spent sixty thousand pounds looking for lead, and perhaps he spent somewhat more, trying to make vitriol outside with the minerals got from within the hill. Our ride being short, we shall need no rest here, but we shall again take the private rather than public conveyance ; we must spend some time on the way.

We drive along first an unpromising wild road, and seem to be rushing among pathless hills, but soon we go down to the plain, and we need not fear, since everywhere the roads are good, and you see that our horses are strong. As we move down we come on an unexpectedly open space, and whilst the wild hills of the deer forest of the Black Mount are on the left, we come on the famous Ben Doran to the right.[1]

Margaret.—It is big but not beautiful, sloping and not varied.

Cameron.—Yet it had power to produce a fine enthusiasm in Duncan MacIntyre, as you will see if you read Professor Blackie's translation of his poem. This to first appearance rather smooth and stony side is long, and if the other is equally so it is a large place not easily passed over by men, except the best of walkers. But listen to MacIntyre and you will hear that behind that too flat side, and perhaps upon it, there are numerous dens where deer can hide and men may be lost.[2]

---

[1] It is often written "Dorain," but I suppose that to be the genitive case.

[2] See p. 162, *Language and Literature of the Scottish Highlands*, by John Stuart Blackie, Professor of Greek in the University of Edinburgh : Edmonston & Douglas, Edinburgh, 1876.

BEN DORAIN.

" HONOUR be to Ben Dorain
Above all Bens that be !
Beneath the sun mine eyes beheld
No lovelier Ben than he ;
With his long smooth stretch of moor,
And his nooks remote and sure
        For the deer,
When he smiles in face of day,
And the breeze sweeps o'er the brae
        Keen and clear ;
With his greenly-waving woods,
And his glassy solitudes,
And the stately herd that fare,
        Feeding there ;
And the troop with white behind
When they scent the common foe,
Then wheel to sudden flight
        In a row,
Proudly snuffing at the wind
        As they go.

.   .   .   .   .   .

'Tis a nimble little hind,
Giddy-headed like her kind,
That goes sniffing up the wind
        In her scorning ;
With her nostrils sharp and keen,
Somewhat petulant, I ween,
'Neath the crag's rim she is seen
        In the morning.

.   .   .   .   .   .

You will never with your ken
Mark her flitting paces when
With lightsome tread she trips
O'er the light unbroken tips
        Of the grass ;

Not in all the islands three.
Nor wide Europe, may it be
That a step so light and clean
    Hath been seen,
When she sniffs the mountain breeze,
And goes wandering at her ease,
Or sports as she may please
    On the green ;
Nor she will ever feel
Fret or evil humour when
She makes a sudden wheel,
And flies with rapid heel
    O'er the Ben ;
With her fine and frisking ways
She steals sorrow from her days,
Nor shall old age ever press
On her head with sore distress
    In the glen.

.   .   .   .   .   .

III.

My delight it was to rise
With the early morning skies,
    All aglow ;
And to brush the dewy height
Where the deer in airy state
    Wont to go ;
At least a hundred brace
Of the lofty-antlered race,
When they left their sleeping place
    Light and gay ;
When they stood in trim array,
And with low deep-breasted cry,
Flung their breath into the sky,
    From the brae ;
When the hind, the pretty fool,
Would be rolling in the pool
    At her will ;

Or the stag in gallant pride,
Would be strutting at the side
Of his haughty-headed bride,
    On the hill.
And sweeter to my ear
Is the concert of the deer
    In their roaring,
Than when Erin from her lyre
Warmest strains of Celtic fire
    May be pouring ;
And no organ sends a roll
So delightful to my soul,
As the branchy-crested race,
When they quicken their proud pace
And bellow in the face
    Of Ben Dorain.

  .   .   .   .   .   .

IV.

For Ben Dorain lifts his head
    In the air,
That no Ben was ever seen
With his grassy mantle spread,
And rich swell of leafy green,
    May compare ;
And 'tis passing strange to me,
When his sloping side I see,
    That so grand
And beautiful a Ben
Should not flourish among men,
In the scutcheon and the ken
    Of the land."

Margaet.—That is certainly beautiful enthusiasm, expressive of poetic joy. Is it really a good translation, or is the poem of Professor Blackie's making altogether?

Loudoun.—I have been particular to ask, as I am not able to judge of the style, and every one says that it is well done, and not superior to the original.

Cameron.—I am a Highlander, and I prefer the original, still I think it well done and wonderfully exact. I have asked our minister also, who is a cultivated man, and can compare the two versions, and he thinks it very well done, expressing the original very closely.

Willie.—I see no room for deer. Let us run up a bit and see.

Cameron.—Well, you may run up this lower part. There must be many smaller glens, ridges, precipices, brooks, and shelter for deer on the great mass of this hill; we see only the face here. Behind is a great region—the glorious region to which only strong men can attain, and which made a poet of the gamekeeper, and which even we who cannot attain delight to revel in so far as he can enable us. Let us take some lunch until Willie returns.

O'Keefe.—I shall sleep among the heather or look up to the sky; I like to see the clouds, they are always changing, growing, and diminishing, and the edges are in everlasting motion, and those which go fast are the most changeable.

Willie.—Here I am after a good run; but I could, after all, find nothing without much more running. It would require a fox or a deer. There is a far beyond.

Cameron.—In old times there were plenty of foxes, and I daresay there are some here still. They have been killed to introduce sheep, and this habit annoyed MacIntyre exceedingly. Listen to his praise of foxes. (*P.* 184, *Dr. Blackie.*)

A SONG OF FOXES.

" Ho ! ho ! ho ! the foxes !
Would there were more of them,

> I'd give heavy gold
> For a hundred score of them !
> My blessing with the foxes dwell,
> For that they hunt the sheep so well !
> Ill fa' the sheep, a grey-faced nation
> That swept our hills with desolation !
> Who made the bonnie green glens clear,
> And acres scarce, and houses dear ;
> The grey-faced sheep, who worked our woe,
> Where men no more may reap or sow,
> And made us leave for their grey pens
> Our bonnie braes and grassy glens."

MacIntyre lived when sheep-farming on the hills was new, so late is the custom.   In old times deer and foxes and free hunting made a happy ground for undisturbed men.

Now we are come among deer foresters and stalkers, men who make thousands of acres desert for the purpose of shooting.   Much of this is wilderness.   There is a house in that wood, and there is an inn at Inveroran, and you see some trees called a part of the Caledonian Forest, but, so far as I know, all interest here is in the wildness and the mountain and the deer.

Loudoun.—And why not ?   Did we leave home to see more chimneys or houses ?   You may travel in England through many counties and scarcely see variety of scenery ; perhaps some difference, not much, in building houses or working farms : here you have land, crops, and animals all different from those where we started, and it is a new world. I think it worth while to lose the sheep for the variety of the sight, even if we are not the favoured ones who possess it. Even the owner may see it little.   Look at the Moor of Rannoch, a desert with danger from water, a place without a track, which a man cannot well cross in a day if he does not know the road. There is no sitting down on warm sand when you are tired, confident in the permanence of the heavens above you. You rather feel sure of a constant perfidy. You need shelter, but there is none until you come to King's house, which stands at the top of Glen Etive and Glencoe looking down each of them.

Cameron.—Nowadays we have some chance of being fed and lodged ; that is, one may rely on the people if the house is not too full.

I took care, by writing ; otherwise we might have been obliged to drive down to Glencoe and so lose our object. Still we shall go down, a little after dinner and some rest.

O'Keefe.—What a wild run to the top of Glencoe ; at this precipice we may stand and look down. It is a beautiful defence against outside men. These walls are magnificent, and were it not for this road I could hold it with one to a hundred. Down there men might live in peace so long as there were sheep to eat.

Sheena.—I shudder at that awful hill ; black caves on the front looking over precipices, and wild clouds covering summits making the passes above as dark as night. What is the name of it ?

O'Keefe.—The forester here told me it was Aonach Dubh. Aonach, I suppose, is *onely, lonely,* and is a name given to a hill, a wild poetic name suiting the solitary spots and the wonders on it. Many people at one time never can be on these hills. Dubh is black. "Black and lonely" is a fine name for it, and behind where you saw an opening there is a pass from Loch Etive to Glencoe, which is called **Larig Oillt,** thé Pass of Terror. It expresses exactly the feeling you seem to have had when looking up to the black clouds moving among the broken rocks and darkening the way.

Loudoun.—I once asked the forester here about this pass of Terror, and he, you know, looks after the deer, and knows the rocks as well as they do ; but he told me that the name wàs Larig Eild, the *pass of the hinds*, and that it related to the habits of these animals.

Margaet.—I prefer Mr. Clerk's view ; besides he has studied Gaelic. The result is more poetical, and I feel that we have hit on a wonderful spot ; besides the word is used elsewhere. This at least is a view of Glencoe new to me, and as we look down on that awful gulf in the darkening night, I wonder that our fellows live there and not a colony of mysterious forms. But there is mystery enough, and a deed of moral blackness has made the whole more famous than even nature has done with time and violence.

Cameron.—Let us return. The hotel stands more in the mouth of Glen Etive than Glencoe, and Glen Etive means the wild or terrible glen. But we must not leave Glencoe without looking at the Cona, the favourite of Ossian, whose harp is called the voice of Cona, on the banks of which he was born. You know I believe in the Ossian published by Macpherson as the real ancient Ossian, and often he must have hunted here and ranged among these hills.

Loudoun.—We shall not dispute here ; but we can all admire this wonderful hill—this conical mass between the two glens—this Shepherd of Etive as it is poetically called, looking for ever down to the loch beside his companion opposité. They both look also over the moor of Rannoch. Wilson has made a beautiful photograph of one. When I was proposing to go down Glen Etive, the landlord of the hotel doubted the propriety of allowing me a horse, because the streams came down with such violence on rainy days, and the day was threatening. However we ran down and up, the foaming torrents from the hills softened into wide streams flowing over the roads, which had no bridges and were liable to be swept away. The two hills are very steep, and look as remarkable here as they do at a distance; whilst this one connects the two glens, it also unites Gaelic, Greek, and Latin, the name of shepherd being nearly the same in both. The Greeks had their *boukolos*, and Virgil wrote his Bucolics, and here we have our *buachaill*—all one word we may say. But more exactly the word does not mean shepherd either in Greek or Gaelic, but cowherd, and bucolics "relates to cow herding," and in Gaelic the word is used for general herding.

Cameron.—Now that we have come out of the dark glen and the clouds have cleared away, it is not quite dark, and I care not to go into the house ; I will go up to my friend the forester, about a mile or more on the Inveroran road, and see a true Highland house, built with comfort. Who will come? The ladies may stay, and we shall expect some tea when we return.

This road is farther than I expected, and it is already darkening. There is only one house, and it is on the right, and we cannot miss it. There is a light, and the dog barks, and we must find our way among stones and holes to the door. I doubt not that we shall find a welcome.

O'Keefe.—It will be dark before you reach the house.

Forester.—I am glad to see you. I wish I could show you

into my dwelling on the hills among the deer ; that would be something to look at.

Willie.—This is novel enough. I thought you would live here in misery, with all these dubs about and the road to the house made only by tramping feet, and the house too looking very dark. But here you have a blazing fire and a good lamp, and shooting and fishing tackle round the wall, and plenty in the pots.

Loudoun.—Yes, and happy faces about : why! here too is my friend from Barcaldine come to chat with you.

Willie.—I like to look up to the mysterious rafters. One wonders what may be there.

Cameron.—Yes, you sometimes see the fowls roosted up there ; but it is not so in this house. It is a very bright and busy house to me coming from the outside darkness.

Loudoun.—It is certainly very different from the houses of the town workmen and far superior, whilst the freedom of the occupation during the day makes the life brilliant. It is living in the world instead of in a prison. What say you, forester ?

Forester—I say that the work is hard, but grand. I am not a machine ; I must use my judgment daily, and that on no small scale, over many hills and over many cattle. I am healthy, I am comfortable, and happy as most men. Indeed I have my days of glorious feeling, and I seem to rise with the mountains, although I sometimes may sink in bogs like those on the moor; but these changes are like the face of nature.

Loudoun.—We must go. Good night. I am proud of your acquaintance, and may we all see you again.

Margaet.—You must have had a dark walk home. Why did you stay so late?

Loudoun.—There is something very fascinating about the darkening in the Highlands. I cannot explain it. I had some of the feeling too in Switzerland. It is caused partly by the hills looking upon you, but partly by the peculiar shades. In a level country the land does not look at you; you are alone; here you are stared upon by all around. It is a rare sensation to us, and a luxury. To-morrow we have another new series of sensations.

GLEN ETIVE.

Cameron.—And now we roll down Glen Etive, with a Buachaill on our right and on our left, although the latter mountain receives also a very prosaic name. I am afraid of telling it. They call it Sron a creis (creesh), and say it means the (promontory or) nose of grease or fat, because it fattens animals so well. But this must be a very modern name—a farmer's name. I prefer the Buachaill (south).

The river rushes down that deep ravine, which it has evidently made for itself, and we pass along this precipitous bank, our lives depending on good driving. Let us stand awhile and look at the deer on the opposite side; they are quite undisturbed; no wanderers come here, except by ones or twos, and a whistle will startle them. See!

Loudoun.—They move off as soon as they hear. One might almost measure the speed of sound by observing their movements; it is only a few seconds, and certainly corresponds closely so far as I can judge of the distance from us. They leap the brooks and sometimes seem to dance. One must quote MacIntyre here, *i.e.* Donncha Ban, to describe the light springing race. Such a solitude—not a farm-house, not a man, not a sheep—and all this in Scotland. Each valley is a new country, and there are thousands, or hundreds at least.

Margaet.—I would look and rejoice if I could walk instead of staring continually down that terrible steep; when it ends I shall think on the scenery.

Cameron.—We now move rapidly down the hill and come into the depth of the valley, where violent storms often meet, since here is a rapid turn to the right, and numerous passages for air are made by the irregular peaks. And see that one standing up like a piece of black iron before us, the end of some Titanic spear. That is a memorial of Deirdre, and I should not have asked you to come had there not been here something to remind you of the sons of Uisnach. It has two names—Ben Cetlin or Kettelin and Grianan Dartheil, the Boudoir of Darthula, a fantastic appellation, just as they call the rugged hills of Loch Long the Bowling Green of the Duke of Argyle. But as the latter indicates the nearness of the Duke, so the former does the power of Deirdre. We must look on her and the whole tribe as spending much time here and living on the deer. Kettel is a Norse name, but this need not have a Norse origin; in Gaelic the meaning might be quite different.

Loudoun.—We are here in a basin, and it is hard to imagine these great hollows filled with grinding ice. However, they are still subject to attacks of water which washes down what little soil it may meet, and makes way for the rolling of numberless pebbles and blocks. Much of the valley below seems at times to be covered, judging from the breadth of the gravel beds of the river.

O'Keefe.—Here is another memorial of Deirdre—that field is called after her. And so we hunt up our heroes in all the surroundings of Loch Etive.

Margaet.—I wish some one would invent a way of describing a scene. I see and feel, but cannot express.

Loudoun.—You said this before ; but there are many ways invented. The geologist will describe this clearly, and have the surveyor to assist him ; the photographer will give you details ; the artist will come from it with a memory on canvass of beautiful effects; but the poet, and he only, can describe the feelings, and even he cannot exhaust them.

Margaet.—I am not satisfied with any poet's description, it is generally a collection of similes, or a number of unrealities which are raised into being in his mind. Still I am not insensible to their beauty, and I confess that Black has had great success in describing scenes in this west in his Highland novels.

Cameron.—We have passed only one house, it was at the bend of the glen, and was a forester's. Now we come to Dalness or Dal an Eas, the field of the waterfall, and our poet Duncan Ban lived close to it for a while, in a cottage of which a few stones are left. I cannot worthily translate his verses, but we can look at the fine broad waterfall.

Here we may have Wilson's poem, part of which I can give. He early found the beauty of this valley. Let us imagine Professor Wilson addressing the deer as he did here at Dalness. His own reading of it to his class was a feast which seems to have fed his students with some of his enthusiasm for the remainder of their lives. To be able to do this is to live not in vain, and I am glad to say this for those who may dwell too much on the author not being in the front rank of poets.

. . . .

" Up, up, to yon cliff ! like a king to his throne,
O'er the black silent forest piled lofty and lone ;
A throne which the eagle is glad to resign
Unto footsteps so fleet and so fearless as thine.

. . . .

There your branches now toss in the storm of delight,
Like the arms of the pine on yon shelterless height,
One moment, thou bright apparition, delay !
Then melt o'er the crags like the sun from the day.

. . . .

Down the pass of Glen Etive the tempest is borne,
And the hillside is swinging, and roars with a sound,
In the heart of the forest embosomed profound.
Till all in a moment the tumult is o'er,
And the mountain of thunder is still as the shore
When the sea is at ebb, not a leaf, not a breath
To disturb the wild solitude, steadfast as death."

Loudoun.—That is fine, and if we do not see the same sight as he describes, he having been himself a hunter on the hills, we are saved the labour We like to see the wild passes that show themselves up these pathless hills, and it is not strange that men from London seek the life of the wild man here, as far as they can endure the imitation. One ought to tame the deer and ride with them over the rocks. We can only follow them with the imagination, but slightly with the eye ; and we have the same want of satisfaction looking at, but unable to follow, the salmon. It is a poor enjoyment eating him, as if we ate his life and his poetic wanderings. Sport is partly a wish to imitate, and eating the game is like a New Zealander eating in fancy the strength and mind of his victim. It is a life of hope only, but that is all our life; and he is not a sound lover of nature that has no sympathy in sport.

The verses you recited give a description of the forests which we may suppose Deirdre alluded to in her song. There are few pines now at Glen Etive, although nominally a forest for deer. The real meaning of forest is not well known; if it comes from *foris*, without, out of doors or outside the walls, then it is easily understood, and its present use by deer-stalkers is more correct than the use by tree-planters.

Cameron.—Another rough road over streams, and in that terrible blast that comes down—unavoidable! We must bow our heads and look up as we dare; now we are at the height and can see the loch. We are at *Druimachothais* (perhaps *Druimachois*, the ridge at the foot), and we shall dash down to the small portion of plain to look for our boat.

Loudoun.—Before we leave this wondrous glen let us think of it so as to remember. It is certainly one of the largest of the narrow glens of Scotland. It may be said to be 30 miles long, as the glen includes the lake. It is certainly one of the deepest, and it has points as terrible as those of Glencoe, in certain kinds of weather. It is larger, more varied, and I imagine in storms almost as terrible. One wonders if the ancient Celts really went up these hills; they speak of them and of the clouds, but I do not know how high they wandered up the peaks.

O'Keefe.—I think they went up, but like the Greeks they do not leave us much description of nature. I can give you a hunting scene from the Dean of Lismore's book, which Dr. M'Lauchlin has translated. It is said to be Ossian's, but the hunt is in Ireland on Sliabh nam ban fionn, *the hill of the fair ladies.* Finn had a hunting dog called Bran, a great favourite.

> " Then Finn and Bran did sit alone
> A little while upon the mountain side,
> Each of them panting for the chase,
> Their fierceness and their wrath aroused.
> Then did we unloose three thousand hounds
> Of matchless vigour and unequalled strength ;
> Each of the hounds brought down the deer,
> Down in the vale that lies beneath the hill ;
> There never fell so many deer and roe
> In any hunt that ere till this took place.
> But sad was the chase down to the east,
> Thou cleric of the church and bells,
> Ten hundred of our hounds with golden chains
> Fell wounded by ten hundred boars ;
> Then by our hands there fell the boars,
> Which wrought the ill upon the plain.
> And were it not for blades and vigorous arms,
> That chase had been a slaughter."
>
> *Book of the Dean of Lismore*, from the 3rd Poem.

The writer evidently wishes to astonish the cleric by the amount of slaughter, and expects the perhaps tame-like preacher to despise his own vocation, before the glory of killing a thousand wild boars; but there is no sentence regarding nature. The name of the hill may relate to nuns with white dresses.

The Greeks were awed by their great mountains, and stood in humility below. Did any one of them ever climb Olympus or Ida ? There is no wonder that men cower before nature.

They fear the darkness in the Highlands even now, in the valleys, and much more a dark passage on the top of a black clouded mountain.

Cameron.—If they did go up they did not live there much; that is, the people who wrote did not; but there is a class living even now on Mount Olympus who rarely come down, and are almost entirely separate from all others. Probably the same class lived with the same habits in old times, unknown to the town-loving Greek, who knew little of topography, and filled the wilds with mythic creatures. When we look at that terrible pass on the western side of the Buachaill, the pass of terror, at the time when the peaks are covered with black clouds, and only a dark cave shows itself below, we have room for the wild beings that were supposed to haunt this valley. You will see a drawing of one of them in J. F. Campbell's *Tales of the West Highlands:* there is a sketch of the wild creature of Glen Eiti (Direach Glenn Eitidh, Mac Callain), he was also a Mac, the son of Colin. The drawing, like the story describing him, gives " one hand out of his chest, one leg out of his haunch, and one eye out of the front of his face."

Margaet.—Is it not said that even the Greeks worshipped mountains ?

Loudoun.—I don't know of any actual worship of mountains, but there is an abundant appearance in the Greek mind of awe and feeling of mystery relating to them.

Willie.—Now this is a fine opportunity to tell a story as we stand under the shed waiting for the boat.

O'Keefe.—As you are near Cruachan, I will tell you a little tale from the Irish Cruachan which is very different from yours.   Near it was the palace of the old Kings of Connaught, and it was not far from Carrick-on-Shannon.   The king and queen, Aillil and Meave, people of whom I told you, who lived about nineteen hundred years ago, were amusing themselves one winter evening with their followers, and they were, I dare say, all bragging of their courage, when the king said he would give his sword, a gold-hilted one, to the man who would go out in the dark and bring a twig that was round the leg of one of two men who had been hanged, and were still hanging. Nera was a spirited youth and went, but on coming back he saw as it were the palace on fire, and a host of men met him who seemed to have plundered it.   They passed but did not take notice of him, and he followed.   They went to a well-known cave on the hill of Cruachan, whilst Nera followed. But he was seized and taken before the king of the Tuatha De Danann.   Now this cave was not visible to ordinary human eyes, but Nera's had been enlightened and he could even show the place to others.   The king said little to him, but ordered him to bring a bundle of fire-wood to the kitchen every day. On one of these days he saw a blind man carrying a lame man and depositing him near a fountain, and they had a dispute about the right spot.   He asked a woman, from whom the king had told him to take instructions, who these people were, and she said they were guardians of the Barr or Mind, a crown of gold which the king wears, and these people were trusted by the king. The fountain was in the cave, and the Barr in the fountain.   Nera told this at Cruachan, and King Aillil obtained the assistance of Fergus MacRoigh and the Ulster champions who had left home because of the murder of the Sons of Uisnach, and plundered the cave and obtained the golden diadem. Fergus, you know, is one of our heroes. This was a mystery of the Irish Cruachan. The story is from the book of Leinster, but taken from O'Curry and Sullivan's 29th Lecture on *Manners and Customs of the Ancient Irish.*

Margaet.—I am unwilling to pass out of the glen proper on to the loch until I have a good description of Glen Etive. It seems deep, lonely, secluded, more than most, with curves that seem like passages to hide the way into the great centre, where I can imagine a tribe living unknown for generations; indeed, who knows this glen even now? The hills are high, but except at the Grianan Dartheil, not so rugged as at Glencoe, although the weird passages through the upper parts seem as wild and ghostly.

Loudoun.—We settle as before. Glen Etive must live in our feelings, and Deirdre is the first person who is said to have discovered its beauty, and to have recorded it in song. Perhaps you will object by saying that the song is put into her mouth. It may be so, but I know of no other author. No one of the outer world has come here to settle until about five years ago, when that new house was built; the summer fishers in the house above, which seems to be a very much improved dwelling, if not a new one, may be another exception; but both are very late comers. Now there is a steamer for the loch and a coach to take people up the glen. It is not easy to go to the shore to find a boat; one must sometimes pass the brook on the west side when it is high. The bridge is only two planks covered with sods, far up and reached only by passing through a bog. It is made for the shepherds; or one may pass over half land half water, to the mouth of the River Etive. It depends on the wind which side is best, but to-day there is no wind, and we have good rowers waiting us, and a long boat by the river side, and we may take the low road.

O'Keefe.—The hills are desolate and rather too plain, I imagine, as we go down the first mile or two.

Cameron.—This view may be so, but on our left is Ben Starrive or Ben Starra, which, by some mistake of a map, has been continued to be called in guide books Ben Slarive, and that is a lofty mountain (3,519 feet); it looks far down the loch, and on coming up it is often taken for one of the Shepherds or Buachaills. It is broken up by streams, and seems almost impassable for man as we see it.

Loudoun.—It is surprising that the water can be even in a small degree salt here, but there is sea-weed after 17 miles of a narrow passage against roaring streams often driving down great floods. Surely it must sometimes be quite fresh in the loch here?

Cameron.—Over on our left, at Inver Guithaiseagan, is a small plain. There is a wild story about a man who had robbed some place and hid his treasure there, but forgot the spot, leaving the gold to lie there still. I think that a probable enough story. Hiding gold was common, and finding it used not to be uncommon, but this may long ago have been found, and we have more interest in such a name as Inver Draigneach, the point of the thunderer, where such rolling stones are driven down from the mountain, making a great river of boulders. They are at rest now, but we see them there lying ready to flow along with the next sufficient stream.

Do not confound the words for the rumbling noise like

with man's innovations ; here is a quarry, and a capital spot for our lunch.

Cameron.—Capital, if it were raining and windy, but I know a better place than this granite cavity. We come to it soon.

Margaet.—Then from what you say, Mr. O'Keefe, there is a Cruachan in Ireland, more famous in story than this one.

O'Keefe.—The hill was more famous, but only because of the palace that was near it. This one is so high that the lower portions receive names of their own, but as we are still in Glen Etive in a sense, it occurs to me that the reason that no really historical event is connected with the deep and secluded and most habitable portion is because of its inaccessibility. There never was a good road, and even the inferior one is not old ; besides there is no road up either side of the loch even now, except for a good walker or rider, and no steamer plied until lately, and it goes only for a little in summer. I conceive Glen Etive about Dalness to have been a very safe place of refuge, and a good hiding place for the Uisnach family at first, and perhaps for many a generation of men who loved peace or who feared detection. It is, therefore, said in the legend that Naisi and his followers went to a wild part of Alba ; and they would have been very safe down here and in the plain of Cadderly, where they could also fish ; and here, if we turn to the right, and just before going into the bay at Cadderly we come to a little island called Eilean Uisneachan, and on that we must certainly land. It is only a rocky spot with a bush or two on it. It was mentioned that the Uisneachs, when hunting, put up booths, which attracted the attention of at least the narrators in the legend, by having three apartments, one for sleeping in, one for cooking in, and one for eating in. One booth is alluded to as having been on an island, and the name of the island remains. A chart lately published gives Uiseagan, but this is evidently wrong, as we may judge from the Old Statistical report, as well as present inhabitants of the district. The latter would mean the Island of Larks, a name most inappropriate, we may say absurd, since it is only a rather flat rock covered with smaller stones, and a few reeds and briers, certainly not for larks. There was a pile of stones of considerable length, but so irregular that it was not certain that it was a heap caused by the fall of any structure, although it was about the length of a couple of cowhouses of a size common enough. Passages were made through the heap, and a rough long hollow was reached, such as might be made when mere boulders are used for building ; but the chief indications of residence were pieces of wood which had been cut into pegs, and various pieces of charcoal and bones. It was such a ruin as might come from " the booths of chase" divided into three. But a still better proof of continued or frequent habitation was outside the island, there being the distinct ruins of a road out of it, and on to the land,—a line of stones evidently was made leading to a good landing. It is easy still to see some of them out of the water ; they are not entirely dry, I believe, at any time of the tide, but they were intended to support a dry walk to all appearance. The island is scarcely a hundred feet in any direction, a mere lake-dwelling, a place protected by the water on all sides, but only partially at this entrance.

And so we may look around in this arm of the sea as if in an inland lake, where only a wild Highlander in old times could go, a place still frequented by seals and cormorants, eagles and foxes; although in summer visited by screw-steamers, it is probably quieter now, and less inhabited than ever it was, even from the first century, or how much longer no one can guess. I have come up here in a mist when the sky seemed to come down and shut us up as with a lid, so that we saw only some fifty or sixty feet up the hills, and to those from the sunnier south it produced fear and a desire to escape never to return.

Loudoun.—Now that these numerous reminiscences of Uisnach have left us a probable interval, I will take you across to another spot; it is Inver **Liebhan** on our left hand, a pretty bay at the mouth of a stream, where, too, is a farm-house and a piece of ground not difficult to climb. I came here thinking to see a great cromlech. We find an enormous stone; but we must first walk up among the trees, which are neither many nor high, although a great ornament to the glen.

It is easy to see that this is no cromlech, or dolmen, or anything but a great fallen rock, which has lighted on three small stones, which for size are somewhat in the proportion of castors to a table; it may be that the rock was lying on the soil, which gradually was washed away, leaving these stones only. It is a geological *lusus*, and many a dreadful fall takes place on these hills capable of explaining such. On the other side of the hill, namely, on the Awe, a boulder was found on the middle of the road, settling one morning just before the coach, so that no vehicle could pass; and on the southerly side of the same river boulders and gravel seem to be rolling all the year, attempting to fill up the stream, which is white with the struggle against them.

O'Keefe.—Now I am tired. There is a want of stories here; you ought to know more about the place. Land me on the North, and I will walk to the quarries and see some activity.

Cameron.—If you stop at the point before the quarries I will show you another Uisnach memorial. We shall be there as soon as you.

Loudoun.—What is that called?

Cameron.—We call it Ruadh nan Draighean, which would be Thorn Point; but some prefer to write it Druidhean, which would be the Druid Point. I confess that the Druids and the thorns have a struggle here, and perhaps in other places. I see no thorns, and the rocks are too protuberant for us to suppose thorns to have abounded.

The remains are apparently those of irregular bothies; some naturally placed stones have been doing duty in a cottage; some of the lines of wall are curved, others straight. These have been dwellings, but we can scarcely now say how rude; we know that stones may somewhat change their places where soil and vegetation and heavy rains are, not to speak of the inclination of the hilly ground. A tradition has been mentioned that a daughter of the King of Ulster came to live here, having run away with a son of the Earl of Ardchattan. Now, I suppose there has never been an Earl of Ardchattan, but that is of little consequence. A lady having run away from the King of Ulster and come to this place may fairly be looked

To face page 331.

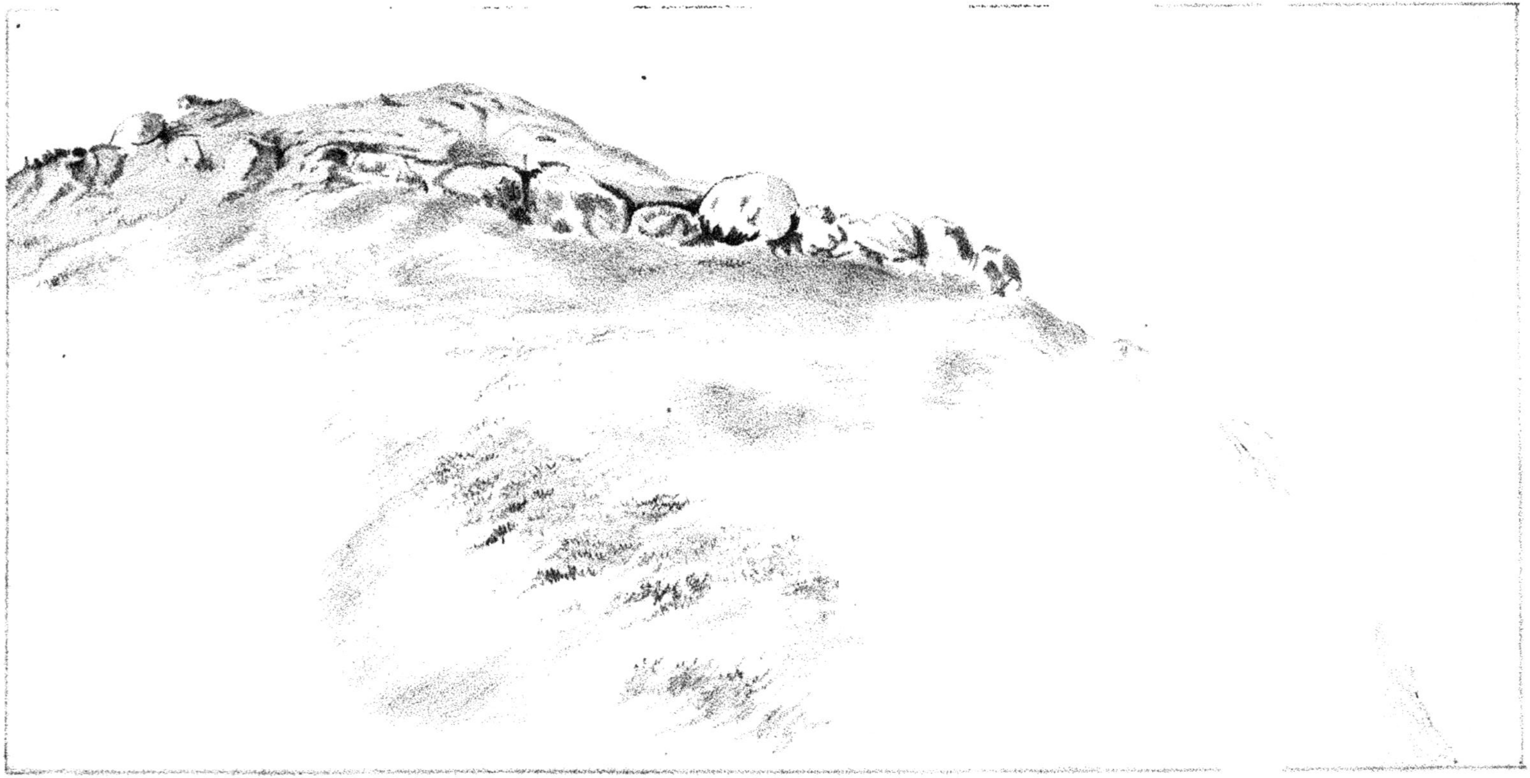

moment in looking at the small remains of a dwelling of one of your country's heroines. As to us, we shall move about among these rocky shores and look for seals, and give you time to examine the quarries, which we can see well enough for our wants from the shore. We shall then take you in, and move onwards.

Cameron.—We have quite time to row to Ruadh na charn, opposite Ardchattan priory, and then on to meet the coach for Oban. The men are not too tired, and they do not require to go farther back than Bunawe.

There is a ferry at this "cairn point." Whether the word refers to the stone circle on the conical hill itself I do not know. The hill is said to be 169 feet high ; it is called Dun Cathich, probably the hill of battle, and the large stone circle may be a burying place as smaller ones are, although the encircling of the top has led people to call it rather a Dun. The stones are large boulders of the Durinish granite, carried over, I suppose, although not arranged by glaciers. They touch each other. It is not a common style of fort, and a drawing has been taken. (See Fig.)

It is said to have been used as one of a chain of beacons, and this may be. There is another small hill on the loch, between this and Connel, called Tom na h-aire, the *mound of watching*, which evidently marks the habit.

Loudoun.—And here we arrive at the Abbot's Isle again, the monks' small kind of lake-dwelling and place of refuge, whilst we run in by Kilmaronaig.

We have passed along the shores of Loch Etive, and·have seen the glen; we must leave others to climb the hills to seek the Pass of Terror, and tell us of the dwellings of the deer, and the summits where the eagles mount. We shall require a lodge in the mountains before we can reach these tops, and must have no daily interruption by descending.

Margaet.—We have seen the principal haunts of the sons of Uisnach, and now I should like to know who these Celts were and how they differed and do differ from other people.

Loudoun.—We may reserve this for a quiet conversation at Oban.

CHAPTER XXVI.

THE CELTS.

As I promised, I will give you some opinions concerning the Celts, about whom people dispute so much. The Gaels are certainly a part of that people, whether they are from Scotland, Ireland, or the Isle of Man, and, excepting those who have emigrated from these islands, there exists no Gaelic speaking people elsewhere; but they are only a part of the great people called Celts. The opinions as to the Celts are so numerous that you would be tired of the word if I ventured to tell you half, and so various and so wild have some of these notions been that the holders have been called Celtomaniacs. There is scarcely any other class of language or people that has such a following, so you have a proof of the interesting character of both. I have known Celtomaniacs and may quote some of their opinions: for example, I have been told by one that Gaelic was spoken in Paradise; and that if you do not allow a child to hear a language it will of itself speak Gaelic. There are milder forms; if you derive Hebrew from Gaelic, or such names as Nile, Nineveh, Nimrod, Sabbath, Abraham, Sarah, and Babylon from Celtic, then I think you are a Celtomaniac. When you say it is spoken among the Berbers you are one; and some will say that it will apply also to those who bring the Greek from it, and I agree with them. But when we come nearer here we are obliged to be more cautious ; for example, who will say that the Latin did not to a great degree rise from or along with the Celtic. There are different degrees of mania, and here we may begin to be cautious. After all who were the Celts? In the time of the Roman kings some of them came to the north of Italy, and they made incursions far south into Italy. They stayed a while among the hills, but how long we do not know, and how many of their people they left behind them we do not know. They troubled the Etruscans, who lived south of the Cisalpine Gauls, and they broke through the Etruscan territory to Rome. It is said that they were all driven back ; but the Romans knew little of Italy in early times, and the hills close to them were inhabited by strangers, perhaps Celtic. The Celts had, if not all Gaul, at least most of it ; apparently all the present France except the extreme south-west possibly. North-east Gaul was Belgic, and probably the Belgæ were a mixed population of Celts. Switzerland, at least the part called Helvetia, was Celtic, and the inhabitants made incursions into Germany, so that Celtic was spoken in some parts there, and it is said even, in some parts, down to the Middle Ages. Germans and Celts fought with each other about the Rhine, as they have done in our day. Spain also had Celts; how far mixed we do not know. And probably all Britain and Ireland were Celtic in Cæsar's time, so far as the speech was concerned. Celts also are said to have peopled Galatia, and there is a saying of St. Jerome that he had heard the same language there as in Treves.[1] Celts appear to have at one time overrun Asia Minor, and there are some reasons for supposing them to have appeared in North Africa.

Now, I have read numerous and wearisome opinions, and have looked carefully for little phrases that would show the Gauls or some class of Celts to have been in Italy, as far south as Rome, before the reputed building of that city; but it is not easy to prove it by quotations from historians, and I wish to search a wider field. It seems to me that the similarity of language speaks decidedly of a connection between Rome and Gaul, and tends to show that Latin was Gaulish to begin with, then tinctured by the Greek of Magna Græcia. It in time developed itself in its own method, by its own character, derived perhaps from the Tuscans and various tribes of Italy.[2]

But, again, what are Celts or Kelts ? I must tell you that the reason for writing the K instead of the C is not so good as many imagine. We obtain C from the Latins ; if we pass the Roman empire and go back to the Greek for our words, we must make a great change. But we must not be bigoted. We say king and kingly, and we think it right at times to say regal, it has something of Roman majesty about it ; but we never say basileus or basilikos, it is a step too far back.

[1] Dr. Karl Wieseler has endeavoured to show that the language was German. This does not oppose the theory here.

If we go eastward we may next meet some Phoenician
dialect, and say *melek* instead of king.

At what stage did the Italians soften their *C?* why do we
pass beyond this period without even knowing where it is?

The question now is, who are the Celts? Philologists can tell
us only that they are those who speak Celtic. This is so far a
very good definition. What is food? It is that which people
eat, is a question with an analogous answer; it is a proof of
ignorance, but there is much of this reasoning adopted for want
of better, and I fear it is that which I must also adopt. The
Celts are said by Cæsar, Tacitus, and others to have been red or
light haired, and to have had blue eyes; others say they had
dark hair; now I have come to the conclusion that we
must not trust merely to the ancient campaigners.

We know what errors travellers make, and how necessary
it is to have statements sifted in all branches of history, and
to do this we must attend to the contradictions of different
historians. For old times we have too few to trust to, and their
knowledge was too limited. Let us look at the countries over
which Cæsar went, and those of which Tacitus wrote, and take
into consideration the great influx of Germans into Europe,
and Franks enough to give a name to old Gaul, also Normans
giving one to a province of France, and we feel surprised to
see that the usual French are not at all like Germans, and that
their appearance is as different as their language and their
character. I believe, whatever ancient historians may say, that
France, as a rule, retains its old races, whilst the old tales of
destruction are mostly boastings of the conquerors or melancholy moanings of the conquered. Now we see chiefly black
hair in west France, and blonde in Germany. Of course some

will say that hair changes. Why has Germany not changed, why have England, Sweden, Norway, Italy, and Spain, not changed? This argument cuts both ways. We know of no time when dark hair prevailed in the former, or light as a rule in the two latter countries.

If we go to Ireland, a true land of the Gaelic, we find both red hair and dark, and the native records speak of a yellow-haired race, a brown-haired and a dark-haired. In the Highlands of Scotland there is the same diversity, the dark preponderating, notwithstanding the influx of the light; but complete statistics have not been taken. In Wales the same thing is found. Spain, Portugal, and Italy have all dark hair; we may except some of the northern Italians, where the invaders were very numerous. In short, if you look at the Celtic countries—*i.e.*, countries in which Celtic was spoken in old time, or is spoken now—or countries on the continent called *Celtica*, you find a predominance of dark hair, and, notwithstanding invasions, this holds good also on the islands.

As to the question of hair changing, I will not say that it is a trifling one. Fair-haired children become dark-haired as the nervous system becomes more active. Take Germans with fair hair into the town, and dark hair increases as the busy life of the town strains the nervous system. I wait for this to be confirmed by the statistics now being collected, but I myself have counted in German town churches a great preponderance of dark hair, and this is a very fair way of taking statistics; so whatever the greater result may be, I know the truth of some cases to be as I say, and this I concluded many years ago. However, I know of no rural light-haired popula-
Y

tion becoming dark-haired, although I do not say that it is impossible.

The argument then is, that the nations alluded to who are dark-haired to a great extent now, were dark-haired to an equal or greater extent when the earliest writers spoke of them ; we know no influx of dark-haired people to change them. If that be the case, the Celts of the early time must have been dark haired to a great extent, and the assertions of several historians must be wrong.   It may certainly be. a daring thing to tell Cæsar that we know better than he did the appearance of a Celt.

Instead of writing this, I might almost quote an article by Dr. Beddoe in the *Journal of Anthropology*, 1870, wherein he shows with remarkable clearness the dark character of the hair of all those countries now Celtic, and Celtic in the Imperial Roman time.   There still remains a difficulty, namely, the fact that several historians ascribe to them light hair.   Dr. Beddoe explains some of this by the contrast which the Romans, accustomed to black hair, would find in men who had not black but such as we should call dark hair, whilst they appeared to the Romans light.[1]   A curious sentence in Stanley's *Journey Across Africa* illustrates this ; having long been accustomed to black faces he looked on the faces he first met at Bemo, in the west of Africa, as exceedingly pale, whereas they were rather of an olive complexion.

Another mode of surmounting the difficulty has been adopted of late.   This affirms that Celts and Teutons are

---

[1] Dr. Beddoe has brought his arguments so fully and fairly that had I seen the article in time I should have relied on it solely, although my own opinions are of long standing on this. point.

all one race; they are all Aryans, and, therefore, we require
no more to account for differences in them than in private
families. The argument that all are one would seem at
first a powerful one. Men, for centuries, have spoken of
the differences, and now, suddenly, the word is passed that
there are no differences. We like, when we understand a
subject, to enter into full detail, to examine it by the
aid of every department of physics, to look into it with
the microscope when our own eyes are deficient, to send
back reflections from history, when the present is not enough,
and to reason with the utmost subtlety over every detail:
but when we can come to no sound conclusion it is pleasant to dash the whole aside, or to cut it like the Gordian
knot, and to determine that, if possible, no man shall solve
it if we cannot. But this mode of acting will not settle
the Celtic question. The Gordian knot was destroyed, but
the Celtic question remained unaffected by the sword.

Although a few men of high position have attempted to
carry the careless view alluded to, it has not been possible to
darken the eyes of historians generally to the great question.
The Celts, that is, the people in countries which have been
or are Celtic, have not been and are not of the same race as
the Teutons in any useful sense of the word. It is wonderful
what difference there is between the dark Frenchman and
the light German, between the small and dark Irish, the
descendants, according to one authority, of the Firbolgs, and
the same great smooth-skinned and fleshy Teuton. It is
marvellous, too, how they differ in character. This difference
is proverbial, and has been so for ages, one may say; to this
day it is plain to all who have had any acquaintance with

both. It is true that we have the same difference in Ireland itself, both in appearance and character, that is, we hear of Milesians with brown hair invading the country, and Tuatha de Danann with light hair, and it is clear, therefore, that Ireland had, in the earliest known times, a mixed population. In those times there was no attempt to prove that the dark, small, and mean were of the same race as the brave, large, and noble, because it would have been simply absurd, and it has been left for bolder men of our day. There was a class, low and degraded in character, another generous, open, and such as bards could admire and sing of. The one small and dark, the other large and light We must, therefore, distinguish between these and name them differently since they are different ; to call them the same is passing those boundaries to which I, for one, confine myself.

It is clear, then, that in earliest times men recognized the difference of races, and that in some Celtic countries the races were mixed, and so mixed that the ignorant people of the time could recognize the difference. Even now these various peoples and others also may be recognized to some extent, although some do say that the Milesian race has gone out.

The people of the Celtic lands were not one, and who can tell the exact character of a Celt? One may ask, is the Celtic character in one section of the mixture only? We cannot shew this, they are not now sufficiently kept separate, but there is a character obtained by the union of all. This does not deny that there may have been a definite and uniform character of body and mind which originally gave rise to the name Celt.

We may suppose, then, that it is scarcely worth proving that Celt and Saxon are not the same, reasoning and feeling, body and mind, are different. Literature, which is the outcome of the inner soul of a people, is remarkably so, and that of the Celts has a peculiar character, such as never has been found among Teutons.

It is scarcely worth while alluding to things so well known. To prove them all requires a considerable time. Now, for example, let us take the last and the most important—the spirit of people in their literature. I shall not trouble you by bringing the arguments forward, they would be very numerous, but I should advise any one interested to read the literature of Ireland, after being pretty well acquainted with that of England and of Europe ; and if the peculiarity of this most Celtic of all literatures is not visible, then, of course, this argument fails more than expected.

Read Dr. Beddoe's accounts, and examine his tables of the eyes and hair of Celtic and Teutonic nations, and see if that argument fails.

It is very difficult, indeed, to remove a population. The boundaries of the Celtic remain in some places in this island, the same, to a few yards, as they were centuries ago. I speak with consideration when I say yards, meaning by this a small portion of a mile. The Comte de Villemarqué, as quoted by Dr. Beddoe, says that the boundary line has been the same for French and Breton for four centuries ; how much longer is not known. I shall mention a similar case in Scotland— one may say that Britain has an example extending all the length of Wales and north Scotland.

It may be said by men who seek a flaw that the argument

only proves that light people and dark exist in a peculiarly Celtic country such as Ireland, whilst there are also light and dark people in the peculiarly Teutonic countries.

At first a loosely-constructed opposition like this sounds well, but we cannot travel in France or Germany without seeing remarkable differences such as are striking to the most careless, and when we enter into details and take the statistics that have been prepared, the result is certain[1] that there is a majority dark in the one and light in the other.

Here I can imagine some one saying, It has been abundantly proved that an Aryan race has peopled Mid-Europe, the languages, with slight exception, being closely allied, and to upset such a well-established theory will require another generation, even if the arguments for the theory are not good, but on the other hand they appear incontestable.

This I believe to be a fallacy which has caused much error. I am not aware of any proof of a purely Aryan race existing anywhere, neither do I know that any one has shown what an Aryan race really is. There certainly is no proof that such a race ever fully peopled Europe, but there are abundant proofs that it never did so in any known epoch. To have such a result we must put the dark-faced hillmen of Italy and the plain-dwellers of Holland and Schleswig into the same category, although they are as different to ordinary observation as negroes and Chinese. We must bring in the Spanish and the Portuguese with the Slav and the German. The Welsh and the Norman become one although so different in type, and the Irish of all kinds, long recognised as different by themselves, and as coming from different countries, must

---

[1] Have just seen a notice of the statistics when this was printing.

be called one. Character goes for nothing in this mode of arguing, as nearly all the characteristics known to us from India to Portugal, with some slight exception, are thrown into one. The shapes of the head are not considered —the broad, square Roman one, the long Anglo-Saxon, and the Irish are all one. This is merely to cease observing. Of course, I am willing to say that all men are one, but there are differences, and it is convenient to call these by names, the word race being very well chosen for the purpose. Whenever two peoples cannot be found to have distinctions we may call them of one race.

It may, however, be asked whether I am intending to deny all the conclusions obtained by comparative grammar, and the results which indicate not only a similarity of language among nations in India and Europe, but a certain identity in many points of thought and tradition. This is not my intention. So far as I see, it is proved that an Aryan language has spread from the East, and, of the whole theory of the language and its relations, it is most interesting to learn the important results obtained. They have been found by men who have devoted their lives to the purpose. It is quite otherwise, however, with the idea of an Aryan race being co-extensive with an Aryan language, and it seems to me that many persons do not see the difference. I have seen no proof of the spread of any one race to such an extent as to people the West, and the differences already alluded to when speaking of the Celts constitute of themselves sufficient reasons.

There remains, then, the old difficulty, how to account for the similarity of language or the Aryan relationship of the languages. Whatever these difficulties be I will not throw them all aside as trifling, and, if I cannot account for them, I will wait for more information.

The permanence of the boundaries of language is enough to surprise us. A German language is found on one side of the Upper Rhine valley, although not on the river itself, and a Celtic on the other, and this is as old as history. The Belgians have their own German tongue, why should that be considered to have changed its boundary more than the other? In the little town of Nairn, in the North of Scotland, a few years ago, I found that Gaelic was spoken in one part and English in another, and it is said that King James I. of England made the same remark 300 years ago. I stood on the pier at Dunoon, and asked a policeman there how far it was across to the other side, in Renfrewshire? He said, "I do not know, I was never there." The distance was about two and a half miles. The oldest people of Dunoon speak Gaelic now; the people in Renfrew have spoken English for centuries, it is not easy to say how many. The conclusion is that language is a *very permanent* boundary or institution if nature helps to separate, as in this case, or even without apparent natural boundaries as at Nairn.

When I was a boy few people at Dunoon spoke English; now a large town exists, and all imported people speak English; we may say the same of similar places around, and miles of pure country district. The conclusion is that language is *not a permanent* boundary. We have these two contradictory and remarkable results from places well known.

Let us apply the lesson to Europe. We see at Dunoon that centuries of an opposing population never changed the boundary. Centuries under one government did not change it, but an influx of an overwhelming number, something like twenty or more to one of the original number, changed the language rapidly. This would lead us to say that no over-whelming invasions had taken place since Cæsar's time, from Germany to France or Spain, nothing to overwhelm the original language, and yet German and Scandinavian in-cursions have been so numerous that one would not have been surprised if the language had changed to Teutonic. If we go back to Roman times, still less do we find that enormous numbers invaded the country, so as to change entirely the population.

It was said that all the Celtic races are rather dark, but it was made clear that even in the supposed most Celtic of countries—Ireland, the colour of the hair and the character of body and mind were mixed. The dark hair, however, was a very general characteristic, and there was the peculiarity of speech besides.

This seems to lead to the conclusion of a pretty general existence of a prehistoric race, or of previous races covering the countries alluded to, and having some similarity. If we go very far back we find men with very little enterprise. Savage nations do not wander far ; the world is small to them, and they lock each other out by their animosities. A country peopled in this way may have districts with many peculiarities as we find in Africa, and if it has a sea coast it may have many strangers coming in, but the tendency with a low civilization and similar original habits is to an estrange-ment. The primitive people then could not be the Celts in the condition in which history brings them to Europe. When we hear of the Celts coming as invaders they are said to have had a civilization which comprised a knowledge of the usual metals.

But if we suppose the historic invading Celts to be only a small portion of the total races called Celtic, we can account for a great deal of contradiction, one part being rude in the extreme, and the other considerably advanced. In this way the invaders might bring a peculiar language called Celtic and impose it, in part, on the people. This would account for a part of the Gaelic being Aryan, and a large part not being proved to be so. The invading people might be light in colour, and large in stature, ruling over a considerable variety of people inferior in weight.

This is one mode of considering the question, but I want to bring in the Romans as having this Celtic tongue also, and as allied to the rest of Europe. We can do this by supposing the Celts to be only a branch of the same people that peopled Latium at a period earlier than we hear of the Celts in Italian history. By doing this we have to pass only a few generations back to the legendary building of Rome, a time which I do not doubt was one of no small commotion, worthy of many a tale even if Romulus and Remus are thrust out. We have nothing in the history of the Italian nations to quite contradict this, and much to make it seem possible, whilst I would revert to my former remarks, and look on the language as making it certain. There is also considerable reason for looking on Celtic nations as existing in Italy very early, but I am not ready to enter on the questions regarding Liguria and Umbria.

It must not be supposed that the Romans were even by this theory only Celts, or the Celts Romans. There is a remarkable difference in their characters and in their languages. The old Roman language has a wonderful firmness, hardness, and definiteness. Every word is as if shaped by a carpenter, every sentence is like a well dove-tailed box. The sharpness of consonants is like their laws and their armies, and the beauty is more of the reason than of the feeling. It is not easy to find from whom the language received this characteristic; it does not seem to be derivable from any known neighbours. The Etruscan may have had some influence, but it is an unknown factor; or quite possibly the peculiarity may have come from a very small knot of men, as the true old Roman head probably existed among few. Had it been common, the ruling class would not have been so small or so readily worn out. One sees the head occasionally in the present day, but if unmeasuring observation is to be regarded as enough, the old Roman head is not the Italian head.

The strong Roman character is in great contrast with the lighter Celtic, and was a matter of early observation. The Celtic may be quicker and more penetrating, but it has not the Roman grip. The languages illustrate this well. It is remarkable how well the Romans have retained the pronunciation of their language, even although the old Roman strength of individual character be rare. The language has kept up the early spirit, and the sound of the Italian is wonderfully clear and near to the Latin as it is spelt and as in many cases it must have been pronounced. Nevertheless there is a change such as the pure Roman of old would certainly object to; but when we go to France the tendency to break down a language is seen in great vigour. One might say that the cause of this was simply the distance from Rome and the mixture with the Celtic, and so far this may be true, but that same inclination to degradation of firm and clear sounds into soft, easy, and uncertain sounds is seen with remarkable fulness in the change and loss of the consonants in the branches of the Celtic called Gaelic.

The German has, like Latin, little flexibility, but the way in which Latin and German roots become hidden in Gaelic is very strange and even amusing. We may compare them to a hard character and a soft, to an active man and an idle, to a stern man and an easy man, and this last is the best comparison. Hard Roman words drop lightly out of Celtic mouths, consonants go away entirely whilst others are changed, and vowels take a form more easily pronounced. The manner in which Latin is broken down in Gaelic is marvellous ; let us look at a few examples.

For example: *liber*, a book ; *leabhar*, pronounced *lyour* in Gaelic Alb. *Gladius*, a sword ; *claidheamh*, pronounced *clai*. *Benefactus*, Latin ; *beannaighthe*, Irish Gaelic, pronounced *bannihe*. *Tectum*, a building or covering, is in Gaelic *tigh*, pronounced *tei*, and aspirated in certain cases to *hei*, Gaelic Alb.

Not only so, but Gaelic itself decays, it has this tendency in it, and it is becoming merely a few sighs and gutturals from its desire to soften. Gobha is pronounced gow, although the *b* was pronounced in old time. Aedh, a king, is ay ; the *d* was certainly pronounced, as it occurs in English in the name Aidan. Cath, a battle, pronounced *ca*, although the pronunciation must have been *cat*, as the stones commemorating them are called cat-stones in Lowland Scotch.

With this great diversity of character in Celt and Roman,

and the great difference in the tendency of language, we have an undoubted similarity of roots, and this we must closely remember. If it were merely an Aryan similarity we might leave it; but we believe it to show that the flow of the two peoples westward was at the same time or nearly the same time, and therefore that the Celts did not make their first appearance in Europe when we hear of them frightening the Romans.

This view makes the immediate pre-historic inhabitants of Europe diverse in appearance and not necessarily alike in language, whilst a new language comes in and obtains the ascendancy, not driving out the old. The invasion of Celtic-speaking people might be succeeded by Teutonic, and the great mixture of Teutonic roots would be accounted for, the substratum of the people remaining little changed, or at least changed less than the language.

Another view would make the Celtic the prevailing language in Europe, by pressure the Celts themselves being driven forward to become a conquering people. This also would connect the Romans and Celts; but it is not easy to suppose all Europe, or even West Europe and the British Isles, to have been inhabited by one people, and then invaded in historic times by such a diversity of races as to cause the present differences, and the languages made similar by invasion. I prefer to make them diverse beforehand. The languages, if diverse, as I think probable, would have an Aryan similarity introduced, either by the historic Celts, or by previous invaders from the East. The original very old substratum would supply the diversity in the language not proved to be Aryan.

Beyond these modes of reasoning it is difficult to go. If we do go we are apt on one side to suppose the Celtic element to grow into Roman with a rapidity quite incredible, and to fall into other great difficulties.

We may put the reasoning in fewer words.

1st. We may suppose a dark-haired race all over Central Europe and Britain, as well as much of Italy, with an uniform Aryan language ; whilst incursions of various tongues to different spots changed it.

2nd. We may imagine a diversity of people over the present Celtic Europe—not forgetting Rome—with a diversity of languages, these being invaded by Celts who imposed much of their language and by Germans who imposed some also.

There are many other alternatives ; but these two account for a great diversity of appearance in the people. In the first case the diversity would be produced by various mixtures made in long periods among a widely extended substratum with one language. In the second the languages and people may both have been different, but the newer race coming in produced the Celtic portion of the language, and extended it in the comparatively known short period to all the lands alluded to. This language is the main, perhaps only one, point joining all people called Celts.

Both theories account for that which we must be prepared to admit, a great diversity of appearance and that which may be called races or sub-races even among Celts, and a still greater separation from the Teutons as a great whole, notwithstanding all similarities of portions. In this we take the Celt as he is known to us in all the fulness of the meaning of the term, and do not confine ourselves to certain observations of the ancients, whose words cannot weigh when contradicted by other ancients, and cannot outweigh well known appearances.

We cannot imagine that, in all the long periods before history, people were so miserable that they died off like Australians before the eyes of the historic Celt; archæological remains seem to contradict this, and history does not support it. If the historic Celt of one type had driven the people out, he would have left only one type in, and one type does not appear alone, for neither are the people one, nor is the predominating people such as is described by Cæsar for example. That the Celt should bring one language or dialect of Aryan is probable enough ; but the remarkable thing is that it is like the Roman. We are compelled either to bring in this language with its speakers to join a number of people diverse in appearance, language, and character, or to bring in the latter to join the former. The mixture in historic times, great as it has been, by no means solves the Celtic mystery.

This one race may have been thoroughly Aryan, and some people may prefer to fix upon it and give it exclusively the title of Celtic ; but it is not clearly the original idea, as the title goes over too much ground, as has been said, and is possibly too old for the invading portion which attacked Rome. We can, however, readily suppose the race to have conquered far and to have Aryanized the words and thoughts of the conquered, who were themselves being lost in the crowd. We can account for any variety of people in this way among men called Celts, and even for the sixty-two tribes which existed in Gaul. We gather up all the wild pre-historic fragments of tribes, and with every variety of face and tongue, give them an attachment to their leaders, who are Aryan, and as much of their Aryan language as will make them be understood whilst the diversity of dialects is also accounted for. We account also for a brilliancy and greatness of character in certain Celts, in contrast with the backwardness of the race generally, in places where the true Aryan had less hold.

This is my view, after reading many volumes.

After all, it may be asked, how does this theory differ from that of others? It differs, so far as I see, from most in this, that it considers the overpowering yellow-haired race to be the minority, whether they brought in the Aryan language or not, and the races before them, however old, still to be in the majority, and to differ distinctly in mind and body from the fair, however diverse among themselves, and united by the one language.

NOTE.—Enquiries now making in Italy may enable us to speak more decidedly of the Celts in relation to that country. See the latest " Die Italiker in Po Ebene, by Wolfgang Helbig, 1879."

CHAPTER XXVII.

CONVERSATION ON THE CELTS.

CAMERON.—Then you think that the language which we call Celtic was spoken in the countries called Celtic, before the first invasion mentioned in Roman history as being made on Italy by that people?

Loudoun.—I think that the countries alluded to must have had a Celtic language, or mixture of languages, and I think that mixture was allied to the Roman. For that reason they coalesced so easily. Those nearest Rome would have the language nearest to Latin.

Cameron.—If it be true that the language spoken by the Celts in Gaul was closely allied to that spoken by us here in the Highlands and in Ireland, it seems to me that we must be all of one race and family, from Rome to Donegal and Sutherland.

Loudoun.—Here you introduce difficulties. I have already shown the great diversity in appearance amongst the nations even now called Celts, and Dion Cassius says that the Gaul of his time contained many tribes. Now, I particularly called your attention to the great continuousness of race upon the ground it first seizes. The long-continued and enormous

z

migration· of Goths into France has not made it Gothic. When lately going from the north down to Nimes by the Bourbonnais Railway, I did not see light-coloured hair at any station till we came near the south, when I saw that the children on the high ground were light-haired. In going up again to Dijon, it was wonderful to see the old Burgundian country with light-haired people, or at least not black, and the whole country population befaced like Germans, with countenances sympathetic for us Saxons, and to find this strong in Alsace, at least where I went, and on to Saarbourg and Saarbrücke, and north to Trier and Aachen.

Margaet.—That makes me think of the poem—

> " Uns ist in alten Mæren,
> Wunders vil geseit
> Von helden Lobebæren,
> Von grôzer kuonheit.
>
> .   .   .   .
>
> Ez wuohs in Burgonden
> Ein Schœne Magedin
> Daz in allen landen
> Niht schœners mohte sin.
>
> Kriemhilt was si geheizen
> Und was ein schœne wip
> Dar umbe muosen degene
> Vil verliesen den lip."

and so on.

Loudoun.—Of course this is no proof that the Nibelungen Lied was written in Burgundy, but it shows the Germanism of the kingdom in the poet's mind. Worms, where, in the German version of the story, the heroine is said to have lived, was far east in Burgundy, and Dijon far west; in the first there is German and in the second there is French spoken; still, I say that in the province of Burgundy, if we do not extend its limits to the extreme limit of its power, at any moment, there is the north-eastern face and hair, yes, and character; and no one who looks at the Burgundians will care much for their early boast, that they sprang from Romans. Language is no final proof. The Franks speak French now, and are not as the old Franks.

Cameron.—You seem to argue both ways—the Burgundians not altered, and the Franks altered.

Loudoun.—This only shows the complex character of the subject. The Burgundians on the side of Germany making constant inroads, destroyed, to a great extent, the Gallic character, but were not the less altered by the Gauls, and made to speak French. The Franks going farther forwards, were absorbed altogether, at least as to appearance and language. Their character may be sought mixed with the present French.

· All who came far enough west became Celtic, because of the strong Celtism in the west, and this Celtism extended to Scotland and Ireland. But this Celtism was a consequence of a great mixture.

Cameron.—Is it not difficult to reconcile these theories with the fact of Rome being separated from the Celts by part of Etruria, even allowing that the languages of Umbria and Liguria were Celtic?

Loudoun.—The first speakers of Celtic came early, in my opinion. The invasions of the Celts spoken of by the Romans were by a later band, and some of these new comers were less civilized than the long resident. It is indeed questionable how far some of the immigrants were Celts, the Romans not distinguishing them well from Germans.[1] But in any case, the Etruscan break into Italy does not alter the case. Even Etruria may have had a population originally as Celtic as Umbria before a Greek, Lydian, Phœnician, or northern race came there and planted civilization, which is difficult to retrace. The similarity of the Roman language, even to Irish and Scotch Gaelic, is too great to be passed over, and we must explain it.

My idea is, that the Celtic language, coming west, ran down into Macedonia in part, but being stopped, pushed on westwards because the road was less occupied, and pressing on, occupièd west Europe, and poured into Italy. Rome thus got its language, which was modified by soon meeting that of Greece. The Celtic was modified in Gaul by meeting an endless number of small tribes. This explains why the Celtic language is not totally Aryan, at least my belief is that it cannot be totally so.

This. explains also why the Celtic nations are not wholly Aryan ; and, indeed, at the root of this argument, you will see why no nation of western Europe is, or at least can be proved to be totally Aryan. Of course we can see, without much observation, that the differences are too great to allow of much pure Aryan blood, but the probability is that there is none pure.

O'Keefe.—Then you will refuse to the West Highlanders the purity of Celtic blood, and even to the Irish ?

Loudoun.—How is it possible to consider even the Irish as pure-blooded ? It required many races to build up your

[1] See Ethnology of Germany, Part II., by H. H. Howorth, Esq.. F.S.A., Journal of Anthropological Institute, February 1878.

Rome, which had Greek and other strange and subtle Eastern blood; but do not be cast down, even if you are mixed with clear German blood, and that of the "powerful azure Gentiles and the fierce hard-hearted Danars," who oppressed you long since: even whilst they killed your countrymen, they were obliged to leave their vigour in your land. We see the mixture already existing, and we read of ancient mixtures; but we must remember that the older mixtures were probably more Celtic than the modern, as the newer waves at least were Teutonic or Scandinavian of a known type. The early people of the west, who lived so long, according to my opinion, without being invaded by the bringers of the Aryan tongue, had probably long been disconnected from Central Asia, so that they formed not merely one separate race, but several races and varieties, in appearance and character, and it might take several invasions to modify the tongue of Ireland, so as to make it somewhat different from that of Gaul. There were men continually prowling about the sea; Fomorians landed on the shores, especially of the north and north-west—by name, "men of the sea" probably. Famhair is a giant, and may also mean "man of the sea." It is true that Faobh Fear is considered a derivation, meaning "spoil man," but this is much strained, and we want the *m*. They were evidently connected with the German and Northern Ocean. I presume they were large men, because the men of the sea, Fear mara, and giants have the same possible derivation. They may have even been of Celtic origin, since there were people in the north of Germany who were not Germans—the gens Æstiorum, for example, mentioned by Tacitus, possessors of Amber. If any one will connect Pomerania with Fomoria, I do not object, although Fear Mara was probably the first form of the word— a man of the sea—it is not so clear that the *F* should become a *P*. I may be wrong. This is a perfectly fair and probable mode of adding fresh Celtic blood to Ireland. There is still an island in the Baltic called *Femern* or Fehmarn, which we know to be near once formidable nests of sea rovers, and here it stands with a Celtic name, or at least one which may be Celtic, and which is closely woven into Irish legendary life, let us say also historical.

There were also people in Ireland called Tuatha de Danann. You see that they came also, perhaps first, to Scotland, bringing wonders (p. 41)—a very wise wily people versed in magic. Although there was no kingdom known as Denmark when they appeared, it is not going far to suppose them to have come from the rest of the Danes who gave Denmark its name, and who, as the Cimbric Chersonesus is supposed to have also had a number of Celts to get rid of, were obliged to run west, as others had done, before the Teutons, or be thrown down among the dregs.

The " black Danars" spoken of in " the wars of the Gaedhil and the Gaill" were clearly Danes, and we have tall, dark-haired men in Denmark still, accounting for a dark colour without small Iberians. In Denmark at present there are more light or red-haired. I have counted in a regiment in Copenhagen two thirds having reddish hair. Thus we have both black and red from Denmark, the second agreeing with a tradition in Scotland that red-haired are Danish, and with a statement, which I give as my own opinion, that there are red-haired people of Ireland who have neither the proper German nor Scandinavian type. They are probably the same as of old, but all called Celts, speaking one tongue.

Of course, we must say a word about Firbolgs—men who have been called *Belgians*, also *bagmen, miners carrying sacks, creeping men*, and lately *men with paunches*. It is not impossible, from their attacks having been made in the south of Ireland, that these men were Belgians, but from their character and appearance it is most unlikely. Still accounts are very different. One says that they were a mean and contemptible race—small, quarrelsome tattlers, slaves and thieves, very numerous and black-haired. I do not recognise such a race in Belgium—a country filled with quiet and remarkably industrious people; but if they were Celts, they had less occasion to emigrate, we would suppose, for if driven west they had Gaul to flee to. Mr. Skene thinks they came from Cornwall, and if so were Celtic. Their numbers may have grown, notwithstanding that in early times they were said to have been reduced to 300 fighting men.

It seems to me more likely that the name had nothing to do with Belgium. It seems better to use a derivation out of fashion now, " men of the quiver"—*Fir*, men, and *bolg*, a quiver —men who used bows and arrows, which were of late introduction into Ireland; possibly the Firbolgs alone used them for a long time. Perhaps you would go back, and say that the Belgians were called Firbolgs or men with quivers; but that is going far, since this arm would surely be well known among other people of the continent: still it is admissible.

Cameron.—And do you think that with these facts you can account for the condition of our language and people?

Loudoun.—These facts are stated generally enough to include; in a similarly general way, some questions relating to Irish and Celtic ethnology; but it is a wide subject, not to be trifled with by throwing it aside, and telling us that all the tribes of Europe are the same.

Cameron.—I have heard that all the country was inhabited by small men called Iberians, and that they were really the true beginning of the Celtic race. Although you have quoted Irish story for making the Firbolgs dark and mean, we can also quote other sayings for making them yellow-haired and large, and Dionysius Periegeta applies ἀφνείος and ἀγαυός to the Iberians, rich, and, shall we say, noble or splendid? Festus Avienus says, "Tellus Europa Columnis Proxima magnanimos alit aequo cespite Iberos." If Eber were the true beginning of the Iberians in Ireland, they would belong to the Milesians. If not, this theory breaks down.

Loudoun.—These opinions are contradictory, but these quotations are not specially applicable to the Kymry, who have been called Iberian, and their presence would agree in confirming diversity of appearance in Ireland in early times, as from present appearances we could confidently argue.

· I take the description of the Firbolgs from MacFirbis' Book of Genealogies, as quoted by O'Curry in his "MSS. Materials," p. 224. These Firbolgs we know little of, but in their external appearance I still consider the evidence to be for the dark and small people. Now we know that small and dark people did not cover all Ireland and Scotland, whether we argue from

the Irish records or the appearance of the descendants of the old Irish. Besides, Firbolgs were not
the only " less noble race " in Ireland ; there were *Gailiuns*
and *Domhnanns,* if these two were not merely a part of the
same race, and we have no evidence of one original race here
any more than in Gaul and Italy in historical or even Irish legendary times. There may, however, have been a race or series
of tribes over Western Europe sufficiently one or sufficiently
mixed up to have a similar language, as has been explained.
I incline, however, as already said, to the belief that this similarity was produced by an invading people, who moulded the
language of all the tribes to their will, absorbing the tribal
language, and thus forming the known Celtic, the Aryan part
being the same, but the tribal part different. This accounts
for the great diversity, as well as similarity, from Rome to
Donegal.

It is more probable that this invading race brought in
the links of union than that these existed before, because
people with small culture spread over a great region have
little communion. The idea accounts also for some people
supposing the Celts to be fair, and others dark. I argue that
the Celtic established nations are dark, although the Aryan
influx that made the language may have been fair-haired. It
gave language and so far cultivation, but if the men were fair
they were to a great extent physiologically conquered by the
dark-haired races, who were in overwhelming predominance
in most places. The German words in the present
Gaelic are numerous, and how can it be otherwise ? Some
of the later races were evidently German or Scandinavian
in our islands, and we do not know if the Fomorians may

not have been German in part, since the Irish could not distinguish the pure Aestian of Pomerania from his neighbour if
they were different. All were great sea rovers and robbers.
It appears that Greek and German, Latin and Celtic are the
two pairs of languages which have dominated Europe, the
Greek being allied in the south to the German in the north,
and the Latin to the Celtic, but all altered by the pre-existent
men and the long-enduring centuries, the least permanent
being in the west, to which the earliest races were more
driven.

Some confusion in the history of the Celts has come from
the Iberians, whom the inhabitants of South Wales are said
to have resembled in the early centuries. This has naturally
led ethnologists to think of similar dark people in Ireland.
Some have, therefore, connected the Iberians with Eber,
who came to Ireland with his brother Eremon. This mode
of putting together the same letters of the alphabet from
different countries and languages is a habit of very early
philologists, Greeks especially ; and it is certainly a great
favourite at present among the Germans. Celtomaniacs have
a great advantage in the peculiar capacity of the Celtic
language to run over letters and leave whole syllables un-
attended to. Eber was an ancestor of the Milesians, and they
were a proud and leading race in Ireland ; and, by one tradition, despised the arrow shooting of the Firbolgs as we do that
of savages ; by another, they were of the same stock. I put
in the arrow shooting without good historic authority, but the
rest is true. The connection with Eber can only be made out
by denying much that is said of his descendants the Milesians.
It would be necessary to show that when the Irish spoke of

Eber as a forefather of Milesians it was a mistake, since he was the father of the Firbolgs. The perversion of the fact might have taken place in the legend, but it is too late to think of this. Still the sound of the name and the connection of both with Spain must be allowed to be of interest.

The contradictions on this point are too many to be solved. At present we may consider the later Firbolgs as a fallen race, enslaved and mixed with slaves. They began as a higher one, and first occupied Tara. The mixture with slaves or a lower dark race might be the cause of their being considered black-haired. But I deny that all the dark men are small. I refer to the black Danars of old times who were large, at least powerful, and to the tall dark men of modern times still more telling in an argument.

We may now return home. We seem to have lived through

O'Keefe.—You look in the right direction ; our literature is unknown, and we have not a sufficient number of men given to its study. The great scholars are dying out, and there are few to take their place. Government fears to spend money on the translations, and England and the world bear the loss, thinking they are gaining. There are men who say that we are the same as the Saxons—as well call us like the negroes. It is true that our literature has not reached the stage of ripeness ; it is full of crude power. It has richness of thought and extravagance, but these are not drilled by the intellect or the taste. It is like the rich yellow gorse of Ireland itself, displaying a beauty that no country can boast of, however rich in flower—a yellow, golden, sunny beauty, that sometimes covers over her fields and clothes them as far as we can see, but conceals the fact that this is caused by want of cultivation. It is as if the land itself had that natural instinct which the people possess of clothing their thoughts in brightness, and looking even on their rags with pride. The soul of Ireland is wild, but think of a youth of such promise. What will be its ripeness in the time when you Saxons will be sinking in old age !

Loudoun.—It may be so, but I prefer to enjoy some of the ripeness of national life, although I sometimes wish for your youthful dancing spirit. We, even in lowland Scotland, have a good deal of the Celtic blood, so that we have great diversity of character ; and, on the whole, I have reason to love my own nation. We are, as the old saying made us, " kindly Scots." In no part of the world will you find people with more sympathy, or more interest in the welfare of others, especially their own brethren. We have been till lately poor, but we have not been less civilized in some aspects. I say it, and with reason and deliberately, the working men of Glasgow were more civilized fifty years ago than now. They had more of the love of man and reverence before God. They had less money, but they had less craving for pleasure; their lives were simpler, and they scarcely knew that they were poor, if they had only their week's wages; and even if that failed, was it not the common lot of man to suffer? and good friends would help them through, as they themselves had helped others. They were ruder, but had higher ideals; civilization is neither science alone, nor refinement of manners nor wealth.

I would I could tell you more of the beauties of our country, but we must leave. The soil is covered with romance: I wish there were a phonograph to utter it, and yet it has one. I might take you home another way, and revel for weeks in Islay and Jura and Gigha—yes, even in that little Gigha; we might wander for a season down Cantire, and live among its saints, its martyrs, and its heroes. We could spend much time in Arran among its tales and its hills, and as long in Bute, which is a miniature of Lowlands and Highlands, with its wild, barren rocks and heaths, and rich, warm gardens; and we might spend a long time in the study even of the Little Cumbraes, which seem quite covered with the names of saints, churches, and men to be remembered, a very treasury of sacred memories. But we must separate, glad to think that even the wild Loch Etive has interest enough for more than a season for us, and will have for ages of men; and if that spot, little habited and little written of, has so much that is interesting, surely a life could not enter fully into the stories that cover all that ground which is now called Scotland. We differ distinctly from

the English, and long may we kéep different.   Assimilation
destroys originality.

O'Keefe.—These memories yóu mention are all Celtic, and
I say Irish, and I was going to leave you by sáying " Eirinn gu
brath," but as you are from the Alban side, I shall include all
the Gaels and use the wider expression " Gaidhealtachd gu
brath." [1]

[1] Gaeldom for ever.

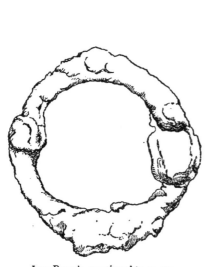

Iron Brooch, mentioned on p. 147

Part of an Iron Sword,
mentioned on p, 150.

APPENDIX.

VITRIFIED FORTS.

THE first observer of vitrified forts was Mr. John Williams, who described them in a small book entitled " On Highland Ruins," published in Edinburgh in 1877. It contains the following letter :—

Letter from DR. JOSEPH BLACK, *Professor of Chymistry in the University of Edinburgh.*

" SIR,—I am much obliged to you for the sight of your letters concerning the vitrified fortresses in the North. I had got formerly from some of my friends, some accounts of extra-ordinary vitrified walls which they had seen in the Highlands; and Mr. James Watt, who spent some time in surveying a part of that country, communicated a number of particular observations which he had made upon one of these ruins ; but we were not enabled to judge with any certainty, for what purposes, or in what manner, these hitherto unheard-of build-ings had been erected. It is very probable that they were executed in some such manner as you have imagined. There are, in most parts of Scotland, different kinds of stone, which can, without much difficulty, be melted or softened by fire, to such a degree, as to make them cohere together. Such is the grey stone, called whin-stone, which, for some time past, has been carried to London to pave the streets. Such also is the granite, or moor-stone, which is applied to the same use, and pieces of which are plainly visible in some specimens of these vitrified walls, which I received from my friends. There are also many lime-stones, which, in consequence of their containing certain proportions of sand and clay, are very fusible: and there is no doubt that sand-stone and pudden-stone when they happen to contain certain proportions of iron mixed with the sand and gravel of which they are composed, must have the same quality. A pudden-stone composed of pieces of granite must necessarily have it.

"There is abundance of one or other of these kinds of stone in many parts of Scotland; and as the whole country was, anciently a forest, and the greater part of it overgrown with wood, it is easy to understand how those who erected these works, got the materials necessary for their purposes.—I am, SIR, your obedient humble servant.

(Signed)   "JOSEPH BLACK.

" Edinburgh, April 18, 1877.

" To Mr. John Williams."

From *Remarks on the Construction of Vitrified Forts*, by JOHN HONEYMAN, F.R.I.B.A. (*Read at a meeting of the Archæological Society held at Glasgow on 10th February,.1868.*)

"The conclusion to which the phenomena exhibited at Dunskeig pointed seemed to me to be this—that the walls were constructed of loose materials, bound together into a solid mass by being grouted with a liquid vitreous cement, composed chiefly of greenstone and other easily fused materials, and that the process was effected *on* the wall, not on either side of it. In this way it would be as easy to construct a wall twelve feet thick as two, and as easy to carry it along the verge of a precipice as on a plain. But, it may be asked, if the agglutination is chiefly effected in this way, how is it that we find so large a portion of the remains bearing the evidence of the action of intense heat? The reason, I think, is obvious. The material could not have been melted at all without the action of intense heat on whatever enclosed the fire, and these enclosures must necessarily have been very numerous. It would, with our present amount of information on the subject; be obviously absurd to dogmatize as to the exact *modus operandi*, but I shall suggest a possible method. Suppose that first a course of loose stones was laid all round the enclosure the width of the proposed wall, across this a series of furnaces about eighteen inches wide and two feet high were formed, closed at each end, and separated by partitions composed chiefly of trap, the ends would form the outside and inside faces of the wall, and would be provided with holes for the passage of air through the furnace. The whole was then covered over with stones (to a considerable extent trap) and probably turf and sea-weed were added. In such a furnace —the means of producing a blast being satisfactory — an intense heat would be produced, and the result would be that the partitions and top would be fused." [1]

Mr. Honeyman makes the following addition to his paper:—

"Having extended my observation much since the above was written, I am able to add that the vitrifaction is generally less perfect towards the outside than in the centre of the wall, that in some forts which I have examined, the vitrified mass rests upon rough building which has never been subjected to great heat, and that in these cases the centre of the wall is vitrified to a greater depth than either of the sides. It

[1] *Transactions of the Glasgow Archaeological Society.* Part I., vol. II.

seems evident therefore that the vitrifaction was effected from the top of the wall, not from the sides. In every wall I have examined there is abundant evidence that the cementing material has *run down* among the loose stones, and the same appearances prove that the dry building above referred to occupies still its original position under the vitrified mass. In the interstices among the unvitrified stones, drops and small streams from above still remain as they cooled.

     " 1879.   J. H."

It is, however, true that some of the loose stones have been exposed to great heat. The fort existing in Bohemia has been remarked to have had alternate layers of wood and stone.

INDEX.

WS - #0022 - 200723 - C0 - 229/152/23 - PB - 9781331829232 - Gloss Lamination